HEALTH SERVICE LAW

AUSTRALIA
The Law Book Company Ltd.
Sydney : Melbourne : Brisbane

CANADA AND U.S.A.
The Carswell Company Ltd.
Agincourt, Ontario

INDIA
N.M. Tripathi Private Ltd.
Bombay
and
Eastern Law House Private Ltd.
Calcutta
M.P.P. House
Bangalore

ISRAEL
Steimatzky's Agency Ltd.
Jerusalem : Tel Aviv : Haifa

MALAYSIA : SINGAPORE : BRUNEI
Malayan Law Journal (Pte.) Ltd.
Singapore

NEW ZEALAND
Sweet & Maxwell (N.Z.) Ltd.
Auckland

PAKISTAN
Pakistan Law House
Karachi

HEALTH SERVICES LAW

By

JOHN D. FINCH, B.A., B.C.L.

LONDON
SWEET & MAXWELL
1981

Published in 1981 by
Sweet & Maxwell Limited of
11 New Fetter Lane, London
Photoset by Promenade Graphics Ltd., Cheltenham
Printed in the U.S.A.
by Edwards Brothers Inc.

British Library Cataloguing in Publication Data

Finch, John
   Health Services law.
     1. Medical laws and legislation — England
     I. Title
344.204'321   KD3395

ISBN 0–421–26460–8
ISBN 0–421–26470–5 Pbk

PREFACE

This is a book about law. But it is not written with lawyers uppermost in mind. The book is intended for use by anyone interested in some basic laws and legal principles about the running of personal health services.

As such, *Health Services Law* is intended for anyone interested in the voluminous legal aspects of the National Health Service. These people include administrators, students of administration and medical and nursing personnel. But this book is not exclusively directed at all those people, being intended for those working in the fast-growing private health care sector also.

This book differs from most law books in its lack of complex and often tedious references to chapter and verse. Statutes, statutory instruments, decided cases and circulars are all referred to briefly and clearly in the text. Fuller references are reserved to the tables and index at the beginning and end of the book. This avoids footnotes, of which there are none in this book. This is certainly not an encyclopaedia of health services law. Such a tome (if one were indeed conceivable) would be ten times the length. But the readership which this book has in mind will want a broad grounding in the vital rules and principles discussed, underlined by a good understanding. As such, this book explains rather than states. There is an array of specific detail, but never at the expense of explanation about what the detail exemplifies. It is hoped that students of health service administration will find this approach particularly useful, especially since the syllabus in Law Affecting Health Services of the Institute of Health Service Administrators is almost completely covered in this book.

I am grateful to my friends at the Institute of Health Service Administrators and in the Education Department of NALGO for the stimulus they have given each in their own way. David Newell of the Law Faculty, Leicester University, read and improved the chapter on Employment Law and I stand in his debt. Brenda Hoggett of the Law Faculty, Manchester University made a number of corrective and updating comments on the two Mental Health chapters, and I am grateful to her also. The Modern Law Review kindly allowed me to draw on material which I first published there. Leicester University kindly made me a small grant in the preparation of materials. The law in this book represents sources to hand at March 5, 1981.

John Finch

Leicester

CONTENTS

TABLE OF CASES

ix

TABLE OF CIRCULARS AND NOTICES

TABLE OF STATUTES

TABLE OF STATUTORY INSTRUMENTS

Chapter 1

HEALTH SERVICE STRUCTURE

I

The provision of personal health services

Any society, and especially an advanced society, has an interest in the maintenance and improvement of its overall health and welfare. The public good includes the aggregate of private interests in wellbeing. Public health has for some time now been governed by legislation specifically aimed at what might be called the public sector. For instance, the Public Health Act 1936 was a landmark in the legislative provision of powers and imposition of public duties in respect of health and welfare concerns expressed on a public scale. More recent legislation on the prevention of noise and the control of pollution provides further examples of the expression of the concern for public wellbeing.

Alongside this public concern there now lies a whole mass of legislative expression of the concern for individual health welfare and care. The powers and duties governing the provision of health care and services on a national scale are to be found in the now very considerable mass of National Health Service legislation, commencing with the National Health Service Act 1946, and including most recently the Health Services Act 1980.

A large part of the contents of this book is equally applicable to the provision of personal health services outside and independent of the national service. Whenever it is necessary to make a distinction between the two sectors, an explanation will be given.

The National Health Service

While the concern of this book is with the law relating to the provision of health services generally, the practical focus of our attention will naturally and very frequently be on the activities of the National Health Service itself. This focus of attention is natural owing partly to the sheer size of the operations of the National Health Service. The total number of employees in the National Health Service, including both whole-time and part-time employees, is in the region of one million. That amounts to a remarkable two per cent. of the total population of England and Wales. From the recipients' point of view the figures are noteworthy also. The average daily number of hospital in-patients is well over 400,000, and the number of in-patients treated per annum is not far short of six million. So the practical incidence of the rights and duties, rules and regulations which we are concerned with in this area is quite enormous.

The National Health Service is a creation of the legislature, or Parliament. The statutory creation of the system is traceable to as recent a date as 1946. Before that, however, the social, economic and consequently political pressures within the community were responsible for surveys and reports, in particular the Beveridge Report of 1942; and these pressures eventually led to Parliamentary action shortly after the Second World War which resulted in the National Health Service finally coming in existence on July 5, 1948. The creation of the service was accompanied by a reconstruction of the social security system, the Education Act of 1944 having already imposed a duty on local education authorities to ensure free medical treatment for school children.

The background

The British health services are largely a product of the nineteenth and twentieth centuries. During the Middle Ages there was evidence of a special concern for the sick, and some religious orders made a point of caring for the sick and the infirm. After the Reformation, the Poor Law Act of 1601 imposed on local authorities a duty to provide for the sick, the needy and the homeless. By the mid-nineteenth century a clear policy was emerging in relation to social aspects of sickness, need and infirmity. The growth of urban living in the towns in the earlier nineteenth century caused epidemics, some on a disastrous scale, and a programme of sanitary reform which was made necessary by such conditions led to the passing of the Public Health Act of 1848. Among other measures this Act initiated steps to clean up the water supply, and in 1866 the appointment of sanitary inspectors was made obligatory.

The work of social reformers culminated in the Public Health

Act 1875, under which a central government department became responsible for environmental health. This statute also provided for the appointment of local authority medical officers of health. Other measures included the obligation to notify infectious diseases. The result of these measures together was the elimination of cholera and the virtual elimination of typhoid fever attributable to contaminated or infected water. The Public Health Act 1875 is the statute upon which all subsequent public health legislation has been based.

While public health regulations grew beneficially it was not until the present century that provision came properly to be made for personal, as distinct from public, health care and treatment. But when improvement in the provision of personal health services came, it came rapidly. The rate of improvement was made possible by progress in medical science and by the increasingly wider availability of medical treatment. In 1907 a school medical service was started under which children were given periodic medical inspections. The National Insurance Act 1911, a triumph of Lloyd George, put into operation in 1912 a compulsory health insurance scheme. The scheme provided free medical treatment for a section of the population by means of doctors being paid a fee for each patient on their list. The scheme gave the right to choose and use a general practitioner and to the free drugs and medicines which he prescribed. The scheme did not, however, extend to hospital treatment, nor to people above a certain (fairly low) income limit. Dependants of the sick and infirm were also excluded from the scheme.

The hospitals service was characterised by hospitals of two types. In 1929 the former Poor Law infirmaries were taken over by the local government authorities to form part of a local authority system parallel to the voluntary hospitals. The voluntary hospitals largely depended on charitable contributions from the public, and from living patients and through past patients' wills. Some such hospitals were in almost constant financial difficulties and many had to be further supported from public funds. The hospital system, which was really no system at all, suffered from at least two major defects.

First, the location and size of the voluntary, charitably supported, hospitals was far from conforming to an overall plan. Some areas, particularly the affluent middle-class areas, were well provided for, and other areas were provided for poorly or not at all. Secondly, much of the legislation authorising local authority services was permissive only; that is, it gave a power to make certain provisions but did not go further and impose an obligation or duty to exercise that power. In other words, local authorities were not compelled to provide certain services. As a consequence, provision varied widely from area to area, some authorities maintaining excellent personal health services, and others having inferior ones.

The apparent deficiencies in the provision of personal health services were highlighted by the conditions of the Second World War, and events precipitated reform.

Reform and legislation

Reform came to a head in 1942 with the Report of the Beveridge Committee. The Beveridge Report presented a plan for social security which implied a security of income up to a certain necessary minimum. The Report stated that the provision of income should be associated with arrangements designed to bring the interruption of earnings to an end as soon as possible. One such arrangement envisaged was a national health service which would ensure that every citizen, however rich or poor, could receive necessary medical treatment without an economic barrier at any point to delay recourse to it.

The Beveridge proposals were accepted by the wartime all-party coalition government. In 1944 the government issued its proposals for a national health service which it described as "the next natural development in the growth of the health service of this country." A National Health Service Act was passed by Parliament in 1946, with corresponding legislation for Scotland and Northern Ireland. The National Health Service came into existence on July 5, 1948. The service was created not just to make services free at point of use but to make them available wherever they were needed. It was designed to provide for a much better and more efficient geographical distribution of general practitioners, of specialists, of dentists and of opticians. An important accompanying measure was the rationalisation of the hospitals, according to which an uncoordinated series of hospitals of varying size, function and quality would be assembled and supplemented into an integrated, rational and coordinated system designed to provide all necessary forms of specialist care.

Under the National Health Service, the voluntary and local authority hospitals were taken over by the State and administered by regional hospital boards responsible directly to the central government health ministers. Teaching hospitals were controlled separately by boards of governors who were also responsible to the health ministers. Family doctor, dental and ophthalmic practitioner services were administered by local executive councils representing the government, the local authorities and the medical professions. Local authorities retained responsibility for maternity and child health clinics, the school health service, immunisation programmes and other preventive services, the ambulance service, and environmental or public health. To summarise, the 1946 Act organised the service on a tripartite basis: the hospital service administered through special authorities and boards created for that purpose; the miscellaneous health and care services which were administered by local authorities; and the general practitioner services under the executive councils. At all points in the new service, priorities were to be established on the basis of medical need rather than on the ability to pay.

Administrative organisation

Before turning to the powers, obligations and duties underlying the present-day provision of personal health services it will be useful to take a brief look at the administrative structure within which health services are operated.

As provided for in the 1946 Act, on July 5, 1948 the National Health Service came into being and the biggest change was in the administration of the hospitals. The great majority of the former voluntary hospitals, including all the teaching hospitals, and all the local authority hospitals were transferred into national ownership. The National Health Service began with 1,143 voluntary hospitals which provided about 90,000 beds, and 1,545 municipal or local authority hospitals with about 390,000 beds. Of the latter figure 190,000 beds were in hospitals for mental illness and mental handicap.

Boards of governors directly responsible to the Minister of Health were established to run and control the 36 teaching hospitals in England and Wales. The other hospitals were placed under the management of hospital management committees, which numbered 388. The planning of the hospital services and the employment of senior medical and dental staff were made the responsibility of 14 regional hospital boards.

On the establishment of the Service a distinction was made between hospital medical practice and general practice. Except in the case of accidents and emergencies, access to specialists would henceforth be only by the referral of the general practitioner. A most important early benefit of the new arrangement was that the principal specialist services became available on a planned basis across the country, instead of being confined to areas in which a variety of factors, not least economic, dictated the pattern of provision and availability of services.

New services, new problems

The introduction of the National Health Service created a social benefit unique in Europe. But new services are apt to create their own problems, and it is perhaps remarkable that the service remained substantially unaltered until 1974. In the 1950s there were reports, surveys and investigations into this and that particular area, but it was not until the 1960s that any move for reform really got underway.

As indicated earlier, the National Health Service had been established in three separate parts: hospital and specialist services, family practitioner services and the local authority services. Even outside this tripartite diffusion of responsibility there existed other health-care services such as the school health service provided by local education authorities, and the port health and environmental health services which were the responsibility of local government. Nor were occupational health services provided by individual employers within the new Service. This division of responsibility, especially between health authorities and local government authorities, was productive of certain difficulties and sources of frustration. In particular, the regional boards which had the responsibility of building up and developing the hospitals were not in an administrative position to control development of the community services which remained the responsibility of local authorities. The latter responsibility included the numerically very considerable problems of providing community care services for the mentally ill and the mentally handicapped.

A strong case arose for health services of these varying sources of responsibility to be brought together under a unified administration. The principal problem was as to how particular services should be classified prior to a reallocation of responsibility. Which areas of service should conveniently remain within local authority control, and which should pass to the control of a new and expanded type of health authority? A government policy document of 1970 announced the borderline between local government and area health authority responsibilities. In general the new area health authorities would match the new local authorities. Health authorities would be responsible for services where the main skill necessary was that of the health professions, while local authorities would be responsible for services which depend principally on care and support. Instead of the regional hospital boards there would be (in England) the same number of regional health authorities occupying a position of responsibility directly between the Secretary of State for Health and Social Services and the area health authorities. At the district level within each area there would be administration but no committees. However, community health councils would be established in each district to represent the views and advance the legitimate interests of the users of the health services in that district.

The 1973 Act

The National Health Service Reorganisation Act of 1973 came into operation on April 1, 1974, when the above proposals for reorganisation were put into effect. Given the relatively short time available, reorganisation of administration was smooth. While the 1946 Act gave local authorities medical, as well as welfare functions, the effect of the 1973 Act was to bring together the administration of local authority medical functions and general practitioner services along with hospital and specialist services. With the exception of the postgraduate teaching hospitals which were left for separate future consideration, the health services including now the school health service were brought together under the management of area health authorities. Regional and area health authorities would henceforth be served by multi-disciplinary teams of officers. District teams were made responsible to the area health authority itself, so that the area health authority was to have an important supervisory role in relation to the key operational level of administration, the district management team.

The operation of reorganisation

As hitherto, the Secretary of State for Social Services continued to be responsible to Parliament for the operation of the National Health Service as a whole. It is the Secretary's responsibility also to decide on national policy. We shall notice in a moment the infusion of politics, even party politics, into health service operations in respect of the so called "pay-beds" issue. In such a case it is the function of the Secretary of State to bring to bear on health service activities the policy, including the social and economic attitudes, of the government of the day.

The location and size of regional health authorities are determined so that each region has at least one university medical school within its boundaries. The new regions are based on the regions previously used for purposes of hospital service administration. The population of the regions varies widely from two to five million people. The chairman and other members of the regional authorities are appointed by the Secretary of State. The membership includes representatives of the main health professions, the universities, local authorities, and health service and other employees. The regional health authority employs regional staff, consultants and senior registrars of non-teaching area health authorities. The regional health authority appoints all area health authority members, except those appointed by the local authority and by the relevant university. The authorities at regional level are responsible for identifying the need for, and for providing, services which necessitate a regional rather than an area-based approach. They develop, with the help of specialist professional advice, an overall regional plan for specialist health services. The same principle remains equally applicable to a situation involving the removal of the statutory area level of responsibility.

The 1973 Act further created, at the lowest level of statutory authority, area health authorities within each of the regions. Area boundaries under the Act coincide with major local authority boundaries, and each area authority became responsible for planning and developing services in consultation with its matching local government authority.

A principal function of the area health authority under the 1973 Act was its duty to establish a family practitioner committee. The four functions of such a committee are to make contracts for services with practitioners; to prepare lists of such practitioners; to pay them; and to deal with disputes and complaints arising out of the performance of their contracts by practitioners. It might be pointed out here that the "contract" in question is drawn up between the family practitioner committee and the individual practitioner. While private or paying patients certainly have a contract with their doctor or other health services organ, no legal contract exists between a National Health Service practitioner and his patient under that service.

All statutory health authorities, as well as family practitioner committees, have a statutory duty to recognise and consult professional advisory committees. The main national advisory body set up by the 1973 Act for England and Wales, the Central Health Services Council, was itself abolished by the Health Services Act 1980. But, importantly, the 1980 Act retains in existence the standing advisory committees set up under the 1973 Act. The professional advisory committees which were established at both regional and area level by the 1973 Act supplement the central advisory committees, and these bodies are consulted before decisions at the relevant local level are made. This system of advice and consultation gives health professions an effective and useful voice at all levels in the planning and operations of the National Health Service. The professions so represented are medicine, dentistry, nursing, pharmacy and ophthalmology.

The operational level of health services as reorganised by the 1973 Act is the health district. These districts, having a population varying normally between 200,000 and 500,000, are in charge of the day-to-day running of the health services. Within each district a single district medical committee represents all family doctors and specialist hospital staff in the district. It is the committee's job to coordinate the medical aspects of health care throughout the district. District administration is in the hands of district management teams of the area health authority, and clinical doctors are represented on these teams. Each district management team is responsible for coordinating most of the operational services of the National Health Service, and for formulating policies affecting the provision of operational services at district level. The team has the job of reviewing the community's needs for health care and the provision of services within the district, with a particular eye to the identification of any gaps in providing for such needs. Priorities in the provision of health care are to be assessed at district level so as to provide within each health district the best possible patient care which is possible with the resources available.

The arrangements, structures and institutions which have so far been discussed are now generally governed by the National Health Service Act 1977. This statute, relating also to the provision of private medical treatment and re-enacting the incidents of the Secretary of State's duties to be discussed in Chapter 2, is a consolidating measure; it gathers together a diversity of legislative provisions relating to personal health services under the umbrella of one compendious Act. Even this consolidating measure is now to be read subject to the Health Services Act 1980, which will be examined in a moment.

Public representation

The 1973 Act carried out the proposal to establish community health councils. The Secretary of State was given the duty to establish for each area served by an area health authority such a council to represent the views of the "consumer" to the area health authority. There is one community health council for each of an area's health districts, and the ambit of the councils corresponds to the health district boundaries. Community health councils consist of about 20 to 30 members half of whom are nominated by local government councils, and a third by non profit-making voluntary organisations interested in the health services.

These councils have the right of access to public information, and have the right to visit hospitals and other health care institutions within their district. Area health authorities must consult them on health service developments, and councils are entitled to send an observer to the meetings of the area health authority. Council members do not have the right to vote at area meetings, but they have the right to speak and to make their views known. Annual reports are published by the community health councils, and area authorities are required to publish replies to these reports, stating in particular the action which has been taken or is proposed to be taken as a result of the comments and suggestions made in the reports of the councils.

Reorganisation again: the 1980 Act

The reorganisation of 1973 into the statutory responsibilities to be exercised by the Secretary of State for Health and Social Services, the regional health authorities and the area health authorities, plus the operational or "consumer" level of districts directly responsible for the provision of health care to patients, attracted almost from the outset a mass of criticism. Such criticism usually crystallised into one of two types: over-administration, and overdelay in the provision of services to patients. The cumulative effect of these factors, according to the criticisms which centred on them, was represented by an imbalanced system in which the balance of advantage did not lie with the best interests and health of individual patients. In particular, wastes of resources and manpower were alleged to detract from the advantages which the money and facilities could provide if utilised in a better and more efficient way.

The eventual outcome of such critical examination of the

health services as reorganised in 1974 (by the 1973 Act), and subsequently provided for by the 1977 Act, was the consultative paper, *Patients First*, issued by the Department of Health and Social Security in December 1979. Administrators in particular have in some cases taken exception to any implications, which the title and tenor of the consultative document might be thought to convey, to the effect that administration has been putting itself before patient care. The object of the document appears, however, to be the wider and more general one of reallocating functions and resources within the health service structure so as to provide the most efficient and effective health care to the consumer, the patient.

In consequence, and following very considerable parliamentary debate, the Health Services Act 1980 was enacted. By the first two sections of this statute the Secretary of State is given power to make certain changes in the structure of the National Health Service if he thinks it desirable to do so. So things are not, as such, changed by the 1980 Health Services Act. It is just that the Secretary of State now has powers, given to him by the statute, to make changes. In particular, the Secretary of State has a power to establish district health authorities. It is to be noted that these authorities are to exist at what we have earlier called a *statutory level*, when that expression was used in contradistinction to *operational level*. But the new district health authorities are to be operational as they always were, as well as having a distinct statutory existence. These new authorities are to replace the area health authorities as constituted under the 1973 reorganisation Act.

A period of change

While, as mentioned earlier, the reorganisation effected by the National Health Service Reorganisation Act 1973 was swift and imposed sudden and considerable administrative burdens which were in the event relatively smoothly discharged, the pace and the nature of change envisaged by the Health Services Act 1980 are different. The machinery by which power is given to a government department, in the figure of the relevant Secretary of State, to effect alterations and changes of emphasis, as well as to make regulations, over a period of time is becoming a familiar device.

The executive power vested in the Secretary of State for Health and Social Services has a number of objectives. These include, principally, the strengthening of health service management arrangements at the local level with greater delegation of responsibility to those in the hospital and the community services; and the simplification of the structure of the Service in England by the removal of the area tier in most of the country with the corresponding statutory establishment of district health authorities. The latter are *statutory* in this context insofar as they are to be created under powers specifically conferred by statute to do so.

Owing to the removal of the area tier of administration and responsibility, consequential changes become necessary. Under the Acts of 1973 and 1977 it was the duty of each area health authority to establish a family practitioner committee for its area. Such is now the duty of the district health authority under the 1980 Act. A certain organisational independence is given to family practitioner committees under the 1980 Act inasmuch as they do not, as some people had wished and strongly argued, have to coincide with each health district of the new structure. While the Royal Commission on the National Health Service, reporting in July 1979, recommended that family practitioner committees should be abolished and their functions assumed by health authorities, the Government decided that the new legislation would not upset the existing system. So the 1980 Act makes it possible for one family practitioner committee, where appropriate, to cover more than one district health authority. Membership, funding and staffing implications of this new arrangement are to be worked out in the course of time by ministerial and administrative direction.

The Royal Commission reported favourably on the very significant and energetic contribution made by the community health councils which were introduced at district level in the multi-tier structure of the reorganised health service following the 1973 Act. The consultative document *Patients First* notes that the new district-based structure will mean that health authority members will in future be less remote from local services that is necessarily the case under the arrangements created in 1973, and concludes that "the need for separate consumer representation is less clear." The Government said that it would welcome views on whether community health councils should be retained when the new district health authority structure has been implemented. An undertaking was subsequently given that they should remain, subject to amendments in their structure.

Regional health authorities have the task, following the legislation of 1980, to initiate and supervise changes in health service structure in the direction of a district-based administration. But Government policy is that the regional authorities should stand back from the actual operational activities of the districts, in other words, keep out of what the newly created district authorities actually do once they have been set up. While, in the long term, government might consider it necessary "to adopt changes in arrangements for exercising the regional role," the regions in the interim (until about April 1982) are seen as capable of providing a vital element of stability to the National Health Service in a time of flux.

Public medicine and private treatment

While the paramount objective of the legislation of 1946 which brought the National Health Service into existence was that health care provision should be based on medical need rather than upon ability to pay, the original legislation nevertheless envisaged the provision of medical services and care on a private basis within the facilities provided by the new Service as well as those services provided privately outside and independent of it. Social and ideological arguments have continued to rage one way and the other, and the Labour Government saw to the enactment of the Health Services Act in 1976 which provided for the running down of private facilities within the national Service. The Health Services Board was established, and its job was to make periodic reports to the Secretary of State as to arrangements which could suitably be made to run down private facilities within the Service.

The new Board expressed difficulties in implementing this policy even as early as its first report in 1977. In particular it said that, in deciding on the phasing out of "pay-beds" and corresponding facilities, one of the most serious difficulties was the lack of information on their use and availability, and on their provision and use in the private health care sector. When a Conservative government was returned to office in 1979 the Secretary of State lost no time in trying to restore a degree of private provision within the national service. The Conservative Secretary of State noted that the Board was still under a statutory duty under the 1976 Act, as consolidated by the National Health Service Act 1977, to continue to consider and to recommend pay-bed closures. But he asked that the Board exercise the discretion permitted to it under the legislation of 1976 and 1977 to "avoid unnecessary difficulty" in view of impending legislation.

That legislation has now come, and the Health Services Act 1980 abolishes the Health Services Board, somewhat inaptly called by some a "quango." The legislation of 1976 and 1977 which had as its object the phasing out of facilities for private treatment within the National Health Service has now given way to a legislative policy which goes in the reverse direction. While the provision of private accommodation and treatment is expressly made subject to the condition that no disadvantage will thereby be presented to non-paying patients in National Health Service facilities, the Secretary of State is authorised to revoke an authorisation for private resident or non-resident provision "only if and to the extent that he is satisfied that sufficient accommodation and facilities for the private practice of medicine and dentistry are otherwise reasonably available (whether privately or at health service hospitals) to meet the reasonable demand for them" in the area served by the hospital in question.

Treatment abroad

On a rather different matter, it may be mentioned that special treatment outside National Health Service facilities can some-times be obtained even at the expense of the State. Providing there are pressing medical reasons, a patient may obtain medical treatment and care in another country within the EEC at the expense of the National Health Service. This provision for health care results from the judgment of the European Court of Justice in the *Pierik* case (1979). The treatment involved must be available under the sickness insurance scheme of the country of treatment.

II

When things go wrong

It was noted in the foregoing section of this chapter that an important role in the maintenance and improvement of personal health care provision within the National Health Service can be played by the community health councils which are established at district level pursuant to powers originally given by the National Health Service Reorganisation Act 1973. The activities of community health councils are broad in scope and are not confined to inquiries which are carried out by them on the basis of individual complaints made to them.

The bringing of complaints is certainly, however, a significant way in which legitimate pressure can be brought to bear on those who provide personal health care and services. When things go badly wrong, and harm or injury is caused to patients, the ordinary law relating to trespass and negligence come into play. These areas of law, and especially the extensive and important laws relating to damages for negligence, are discussed in later chapters of this book. Furthermore, in the next chapter following this there is a brief discussion of the judicial attitude to recent actions against the Secretary of State himself (in his official capacity, of course) in respect of alleged failure to provide sufficient services and resources to avoid long waiting-lists of patients who are often in some pain.

The rest of this chapter is about official investigations and enquiries, of one sort and another.

The Health Service Commissioner

An action for damages is one way, but by no means the only way, of obtaining some sort of satisfaction in response to a complaint. Other ways which can, according to circumstances, be equally acceptable include the receipt of an explanation or an apology or both. We saw earlier that an important role is played at health district level by community health councils, which have the job of investigating and commenting on practices and conditions in their health district.

On a national scale there is a further important source of the redress of grievances. By the National Health Service Reorganisation Act 1973, the same statute which provided for the appointment of the community health councils, provision is also made for the appointment of a Health Service Commissioner whose function it is to investigate and report and make recommendations on complaints about the activities of health authorities and those for whom they are responsible.

The office of Parliamentary Commissioner for Administration, or *Ombudsman* as he is sometimes called, was created by an Act of 1967. His functions are to investigate and report on complaints of maladministration by or on behalf of government departments. Originally there was no provision for the Parliamentary Commissioner to investigate also the actions of health service authorities; but pressure for the appointment of a similar official grew, particularly in the wake of reports of inquiry into conditions and activities in a number of hospitals including certain mental hospitals. The National Health Service Reorganisation Act 1973, as now consolidated in the National Health Service Act 1977, makes provision for the appointment of separate Health Service Commissioners for England and Wales; and the National Health Service (Scotland) Act 1972 provides for the appointment of a Health Service Commissioner for Scotland. Although legally there are three separate commissioners (one each for England, Scotland and Wales), all three offices are held by one and the same person. That person is the Parliamentary Commissioner for Administration himself (who just gets the one salary!). He is assisted by a deputy health service commissioner, being empowered by statute to make such an appointment with the approval of the Minister for the Civil Service.

The Commissioner's jurisdiction

In an organisation as enormous as the National Health Service, caring for many hundreds of thousands of people every day, it is always possible that an individual member of the public may feel that, because of an administrative oversight or mistake, he or she has been less than fairly or properly treated. The Health Service Commissioner's job is to investigate complaints from members of the public who feel that they have suffered injustice or hardship as a result of failure in a service provided by a health authority, or failure by an authority to offer a service which it has a duty to provide, or as a result of maladministration. In the following chapter we shall note the failure of a court action for a declaration as to the complainant's rights and for damages when individuals complained about the failure of a health authority to provide a service which, it was alleged, it had a duty to provide. But the jurisdiction of the Health Service Commissioner has different and broader objectives. Its exercise may therefore result in some satisfaction in cases where an individual court action might result in none save the well-meaning sympathy of a judge.

Before the Commissioner can investigate he must receive a complaint in writing from the aggrieved person, and the complaint must normally reach the Commissioner within one year of the event to which it relates. The Commissioner's investigation will normally be carried out only after the relevant health authority has received the complaint and has had a sufficient opportunity to make its own investigation and reply to the complainant. The Commissioner also investigates complaints which are referred to him by the health authorities themselves.

Limits to jurisdiction and opportunities for change

As a result of the statutory powers vested in him, the Commissioner's chances of investigation are curtailed in a number of instances. Some matters remain outside the jurisdiction of the Commissioner, in particular action which, in his opinion, is taken solely in the exercise of clinical judgment. Furthermore the actions of family doctors, dentists, opticians or pharmacists are also outside the Commissioner's jurisdiction. The actions of the latter are investigable by means of a different procedure, through family practitioner committees (or health boards in Scotland). A complaint is also outside the jurisdiction of the Health Service Commissioner if the complainant could reasonably be expected to pursue the complaint through the courts in the first instance by way of the ordinary judicial process. The Health Service Commissioner has no jurisdiction to investigate staff appointments.

The untutored reader of the statute (now the National Health Service Act 1977) giving these powers in limited and defined form to the Health Service Commissioner could well conclude that the Commissioner's jurisdiction makes him legally impotent in certain areas which many would regard as properly deserving of investigation, inquiry and recommendation. The Commissioner himself is clearly aware of possible opportunities for change in his investigatory powers, as is evidenced by his Annual Report for the year 1979–80 published by the Stationery Office in July 1980.

Under section 115 of the National Health Service Act 1977 the Commissioner may investigate a complaint from someone who claims to have suffered injustice or hardship as a result of alleged failures or maladministration on the part of a health service authority. So before he can accept a complaint for investigation he must, besides being shown evidence of what appears to be a failure in the service, be satisfied on two counts: first, that the person making the complaint is the person who has suffered the injustice (unless, as provided by section 111(2) of the 1977 Act, he is for some reason unable to act for himself); and secondly, that he is provided with apparent evidence that injustice has resulted from the maladministration complained of. In the great majority of the complaints received by the Commissioner, and which he may therefore investigate, these two conditions are met. But in the course of 1979, the Commissioner received one complaint where he considered that an investigation by him would have been in the public interest, but which he was unfortunately obliged to reject because neither of the statutory requirements mentioned above was met.

The complaint arose from the employment by an area health authority of a bogus doctor who operated on a number of patients during the latter part of 1977. Following his discovery and subsequent conviction by the courts, the authority concerned reached the decision that it would be in the best interests of the patients involved not to tell them that their operations had been performed by the "doctor" concerned. This decision led the Patients' Association to refer the case to the Commissioner as a possible instance of maladministration, on the grounds that the patients concerned had a right to be informed of the circumstances surrounding their medical treatment.

After carefully considering the complaint he had to conclude, however, that, as presented to him, it failed to comply with the two provisions of the Act referred to above and that consequently it was outside his present jurisdiction. For while he was in no doubt that the reasons which led the area health authority to decide not to tell the patients concerned were investigable by him, the legislation makes it quite clear that the complainant must have been personally aggrieved by the action taken. He could not conclude that the Patients' Association met this requirement, nor was he given any evidence to indicate that the Association had been asked to refer the complaint on behalf of any of the patients involved in the belief that they had suffered injustice or hardship. As the law stands the only way an investigable complaint about the area health authority's actions could have reached him (other than if by chance one of the patients concerned had become suspicious), was if one of them had suffered hardship and the facts of the case were subsequently revealed to him. The Commissioner could take no action to initiate an investigation into the area health authority's action prior to being asked to do so by one of the individuals involved — despite the fact that the area health authority's action had the effect of securing that the people who were affected by it remained ignorant of their involvement. Whether or not that action was sound the Commissioner was of course not in a position to determine. The only step he could, and did, take was to obtain an assurance that the patients involved had subsequently been seen by medically qualified staff of the authority.

As a result of this situation, described in detail in the Health Service Commissioner's Annual Report for the year 1979–80, he was moved to comment thus:

> "The circumstances of this case highlight the fact that I can only investigate cases where there is prima facie evidence of injustice to a named individual. This limitation on my

jurisdiction, which appears to conflict with the public interest, has caused me some concern and I believe it is one which deserves to be examined closely and critically, with a view to considering whether I should be empowered to initiate investigations where in my discretion I think that an investigation would be in the public interest, and to report my findings to Parliament."

Clinical judgment

The fact that the relevant legislation does not empower the Commissioner to investigate matters which appear to consist in the exercise of clinical judgment has also received some recent attention. In March 1979 Mr. Jack Ashley, Labour M.P. for Stoke-on-Trent South, introduced a Bill under the "ten-minute rule" which had the effect of drawing Parliamentary and public attention to what he saw as this gap in the Commissioner's jurisdiction.

Such complaints are now dealt with through health authorities. The British Medical Association is proposing a modified form of procedure. But an association spokesman said in February 1980 it was opposed to the ombudsman being given powers to judge a doctor's clinical judgment. "It would create a situation in which the doctor would be constantly looking at his decisions in the light of whether they could be defended to an external authority. This would be impracticable and not be in the interests of good medicine."

The matter has now received detailed comment from the Health Service Commissioner himself in his 1979–80 Report:

"The issue whether complaints arising from the exercise of clinical judgment should be within my jurisdiction—as recommended in the Report of the Select Committee on the Independent Review of Hospital Complaints in the National Health Service (1978) is now being considered further by the Secretaries of State, following the submission to them of alternative proposals by the Joint Consultants Committee.

While I do not consider it is for me to comment at this stage on the various proposals which have now been made, the subject itself is one which raises a number of complex questions and the implications for my office are potentially far-reaching. I am particularly concerned about the difficulties which appear to me to be inherent in a parallel jurisdiction between my office and the courts with respect to medical negligence.

There is an obvious danger that if my jurisdiction were to be extended to include clinical judgment then a person dissatisfied with some aspect of the medical treatment he has received might take advantage of my office to obtain a 'free' investigation into the merits of a possible case against a Health Authority. If I issue a report in his favour, this report might then be used as the basis for obtaining legal aid for a subsequent action and generally as a means of bringing pressure to bear. While I would see this, in itself, as an abuse, unintended by Parliament, of the service I provide, there is the further—and, in my view, more fundamental—danger that if such an action were subsequently decided against the plaintiff, perhaps on different evidence, the standing of my reports, and hence of my office as a whole, might be diminished. Conversely, if the courts decided for the plaintiff, there might be the equally undesirable suspicion that my report had somehow prejudiced the trial against the Health Service and its employees. And, last, but not least, the co-operation and frankness which I enjoy in my investigations might be seriously lessened if NHS staff thought that my reports might somehow be used to found legal actions against them.

The solution, which has been considerably canvassed elsewhere, might be to offer aggrieved persons a statutory choice: to complain to me, or to take legal action—but not both. I believe this would be acceptable to the great majority of people, since in many of the cases I see the aggrieved person is genuinely not wanting money but a simple, factual explanation of some unexpected death or complication and an assurance that an attempt will be made to prevent a recurrence.

Even if the other serious problems associated with the proposal to extend my jurisdiction to include actions stemming solely from clinical judgment were to be solved, I would regard it as essential to provide also for the matters raised in the preceding paragraphs. And I would still wish to retain, in matters of clinical judgment, my discretion not to investigate a case if, in all the circumstances, I did not think it desirable or useful to do so.''

While the issue of the absence of jurisdiction to intervene in matters bearing on, or directly affected by, the exercise of clinical judgment is still unresolved at the time of going to press, no change in the relevant law having yet been made, it can now conveniently be briefly demonstrated that the powers in respect of communication and transfer of information effectively give considerable strength to the Health Service Commissioner's elbow. While he cannot, as yet, go through the door marked "clinical judgment" he can nevertheless walk right up to it and knock on it hard.

Communication problems

The reports of the Commissioner, laid before Parliament and addressed to the Secretary of State for Social Services, are given very serious consideration. The influence of the reports on systems and the manner of providing for personal health care and incidental and necessary information is substantial and adds a new dimension to the consumer view of personal health services in the national system.

A large proportion of recently investigated complaints resolve themselves ultimately into difficulties caused by deficient, if any, information given to patients or relatives, and by the lack of communication between staff, patients and relatives. Such difficulties are inherently capable of producing annoyance and distress, and consequently complaints. But information and communication problems can also lead to errors or mishaps in the very medical treatment given to patients in consequence.

One complaint which was recently investigated by the Health Service Commissioner resulted from an allegation that deficient and inadequate information had been given within a hospital with the result that a patient died after having been prematurely discharged from the accident and emergency department. The Commissioner in his report was most careful to avoid adverse comment on the exercise of clinical judgment. But nevertheless a very strong recommendation was made in respect of the available means of improvement of communication of vital information in order that such a mishap might be avoided in future.

The legal problems which are apt to result from difficulties or obstacles in communication are by no means confined to situations such as the one just discussed. In a later chapter we shall examine the so-called doctrine of "informed consent" to medical and surgical treatment. Important legal consequences follow from whether or not a patient can be said to have fully and knowledgeably consented to a medical or surgical procedure, for such procedures without such consent may be unlawful and lead to the patient's being able to bring an action for damages against the doctor and the health authority concerned. While, again, it is not the function of the Health Service Commissioner to investigate a complaint of this nature insofar as it could reasonably be expected to lead to judicial proceedings, it is fully within the Commissioner's jurisdiction to comment on and make recommendations about the methods by which information about medical or surgical procedures is communicated to patients. This question appears to concern systems and organisation rather than the clinical judgment which he cannot examine.

Language and communication

A matter of some importance in the day-to-day operation of health services in this country is the adequacy of the command of the English language on the part of the many overseas staff who perform such a valuable role in the British health services. While not being finally determined by it, all questions of communication are basically dependent on the adequate and comprehensible use of language. Health service legislation has responded to concern recently expressed in regard to language difficulties occasionally found in health service staff in a variety of occupations, and it is convenient to mention here the relevant legal provisions as to linguistic proficiency in the medical and nursing professions.

In the case of doctors, section 29(1) of the Medical Act 1978 makes a satisfactory command of the English language a condition for registration. It reads: "An applicant for registration shall not be entitled to be so registered unless he satisfies the Registrar [of the General Medical Council] that he has the necessary knowledge of English, that is, the knowledge which, in the interest of himself and his patients, is necessary for the practice of medicine in the United Kingdom; and for the purposes of this subsection the General Council may provide facilities for testing the knowledge of English of such applicants." Unlike other cases of refusal of registration there is no appeal against refusal on grounds of lack of linguistic proficiency, but there is nothing to prevent an applicant for registration from applying again in the course of time when command of the English language has improved.

Exceptions for EEC doctors

In September 1980 an important prospective change was announced by the Department of Health in respect of more favourable treatment for EEC doctors. Regulations relating to language requirements in the case of other foreign and Commonwealth doctors remain, remarkably, unchanged (or perhaps the remarkable thing is the EEC exemption).

Doctors coming to Britain from countries in the EEC will no longer have to take a language test before being granted full registration.

The decision has been forced upon the Government by the European Commission, which formally notified it in 1979 that in its view, the language tests applied to doctors from community countries were contrary to community law.

The Department of Health and Social Security said in September 1980: "If the commission had referred the matter to the European Court, the ruling of the court would have had legal force in the United Kingdom."

Doctors from the EEC applying to work in the National Health Service will have to satisfy the health service authorities, however, that they have the necessary knowledge of English for the work they will have to do.

The Department of Health emphasized that the numbers coming from Europe were relatively small. Only 380 have been given registration by the General Medical Council since the tests were introduced in June 1977.

The language tests for the larger number of doctors coming from the Indian subcontinent and elsewhere will continue. In 1979, limited registration was granted for the first time to about 1,400 overseas doctors from outside the EEC and full registration to another 1,814.

The Department considers that by announcing that it is going to change the requirements before being made to do so by the European Court, it will give health authorities time to introduce effective alternative arrangements to replace the registration-linked requirements.

The British Medical Association said:

> "The BMA has made it clear that it thinks the discontinuance of the present arrangements for language tests for EEC doctors is regrettable.
>
> We had been told that the Government might be forced to abandon language testing and have already asked the Government to ensure that when this happens there should be adequate safeguards for the public."

A substantial number of the 400,000 nurses in the health service are from overseas, and English may sometimes be a problem. The Nurses, Midwives and Health Visitors Act 1979 creates a register of nurses, midwives and health visitors which replaces earlier registers. Section 11(4) gives the Central Council for Nursing, Midwifery and Health Visiting the power to make rules which are reminiscent of the rules for medical practitioners but which take a rather different form. The rules may either make it a condition of a nurse, midwife or health visitor's being registered that he or she "has the necessary knowledge of English," or may require such a person to have that knowledge within a period to be specified by the rules, failing which registration will lapse at the end of the period. The Act provides for linguistic facility for reasons stressed in the parliamentary debates which preceded its enactment that, despite the excellent qualifications which overseas nurses and allied professions bring to the British health service, it is a fact of life that the ill and the dying may have delicate feelings to impart, and if the nurse cannot understand them or respond suitably in the patient's language, the patient may suffer as a consequence.

Investigations and inquiries

It has been noted that a health authority should be given a reasonable opportunity to make its own investigations into complaints and to take appropriate action. Failing such satisfactory action a member of the public affected by failure to offer or to provide services, or by maladministration, may make a formal complaint to the Health Service Commissioner whose function is to investigate and to recommend action, if appropriate. A recurrent feature of reports of investigations into complaints which the Health Service Commissioner has found to be justified is the inadequacy of the manner in which the patient's or other's complaint has been handled by the relevant health authority. So procedures for the making of informal investigations at health authority level are important.

In HM(66)15, a memorandum about procedures for informal investigations, the then Ministry of Health said: "Two general principles apply. First, all complaints should be dealt with as promptly as the circumstances require. Secondly, not only should complaints be investigated, but it should be made evident to complainants that their complaints have been fully and fairly considered." Complaints by word of mouth which cannot be satisfactorily dealt with right away should be reported to a senior member of staff in the department to which they relate, who should make a brief note of the complaint and of the circumstances. If any appropriate action which is then proposed should not be satisfactory to the complainant he should be invited to take the complaint to a higher level and to put it in writing. Complaints which are made originally in writing should be seen by a senior administrator who should then consult with the head of the department which is concerned by the complaint as to appropriate action. Any complaint which cannot properly and satisfactorily be dealt with in any of these ways should be referred to the appropriate health authority.

In the small number of cases which cannot be satisfactorily dealt with even in this way the investigation should be referred for independent enquiry. Action to refer such serious cases should be taken by a board of governors or regional health authority concerned on a reference from the appropriate subordinate authority. The general rule should be that an independent lawyer or other suitable person from outside the health services should conduct the enquiry, or preside over a small committee set up for the purpose. The membership of such a committee or board of inquiry should be independent of the authority concerned and should include a person or persons competent to advise on any professional or technical matters. The complainant and any persons who are the subject of the complaint should have an opportunity of being present throughout the hearing, and of cross-examining witnesses. Both sides involved in the issue should be allowed to make their own arrangements for legal representation if they so wish.

Furthermore, under section 84 of the National Health Service Act 1977 the Secretary of State for Social Services may cause a formal inquiry to be held in any case in which he considers this to be an advisable step and which concerns any matter arising in connection with the powers, duties and organisation provided for in the 1977 Act.

Chapter 2

HEALTH SERVICES LAW

I

Health services law

In a sense, there is no such specific area of law as "health services law." The laws and regulations which govern the great varieties of activity in the operation of health services relate to widely different objectives. The rules governing negligence, the law of wills, employment law, the regulations governing the control of drugs, and the law permitting the detention of mental patients, are just some of the laws which affect widely varying activities within health services. There are, it is true, statutes which create and govern the general operation of the National Health Service. There are other statutes, other legislation, governing specific areas such as drugs and medicines control, the treatment and detention of the mentally disordered, and the regulation of professions active in health services. But when we add to such specific laws and regulations the legal rules affecting such areas as negligence, professional confidence, consent to treatment, the sanctity of human life, we have a great mass of law which affects the population at large and which is not confined in its effect to specific activities within the National Health Service.

Nevertheless, since our concern is with health services law, and since this country enjoys a National Health Service, the rules and regulations affecting the national health services system must clearly be objects of our attention. The creation of a national health service was motivated by a desire to provide better, and cheaper, facilities for the acutely and chronically sick. An important though secondary objective was to provide conditions of work and treatment which enabled employees, of a wide variety of responsibilities, to function in an environment which is conducive to good and efficient treatment of the sick, infirm and disordered. So our concern will have to be wider than with rules and regulations affecting patients of health services.

Our attention must also be directed to areas of regulation such as employment conditions and the health and safety of health service employees. The law relating to health services therefore relates to the claims and expectations not only of the recipients of treatment and care but also of those whose job it is to provide those services.

Sources of health services law

Statutes have been mentioned. When a piece of legislation, or statute, is enacted by Parliament a new body of rights, duties, powers or liabilities is apt to come into existence. The Parliament of this country is the highest law-making body of the legal system. Any decision of a court of law which conflicts with what Parliament has clearly laid down must bow to greater authority and be considered to have been superseded by the Act of Parliament. The trouble is that there are many occasions on which the provisions of an Act of Parliament are less than abundantly clear. Even if, as is very often the case, complete clarity (except for the jargon!) is achieved, the most that legislation can normally hope to do is to create a general framework of rights, duties, powers and liabilities which can then be supplemented by rules and regulations much more specific to particular situations and particular problems. There are two main ways in which this can be done. One is by the activities of the courts, who give judicial decisions on the law involved in the particular cases which come before them. The other is by what is often called "secondary," or subordinate, legislation. An Act of Parliament is the highest source of law in our system. And since Parliament is the supreme legislative, or lawmaking, body in our legal system, it has the power to give others the authority to make laws and regulations. The most frequent example of the exercise of this important power is the authorisation of government departments to fill out the general framework of the statute with specific rules and regulations in particular areas of activity specifically envisaged by the overall general legislation. Such powers as are given the Secretary of State for Social Services or to the Minister of Health will be of special concern to us.

Courts and the law

A different but no less important way of filling out the general framework of a statute with particularities is by way of so-called "judicial interpretation" of statutes. It can happen that a statutory provision is less than clear; or that, even if it appears at first sight clear, its application to a particular set of circumstances is less than completely evident. So a case may come before a court of law which has as its purpose the clarification, for the particular set of circumstances in issue, of the terms and provisions of the legislation. This can happen also in the case of the so-called "secondary," or subordinate, legislation just mentioned.

But the principal lawmaking activities of the courts relate to those many and wide areas of law which have not been heavily influenced, if at all, by Parliamentary legislative intervention. The decisions of courts of law in series of cases build up precedents, which in some circumstances other courts must follow in their decisions on problems presented in later cases. One most important topic, and one which has been much in the news lately, is that of negligence and especially "medical negligence." This is an area of the law which legislation from Parliament has hardly touched, so that the courts have by and large had their way in determining what sort of conduct it is which will amount to negligence in law, and what sort of conduct will not. A principal distinction between legislation and judicial decisions as sources of law is that legislation is generally prospective in effect—that is, it provides a general framework within which future activities may be regulated; while judicial decisions, the decisions given by courts of law to determine individual disputes, are by nature particular. They relate specifically to the particular problems thrown up by the circumstances and allegations and claims in the particular case in issue. While courts and judges do not shrink from making general pronouncements on law and, in a more veiled form, on policy which other courts may keep in mind in later cases, their principal function is to determine (that is, to put a determinate end to) the particular dispute or issue which has been presented to them. Lawyers sometimes speak of the "solution" to a dispute or issue. The description "determination" is preferred here since the person who loses the dispute, and usually some money in the process, can only in a strained sense be said to view the adverse outcome as a solution. His problems may only just have started!

Circulars and associated literature

A variety of guides, instructions, memoranda, policy statements and other similar literature issues in some profusion from government departments, in our field particularly from the Department of Health and Social Security. This form of guidance is in yet a different form from those which have been mentioned, and it has yet a different status from the sources of regulation so far considered. This literature is of considerable importance at the operational level to all health service staff employed in administration and the implementation of policies, for it frequently details considerations and instructions which are vital to the everyday running of health services.

Some such literature summarises recent legislation, including secondary legislation such as statutory instruments, and occasional comment is made on judicial decisions which lead to the necessity of administrative changes. An example to be met in a later chapter concerns the arrangements which should now be made in respect of voting facilities for long-stay patients in mental hospitals who are no longer considered to be mentally disordered but who now, owing to a variety of circumstances, have nowhere else to go. Other such literature may summarise procedures to be adopted and action to be taken in specific problem areas such, for instance, as the treatment and handling of violent hospital patients, or the care and management of medicines and drugs.

These circulars and other such literature are not "law" in the sense in which most lawyers would use the term. Nevertheless they are highly important guides to conduct and practice within a wide variety of health service activities. Reference will therefore usefully be made from time to time to this type of literature when we come to consider the points at which principle and practice meet, as they ultimately must do.

The following extract from a circular of December 1975, reference HSC(IS)219, is instructive as to the principal distinction, in the classification of this literature, between Health Circulars (HCs) and Health Notices (HNs):

"*Health Circulars* will be the formal means of conveying instructions, guidance, or information to health authorities (and, where appropriate, to local authorities on a 'for information' basis). The general aim is that communications covering policy matters or giving long term guidance, and specifically those intended for circulation to organisations outside the NHS, will be issued as Health Circulars, whilst matters of an ephemeral nature will normally be appropriate to Health Notices.

Health Notices will provide an informal means of communicating with health authorities, usually on matters of a short-term or routine nature; they will not normally be distributed outside the NHS. A main purpose of Health Notices will be to permit the speedy issue of guidance or information, *e.g.* statistical or costing returns, from all health authorities or all of one type or category of authority. The scale of distribution will be considerably lower than that for Health Circulars. They will not be used to cancel or modify advice issued in a Health Circular."

Rights and duties in health services

Enough has now been said about the sources from which "health services law" is to be drawn, and of the variety of rules and regulations which affect health service activities, for us to be aware that these laws confer rights on some people, impose duties on others, give certain people or authorities powers and render others subject to certain liabilities. These rights, duties, powers and liabilities now require more attention. It is important to have some idea of their nature and their variety in order properly to appreciate issues in which their specific application is to be examined. Let us briefly consider some of these rights, duties, powers and liabilities as they occur in specific areas of health service activity to be considered in more detail at a later stage. In so doing, let us be well aware that the individual terms "right," "duty," "power," "liability" do not always have a constant meaning in each and every context in which they are employed. The variation in meaning is particularly evident in the case of "right" and is also apparent in relation to "duty."

Varieties of rights and duties

The Minister has a duty under the legislation creating and defining the structure of the National Health Service to provide health services and facilities. A surgeon is under a duty to take reasonable care to see that the patient who is undergoing surgery is not harmed as a result of carelessness. Medical practitioners are under a duty to preserve the confidentiality of information given and received in the process of patients' treatment. Social workers and hospital staff are under a duty to ensure that the requisite procedures have been followed and properly observed if a mentally disordered person is to be lawfully detained against his will. A nurse has a duty to be kind and courteous to a patient.

All these are instances of "duty." But all are, legally speaking, different. The fact that we conveniently use one and the same word, namely "duty," to describe all these varied circumstances must not mislead us into thinking that it always means the same thing, or that exactly the same consequences flow from a breach of each of these duties. Not so. Let us examine these different instances further, to see why.

Duties and the provision of health services

The duty of the Minister, the details of which we shall examine shortly, is to provide health services and the premises, staff and facilities requisite to the provision of services. What if a patient is mistreated, or not treated at all, or has to wait for a very long period before receiving treatment, when perhaps in acute or recurrent pain? What, if anything, can such a person actually do about the so-called "duty"? If a surgeon or other practitioner in health services treats a patient in receipt of treatment with want of proper care, he may be in breach of a duty of care which the law says he owes to the patient. Detailed discussion of this duty of care, and of the law of negligence which includes this duty as a principal ingredient, comes later. Suffice it to say at this stage that a proven breach of an established "duty of care" may give rise to an action for damages, for compensation, by the patient against the person whose conduct is the subject of the complaint.

Does this mean that, by the same token, a patient who goes without treatment for a long time can bring an action for damages against the Minister, or at least against his Department and thus obtain monetary damages for the pain, suffering, anguish and anxiety which the prolonged wait has caused? We do not have to guess at the answer, for a case has recently come before the courts in which this complaint was the very one in issue. The outcome, as we shall see in more detail shortly, was that the individual patient has no such right of action as he would have against a person or an institution whose *negligent* conduct had caused him suffering or harm, or a prolongation of these. Perhaps that might seem unjust, for the pain and suffering is just as much a problem for the patient in both cases. The result of the court case, the judicial decision, is perhaps not surprising, however. For the usual reason for a prolonged wait is an insufficiency of facilities, such as hospital beds or specialised equipment; and the reason for an insufficiency of facilities is an insufficiency of resources. In other words, there are many individuals who suffer, or suffer further, because there just is not enough money to extend treatment or more speedy treatment to their particular case. Ironically, if every such patient had a right of action against the Minister, or his Department, with a view to obtaining monetary compensation, there would be still less money in the coffers for the provision of health services and facilities. So the result may not seem so unjust after all.

The case of actual mistreatment of a patient, say by a wrongful negligent or malicious act, is different. In such an instance the health service employee who did the wrongful act which produced the harm, suffering or damage may bring liability on the shoulders not only of himself but also upon those of his employing authority. Such cases are brought against area (or, now, district) health authorities, in the case of wrongs done by their employees. Again, more of this later, under the heading of what is called "vicarious liability."

Legal and ethical duties

What about the duty of a medical practitioner, of whatever variety, to maintain secrecy and confidence in relation to the information which has been received from and about a patient in care. The efficacy of treatment by, for example, a general practitioner, is often largely dependent on the open and frank nature of the discussion between doctor and patient, and on the fullness and sufficiency of the recorded information to which the doctor has recourse in considering the best form of treatment for the patient. In what does the "duty" to maintain secrecy and confidentiality consist? Can a person whose confidences are wrongly divulged get damages, or any other form of legal remedy? These are questions we shall have to examine more specifically in due course. But we can notice here that the "rights" of patients in respect of the maintenance of professional confidence, and the accompanying "duties" of practitioners and other health services staff who come by confidential information, are much more clearly moral or ethical rights and duties than they are legal ones. The wronged individual may have to be satisfied with a complaint to the appropriate disciplinary body, in the case of general medical practitioners the General Medical Council, rather than a personal action for damages in the courts.

The duties of the nursing profession to maintain a kind and courteous attitude to patients can hardly be said to be legal duties, except in extreme and unthinkable cases in which unkindness so great as to be positively cruel might cause or exacerbate actual physical suffering or harm. Within the nursing profession such duties can be regarded as ethical duties appropriate and requisite to the profession of nursing. From the patient's point of view these duties in respect of nursing behaviour could be regarded as social or personal duties, owed by the givers of medical care and treatment to recipients who occupy what sociologists might call a "sick role" in society.

Duties and powers

Finally, by way of example, what about the duties which the law provides in relation to the involuntary detention of mentally disordered patients? As we shall see when the law relating to the treatment of mental disorder is examined in more detail, no one is under a legal duty to detain mentally disordered persons against their will, save in specific cases such as in the exercise of police powers or in response to the order of a court of law, say, in the case of a mentally disordered offender against the criminal law. But in order validly and properly, indeed legally, to exercise the powers which are given to certain people such as doctors, psychiatrists, social workers and certain relatives, certain obligations or duties must be borne in mind. There may not, in most such cases, be a duty to exercise the power. But if the power is exercised, it must be exercised properly, with reasonable care and with proper and accurate regard to legal requirements. Here, then, is yet another different instance in which "duty" is used to described the relevant legal requirement.

II

Standards of care

The standards of care which are rightfully expected of all those engaged in the provision of personal health services are high. Those who treat and care for patients in a variety of direct and indirect ways, aspire to standards of care and efficiency which should be applauded by those who receive it. It is in this sense that both patients and employing authorities may expect high personal and professional standards in the supply of health care and services.

When the law enters the arena some different considerations come into play, or at least in some important areas of the law's proper ambit. We shall see in relation to the law of negligence that recurrent expressions include principally "duty of care" and "standard of care." Does this mean that any person, or body or authority, who does not at all times show proof of a desire to aspire to the highest personal and professional standards can be sued in negligence? Certainly not. For the law in its application to disputes between persons or bodies is not concerned to penalise an omission to aspire to the highest standards but rather to award compensation to those who suffer as a result of another's failure to keep above a certain minimum level of care and conduct. It is true that those minima can be demanding, and properly so. For a surgeon is expected to take care not to fall below a certain basic standard of care which is accepted and approved in relation to the surgeon's profession generally, and of which the courts and judges also approve.

So, while doing one's incompetent best is not enough to avoid a finding of negligence, care not to fall below a certain minimum required standard of conduct and efficiency is all the *law* requires of people who in fact spend most if not all their lives aspiring to standards greatly in excess of the minimum. This, at least, is the position in civil actions for damages on account of negligently caused harm, a duty being owed to other private individuals to measure up to a certain standard of care. What of the standards expected by the public in relation to duties and standards which are laid down, as a result of the deliberations of Parliament, in National Health Service and associated legislation? The standards in issue here are those expected by the public, including the private individuals who make up the public as a whole; and they are expected from health authorities, including in that generic title the Secretary of State for Health and Social Services.

Standards and the consumer view

Consumer representation, in the form of community health councils established in the reorganisation effected by the 1973 Act, affords some kind of outlet for, amongst other things, the kind of complaints which patients may make about their treatment or accommodation, or both. It was observed earlier that the councils will continue in existence, though with an amended form and membership, once the reorganisation envisaged by the 1980 Health Services Act comes to be implemented. Councils can be said to provide individual representation, though on a public scale.

The opportunities for individual complaint are threefold. First, a patient or his representative may make a complaint direct to a hospital or health authority, and maybe additionally to the person or group whose conduct or care is the subject of the complaint. Second, legal action may be commenced against individuals, against health authorities or against the Secretary of State for Health and Social Services, and sometimes all of them together as joint defendants. Third, as we have seen, complaint may be made to the Health Service Commissioner, whose office was created by the National Health Service Reorganisation Act 1973.

We have mentioned the standards required if a finding of negligence is to be avoided. Negligence, including what is often referred to as medical negligence, is discussed in detail in Chapter 6. Complaints to health authorities and other employers as being responsible for some of the wrongful actions of their employees are examined in Chapter 4. Duties and standards in relation to the health and safety of employees at work will be discussed in Chapter 5. What we may now do is to examine the duties and standards which have been made the responsibility of the Secretary of State under legislation specifically concerned with the National Health Service, the most recent legislation in this regard being the National Health Service Act 1977.

The duty of the Secretary of State

It is one thing to have a complaint; it can be quite another thing to know how best to make the complaint, and the channels through which to direct it. Methods of complaint to a government minister include lobbying or petitioning and getting Members of Parliament to table questions for the minister or to put them in debate or at question-time. But sometimes people adopt a much more direct course than that: they sue. Sometimes they are successful in their action, and sometimes they do not get very far at all. What, then is the duty of the Secretary of State in relation to National Health Service provision, such that people might have cause for individual complaint?

The duties of the Secretary of State in relation to National Health Service provision generally are laid down in the first three sections of the National Health Service Act 1977. Section 1, re-enacting the 1973 Act on this point, provides that it is the duty of the Secretary of State to continue the provision in England and Wales (there is separate legislation for Scotland and Northern

Ireland) of a comprehensive health service designed to secure improvement in the physical and mental health of the people of those countries, and in the prevention, diagnosis and treatment of illness; and for these purposes to provide or secure the effective provision of health services. Such services are expressed by section 1 to be free of charge except so far as the law otherwise provides. A principal exception to the free nature of the health service, being in general free at point of use, is the charge made in respect of medical, dental and ophthalmic prescriptions.

By section 2 the power is given to the Secretary of State to provide such services as he considers appropriate for the purpose of discharging his duties, and also to do anything else which is calculated to facilitate, or to be conducive or incidental to, the discharge of his duties. It has been indicated earlier that very important differences exist between duties and powers. The performance of a duty may be compelled, or breaches of it sanctioned, by means of the law. On the other hand a power may be exercised but is not normally the subject of compulsion. Powers have to be exercised reasonably and with care, but subject to those broad basic constraints the power-holder normally possesses a considerable discretion as to precisely how the power is to be exercised.

Furthermore, according to section 3 of the 1977 Act it is the Secretary of State's duty to provide throughout England and Wales, to such extent as he considers necessary to meet all *reasonable* requirements, hospital accommodation; other accommodation for the purpose of any service provided under the 1977 Act; medical, dental, nursing and ambulance services; such other facilities for the care of expectant and nursing mothers and young children as he considers appropriate as part of the health service; such facilities for the prevention of illness, the care of persons suffering from illness and the after-care of persons who have suffered from illness as he considers are appropriate as part of the health service; and such other services as are required for the diagnosis and treatment of illness.

What is to be done if a patient, or other person, is in some way dissatisfied with the personal health services which have been provided, or dissatisfied by the fact that such services have not been provided? What is the nature of these duties which are imposed by legislation on the Secretary of State? Can they be enforced, and can an individual patient or group of patients expect any degree of success in legal proceedings instituted against the Secretary of State for failure to provide services of a satisfactory standard, or indeed at all? A recent test case is instructive.

A test case

On January 15, 1979, four patients commenced legal proceedings against Mr. David Ennals, the then Secretary of State for Social Services, alleging that he had failed in his duty to provide an efficient and comprehensive Health Service. In the case of *R.* v. *Secretary of State for Social Services, ex p. Hincks* (1979), the people making the complaint were orthopaedic patients at a hospital in Birmingham who had waited for treatment for periods longer than was medically advisable. The protracted wait was caused by a shortage of facilities which arose, in part, from a decision not to build a new block on the hospital on grounds of cost. They brought a complaint against the Secretary of State, the regional health authority and the area health authority and applied for declarations that these were in breach of their duty under section 1 of the National Health Service Act 1977, and of the duty under section 3 to provide the accommodation, facilities and services appropriate to the health care which it is the authorities' obligation to provide.

The objectives of this action were threefold: first, to ask the judge to rule whether patients had a legal right to bring such proceedings; second, and if so, that a declaration be made by the court that the named authorities had failed in their statutory duty; and thirdly, if the authorities had so failed, to obtain an order to compel them to perform their duties, and to obtain an award of damages against the Secretary of State and the authorities in respect of the pain and suffering caused by the long wait, the orthopaedic patients having suffered considerably during the time complained of.

The four patients failed in their objectives. While the judge, Mr. Justice Wien, said in giving his decision on the case that he sympathised with the pain and distress which the patients had experienced, he continued: "I have come to the conclusion that it is impossible to pinpoint anywhere a breach of statutory duty on the part of the Secretary of State . . . . It all turns on the question of financial resources. If the money is not there then the services cannot be met in one particular place." He said that it was for Parliament to decide how much money should be allowed to the National Health Service, and for the Minister (or Secretary of State) to decide how much should go to the regions and health authority areas. The Act says that the Secretary of State's duty is to provide services in respect of his statutory health care obligations "to such extent as he considers necessary," and the judge pointed out that this formula gives the Secretary of State a clear discretion as to how financial resources are to be used.

The court could only interfere if the Secretary of State had acted so as to frustrate the policy of the Act, or as no reasonable minister could have acted. No such breach had been shown in the present case. Nor, even if such a breach of the statutory obligations had been proved, does the Act give the right to sue for damages in respect of pain and suffering experienced by individual patients. So here was an example of a duty which certainly exists and which represents an obligation of immense social importance. But owing to the court's attitude to this duty, its nature must be distinguished from that of the duty of care which is owed as between individuals and the breach of which, by lack of proper care, is a vital step on the way to a remedy by way of monetary damages.

The Court of Appeal's view

An appeal from this decision was taken to the Court of Appeal (Civil Division) in April 1980, but again the plaintiffs fell at the first fence in that no right of action was held to exist on the part of an individual aggrieved patient to sue for a declaration and damages in respect of protracted pain and suffering alleged to have been caused as a direct result of a failure to provide fuller services within the Health Service. As frequently happens in grey areas of legal regulation the case turned in part on the Court's construction of the word "reasonable" in section 3 of the 1977 Act.

It will be recalled that section 3 imposes a duty on the Secretary of State to provide facilities and services "to such extent as he considers necessary to meet all reasonable requirements" of patients seeking National Health Service treatment. Lord Denning, the Master of the Rolls and senior judge of the Court of Appeal, was content to say that the Minister could be considered to have failed in his statutory duty only if his exercise of discretion was so thoroughly unreasonable that no reasonable Minister could have reached it. However, a more convincing reason was given by Lord Justice Bridge, himself once the senior Treasury Counsel and thus highly cognisant of the workings of governmental finance.

It had been argued on behalf of the four patients that nothing in the statutory definition of the Secretary of State's duty to provide facilities and services mentioned any constraint on the limits of this duty based on the requirements of longer-term government financial planning; and that, if the Secretary of State's duty had been intended to be so limited, the statute would have expressly included such a proviso. Lord Justice Bridge rejected this argument, which he admitted was an attractive one, saying that it went too far. If no limits in respect of longer-term financial planning were to be read into public statutory duties such as this one we should be faced with the economics of a bottomless (or at least ever-deepening) pit. The argument put forward on the patients' behalf is even more difficult to accept as a realistic claim when it is realised that the further the medical and technological advances go in the direction of an even more comprehensive patient care, the greater would be the financial burden placed on the Secretary of State if he were to avoid a dereliction of his statutory duty under the National Health Service Act.

As a postscript to this case it is interesting to note that Lord Justice Bridge asked during the course of counsel's argument: "What is the purpose of this litigation other than to get publicity and to vent a grievance?" Counsel replied: "It is a very serious matter. It affects every citizen of this country." So it does, and the litigation will have served a useful purpose even if it has only shed light on the overriding economic considerations which frequently conclude arguments as to the nature of public duties and public standards of care.

III

Liability and status in the National Health Service

We have seen that other varying duties exist in addition to enforceable legal duties. It has also been noted that the existence of a legal duty does not always lead to the same consequences in all cases. English law has always relied much more heavily on available remedies than on general declarations of rights. The issue, discussed in the foregoing section, which recently went to the Court of Appeal for decision as to the nature and ambit of the Secretary of State's duties under National Health Service legislation was essentially an issue about remedies. The plaintiffs were unlucky: they did not get the form of remedy which they sought, despite the publicity which the legal action engendered. The result was possibly a fair compromise in the event, the proceedings not having been pursued entirely in vain.

Had the Secretary of State negligently driven his motor car

into one of the plaintiffs while both were on their way to the court
(the Secretary of State was in fact *represented* in the action),
there is no question but that he would have acted in breach of a
duty of care which he owes to pedestrians and other roadusers,
and that he would have been liable (this time personally) in
damages to the person injured. This simple if unlikely example is
enough to show that the law is concerned not with the confronta-
tion of persons or personalities but with the operation and
balancing of a variety of interests in the community which
achieve reality through the interests and status of particular
persons or bodies.

It comes as no surprise to learn that an operation as enormous
as the National Health Service spans a variety of interests and
incidents of legal status. In this section we can conveniently note
some examples of this variety of responsibilities, capacities and
legal liabilities by way of preface to further and more detailed
treatment in the immediately ensuing chapters. The law is a
means to an end, and not an end in itself. It has no independent
existence but is a part of the social regulation of a community,
serving its needs for better or for worse. The pattern of liability
and status which will now be outlined is simply the manner in
which English law has chosen, by statutes and judicial decisions
to effect that regulation to date. There is nothing magic about it,
nor is any of the legal position unchangeable.

The constitutional position

It is convenient at this point to refer to the constitutional position of health authorities within the National Health Service.
The legal status of bodies which provide personal health services
outside the National Health Service is no different from any
other body, and the legal status of those who are employed by
them no different in general from any other persons, save that in
both instances there may be statutes imposing special duties or
special prohibitions on particular bodies or persons engaged in a
particular pursuit which it is the object of the legislation to
regulate. But that is something which can happen to any of us
ordinary folk!

The constitutional position of National Health Service
authorities was in issue in the case of *Pfizer Ltd.* v. *Ministry of
Health* (1965). The facts were that Pfizer owned a patent grant-
ing them the sole right to make and use the drug tetracycline. In
1961 the then Ministry of Health invited tenders for the supply of
the drug in National Health Service hospitals. The successful

tenderer, Fraser Chemicals Ltd., imported the drug from Italy where it could be bought at far lower prices than here. Its use here without a licence from Pfizer would have been an infringement of their patent rights. However, under the Patents Act 1949, any government department might use any patented invention *for the service of the Crown*, subject to a payment to be agreed with the patentee or, in default of agreement, a payment to be determined by a court of law.

The Ministry authorised the use of the drug in National Health Service hospitals. Pfizer argued that this was not a use *for the service of the Crown* and that therefore their patent had been infringed. The House of Lords (the supreme appeal court in our legal system) rejected this argument. By a majority of three Law Lords to two it was decided that the Minister was entitled by virtue of section 46 of the Patents Act 1949 to authorise Fraser Chemicals Ltd. to import tetracycline from abroad for the use of hospital patients in National Health Service hospitals because the words "use . . . for the services of the Crown" in section 46 meant use by the members of such services which, the plaintiffs admitted, included doctors and nurses of National Health Service hospitals, for the fulfilment of their duties, and was not confined to use of the drug for the benefit of the members of such services themselves. The basic ground of dissent by the two Law Lords in the minority did not affect the issue as to the constitutional status of the National Health Service. It seems to have taken the form of the narrower reason that section 46 of the Patents Act 1949 should be construed or interpreted narrowly, so as to except from a patentee's monopoly of vending the patented product one potential customer only, namely the Crown, and not as authorising the Crown to enter the field of supply.

The effect of this important decision on the constitutional position of the National Health Service is that it constitutes a *Crown service*, and that health authorities are Crown bodies. This position has a number of consequences. For one thing, there is a rule of our constitutional law that the Crown is not bound by an Act of Parliament unless the Act either expressly applies to the Crown or (in rare instances) includes the Crown by necessary implication (in other words, that you could not read the statute in any other way than as applying to the Crown). Furthermore there are special rules of law and procedure in relation to aspects of the civil law, including the law of tort and the law of contract as they apply to the Crown. Certain special privileges may also be claimed in relation to the giving of evidence in judicial proceedings where the interests of the Crown are alleged to be involved.

Statutes and the Crown

The rule has been mentioned, that legislation does not bind the Crown unless expressly stated in so many words to do so, or unless the wording of the relevant Act would admit of no other interpretation but that the Crown was bound by its provisions. Given that the operations of the National Health Service are carried on by and on behalf of the Crown, as indicated by the decision in the *Pfizer* case discussed above, this rule in respect of statutes and their ambit applies to the National Health Service. Thus the Occupiers Liability Act 1957, which lays the foundation for the present law of the liability of occupiers for the safety of lawful visitors to their premises, is specifically stated by section 6 to bind the Crown. As a result, there is no doubt that premises occupied in respect of activities carried on within the National Health Service are covered by the provision of this statute. The Act and its provisions will be discussed in more detail in a later chapter.

On the other hand the Contracts of Employment Act 1972 does not bind the Crown. This Act, the provisions of which in relation to written particulars of employment have been re-enacted and expanded in the Employment Protection (Consolidation) Act 1978, is not expressed to apply to the Crown. Separate and independent rules exist through the National Health Service Acts and the Whitley Council joint negotiating machinery in respect of such particulars and conditions, and these are discussed in Chapter 3 following.

The Crown and employment law

At the beginning of this section a word was said about varying incidents of status, and it will now become apparent that the constitutional position of the National Health Service is an example of such a variation. We have noted and briefly examined the *Pfizer* decision. But what of employment law? Are we to assume that, as a result of the *Pfizer* decision, all the legal incidents of National Health Service activities, including the employment of staff to operate the service, are automatically conditioned by the special and particular constitutional position of the Crown? Our conclusion will be that we certainly cannot make such an assumption. But first let us note the case of *Wood* v. *United Leeds Hospitals* (1974).

Mr. Wood, a member of NALGO and formerly vice-chairman

of the Leeds Branch, was a technical assistant employed by the defendants. He made an application under the Contracts of Employment Act 1972 to an industrial tribunal for a ruling as to his rights under the Act, but the tribunal dismissed his application on the ground that he was a Crown servant (or employee), and that the Act did not apply to the Crown. He appealed to the then National Industrial Relations Court which upheld the decision of the tribunal that it was correct. Referring to the *Pfizer* case the Court said: "It follows that Mr. Wood, although he did not know it, is in fact a Crown servant." The Court also referred to the rule that the Crown is not bound by statute unless expressly said to be or by necessary implication, and said: "The 1972 Act is wholly silent about the position of Crown servants, and accordingly the general rule prevails."

A point of some apparent difficulty, though one which can easily in the event be explained, is raised by the provisions of the Employment Protection (Consolidation) Act 1978 in respect of rights to redundancy payments and rights in relation to protection against unfair dismissal from employment. Mr. Wood's case turned on the court's application of the *Pfizer* decision to the facts of the issue before them, with the result that he came to be regarded as a Crown servant or employee and thus outside the purview of the Contracts of Employment Act 1972. But a statute can always alter what a court has done, and more recent employment legislation provides an interesting example of just such an occurrence.

Since a statute can choose whether or not to apply to the Crown at all, it is perfectly capable of deciding precisely who are, or who are not, Crown servants or employees for the purpose of the application of its provisions. Just such a task is performed by the combined effect of section 138 and Schedule 5 of the Employment Protection (Consolidation) Act 1978. Section 138 states generally that the Act applies to the Crown, but it makes a substantial number of specific exceptions. That section states that for the purpose of certain parts of the Act, which include the provisions relating to itemised pay statements to be given to employees and to rights in respect of unfair dismissal, but not in respect of other written particulars of employment or in respect of redundancy payments, none of the bodies specified in Schedule 5 of the Act shall be regarded as performing functions on behalf of the Crown; and that, accordingly, employment by any such body shall not be Crown employment within the meaning of section 5. Schedule 5 is terse and simply recites the titles of a number of types of health authority, including principally Regional Health Authorities, Area Health Authorities, the

Dental Estimates Board and the Public Health Laboratory Service Board.

The position thus arises that, for the purpose of this statute, the National Health Service through the authorities by which staff are employed is to be regarded for some purposes as performing functions on behalf of the Crown, but not so for other purposes. More discussion of employment in the National Health Service is given in the following chapter.

Crown liability in tort

The legal position as regards liability in tort for wrongs done to third parties as a result, for instance, of negligence, trespass or nuisance is now effectively the same as any other body or individual. This has been the case only since 1948. But since the implementation of the statute which produced this result was almost contemporaneous with the emergence of the National Health Service in 1948 (following the National Health Service Act 1946), no problems have been created in this particular regard.

As to liability in tort the position immediately prior to the coming into force of the Crown Proceedings Act 1947 was that the Crown, as an employer or otherwise, could not be sued in respect of civil wrongs which it had expressly authorised. Nor could it be sued in tort in respect of wrongs committed against third parties by employees of the Crown acting within the course of their employment. To mitigate the harshness which this rule might otherwise have caused in practice (since, as now, a vast number of activities were carried on by or on behalf of the Crown) the Crown would in practice normally, through a department of government, nominate a defendant who could receive the writ commencing the action in tort, even though such nominated defendant could not personally have been liable for the wrong.

While further and more detailed attention will be given to the law of negligence in a later chapter and while the liability of the Crown in tort through the actions of its employees is also separately pursued in Chapter 4, it is worth noting here that certain activities of the Crown, albeit carried on in the public interest, may carry certain special risks. Health service activities may on occasion be among those risky activities. One special problem might arise from the detention, whether voluntary or involuntary, of mental patients. A decision of the House of Lords in 1970, *Home Office* v. *Dorset Yacht Company*, involved a claim for damages by owners of yachts which were damaged by boys absconding from an open borstal. The claim was made against the Home Office in this particular instance as employers of the borstal officers who were (successfully in the event) alleged to have caused the escape attempt as a result of their negligence in failing properly to guard them. It was strenuously argued on behalf of the Crown that the public interest in the rehabilitation of young offenders at such an institution overrode a duty of care in respect of the property of private individuals. This public interest argument failed and damages were awarded by way of compensation to the owners of the damaged yachts.

While National Health Service authorities exercise their functions on behalf of the Crown, regional health authorities and district (or formerly area) health authorities can commence legal proceedings, and have legal proceedings brought against them, in their own names.

Procedure and Crown activities

Damages and costs may be awarded against the Crown. However, execution of a judgment cannot be levied against Crown property as it can against the property of a private individual or other body; but this is not a matter of any practical consequence since the Crown does in fact comply with judgments against it. However coercive orders for the specific restitution of land and property, for the specific performance of contractual obligations, and injunctions cannot issue against the Crown. Instead the court may make an order declaratory of the plaintiff's rights. One possible defect in this partial cause of satisfaction to a complainant is that, while courts can issue interim injunctions prior to the hearing of proceedings for a trial injunction, there is no parallel procedure for obtaining an interim declaration, only a final one. Therefore, unless the Crown consents to a specially expedited hearing of a declaratory action (action seeking to obtain a declaration as to the complainant's rights), a person aggrieved may be unable to invoke the jurisdiction of the courts as a matter of urgency to restrain the Crown or those acting on behalf of the Crown (and that includes for this purpose National Health Service employees) from inflicting irreparable damage on private rights by unlawful conduct.

Procedure in the context of health and safety at work laws is worthy of a brief introductory comment at this point prior to a more detailed treatment of health and safety in Chapter 5. Legislative provisions affecting the creation and maintenance of health, safety and welfare standards at work are specifically expressed by statute to be binding on the Crown. Since the National Health Service alone of all the many Crown activities is the employer of something like one million full and part-time employees it would be remarkable if the legal position were otherwise. However, since it is also agencies of government which see to the practical implementation of standards of health and safety at work, and since it is really another agency of government which is centrally responsible for the operation of the National Health Service, certain understandable procedural modifications exist in relation to enforcement by way of improvement of standards or cessation of practices. The position in relation to enforcement has recently been amended by the introduction of Crown improvement notices.

Since 1978 a procedure has been adopted whereby inspectors may issue either improvement or prohibition notices to Crown undertakings, including NHS hospitals. The Crown cannot be fined under the 1974 Act, either for a serious breach of safety standards or for refusal to comply with an improvement or prohibition notice. Nevertheless, failure to comply is taken as a serious matter and senior officers of the Department would be consulted if difficulties arose.

Chapter 3

EMPLOYER AND EMPLOYEE

I

Employment laws

It is nothing new for the law to look to employers for a degree of concern in respect of their employees' working conditions. At the end of the nineteenth century it was already clearly the law that an employee did not consent to the risk of injury at work, and thus of getting no compensation for the injury, merely because the job was known to contain a degree of danger. Any damage or injury which was wrongfully caused by the employer would attract damages. Even in the face of knowledge of the risk, an employee could bring an action in tort for damages against his employer if the risks materialised into injury in consequence of the employer's negligence.

It was not, however, until as recently as 1948 that the doctrine of common employment was abolished. That doctrine, which had existed from around 1837 onwards, established that an employer was not vicariously liable for injuries to an employee which were caused by the negligence of a fellow employee also in the employment of the employer. Conditions at work, and the duties of employers and employees in relation to health, safety and welfare at the workplace are discussed in Chapter 5.

But it is only very recently that the flow of legislation affecting such aspects of employment as pay, conditions of service and continuity of employment has developed into a veritable tide. Some of the earlier examples of this employment legislation do not specifically apply to the National Health Service as an employer, but parallel arrangements have been made in respect of health service employees which are as advantageous as the normal statutory arrangements, and in some cases more advantageous. The more recent legislation, including the rules and principles affecting unfair dismissal, applies to health service employees in the normal way. The National Health Service as an employer thus owes the normal legal duties to its employees in respect of job security. Redundancy, however, is separately governed by ministerial direction in connection with the arrangements made by the health service Whitley Councils.

The ordinary law relating to pay and conditions of service, and security and continuity of employment, applies in its entirety to employment relationships established outside the National Health Service. Thus, voluntary and private hospitals, clinics and nursing homes outside the NHS owe their employees the duties which are owed by employers in general. Furthermore, general practitioners, who are independent contractors to Family Practitioner Committees, are subject to normal employers' obligations in respect of the employment rights of such people as medical secretaries and also ancillary staff such as cleaners and gardeners.

Contract of service and contract for services

It is important to differentiate between an employment contract, which is a contract of service, and a contract for services by which an independent contractor is engaged. This distinction will be raised again in the following chapter in relation to differing civil liabilities of an employer and an engager of services, respectively.

The point to notice in the context of the law relating to the respective rights and liabilities affecting the employment or engagement relationship itself is that in order to qualify for the statutory and other benefits enjoyed by an "employee," the person claiming them must show that a contract of service exists. It may happen that an employee, so qualifying, enters into a contract for services with another, but he will nevertheless remain, for the purposes of employment law rights, the employee of the person (or body) with whom a contract of service exists. The law relating to vicarious liability is tort, discussed in detail in Chapter 4, follows the same general principle.

Contracts of employment

It is only very recently that our employment law has firmly espoused the notion of a status relationship between employer and employee. As we shall see in a moment, important rights and privileges have been granted by legislation in respect of continuity of employment and freedom from unfair dismissal, on the basis of the status enjoyed by an employee. Nevertheless the individual contractual relationship still remains relevant.

The basic requirement for an enforceable contract is that there must be an agreement supported by consideration. The law of contract relating to the concept "consideration" is quite complex, but it can generally for our present purposes be described as "the price of a bargain." Thus in the employment context the usual situation is that a promise to pay wages is "bought" either by the actual performance of work, or more often by a promise to work. Mutual promises, here one to pay and the other to work, are necessarily assumed in law to be "good consideration" for each other. The promises on either side may be express or implied, and the exchange of promises can be analysed in terms of offer and acceptance. In an employment situation the offer is usually made by the prospective employer, but there is no reason in law why it should not be made by the prospective employee.

The agreement must be sufficiently certain for the courts to give it a meaning for the purposes of attaching legal consequences to the employment relationship which is sought thus to be created. However, recent judicial decisions have leaned in favour even of ambiguous terms, provided the lack of clarity or of certainty is not too great. The requirement of consideration, the "price of the bargain" means that a promise to perform gratuitous services is not legally enforceable. This principle also extends to volunteers who actually do work or perform services on another's behalf and who have thus no legal claim to be paid for them. Thus voluntary workers in the health and care services, of whom there are fortunately a great many, do not have a legal claim to be paid for their assistance even in the highly unlikely circumstances of changing their minds and deciding that they now want to be paid for what they have done.

Work rules

Among the contractual terms which may either expressly or impliedly become part of the employment agreement are work rules. Many employers in a very wide variety of pursuits and enterprises issue their employees with a book of rules, or some other such document, either at the time of engagement or subsequently. Some employers display notices at the place of work. Some such rules result from collective bargaining pursued by and on behalf of the workforce or larger groups, but more often these work rules are drawn up by the employer without the aid of collective bargaining. These rules are frequently of a disciplinary nature, such as the right to suspend without pay or summarily dismiss the employee for a wide variety of offences or misdeeds such as bad timekeeping, drunkenness, gambling or other misconduct likely to be prejudicial to the employer. The rules may lay down methods of payment or mention restrictions, such as a duty to wear clean overalls or protective clothing, to work overtime as required, and not to engage in spare-time work. Grievance and disciplinary procedures may also be set out.

It is a matter of interpretation in each case whether or not work rules, notices, collective agreements and the like are sufficiently certain to be construed as terms of the contract, and whether or not they have actually been incorporated into the contract of employment by the parties either expressly, or impliedly by conduct or by custom.

Written particulars of employment

It may come as a surprise to some that, apart from certain exceptional cases which need not detain us here, the contracts of employment need not be in writing. Indeed, contrary to common misconception, the general rule of the law of contract is that an agreement supported by good consideration need not be in writing to be legally enforceable. If a contractual agreement is in writing it will, of course, be easier to prove in any dispute as to terms and conditions. But that is a procedural point and does not affect the substance of the issue, which is that an agreement supported by consideration, the price of the bargain, has been reached.

However, the Employment Protection (Consolidation) Act 1978 obliges an employer to provide an employee with a written statement identifying the parties to the agreement, specifying the date when the employment began. This is not a written contract of employment. It is merely strong evidence as to what the terms of the contract are. These necessary written particulars must also state whether any employment with a previous employer counts as a part of the employee's continuous employment with him, and if so, specifying the date on which the continuous period of employment began, and giving particulars of certain terms of employment which are listed in a moment. The written statement must be given to the employee not later than 13 weeks after the beginning of his period of employment with the employer, and must represent the terms of his employment as at a specified date not more than one week before the statement is given. This means, in other words, that the statement of written particulars must contain details of terms which formed part of the contract before notice of the terms was given. But a practical problem arises if the written particulars differ from the original agreed terms. In this event the original terms take precedence.

The specific terms of which the 1978 Act says that particulars must be given, if they are to form part of the employment agreement, are as follows:

(a) the scale or rate of remuneration, or the method of calculating remuneration,

(b) the intervals at which remuneration is paid (that is whether weekly or monthly or by some other period),

(c) any terms and conditions relating to hours of work (including any terms and conditions relating to normal working hours),

(d) any terms and conditions relating to:

    (i) entitlement to holidays, including public holidays, and holiday pay (the particulars given being sufficient to enable the employee's entitlement, including any entitlement to accrued holiday pay on the termination of employment, to be precisely calculated),

    (ii) incapacity for work due to sickness or injury, including any provisions for sick pay,

    (iii) pensions and pension schemes, and

(e) the length of notice which the employee is obliged to give and entitled to receive to determine his contract of employment,

(f) the title of the job which the employee is employed to do.

Such a statement may, for all or any of the above particulars to be given by the statement, refer the employee to some document which the employee has reasonable opportunities of reading in the course of his employment or which is made reasonably accessible to him in some other way.

If it happens that, in the circumstances of some particular agreement, there are no job particulars to be given either expressly or by implication, such fact must be stated. An employer who states that there are no particular terms of employment, express or implied, under one or other of the headings listed above must be careful. Widespread or general practices in relation to many of the listed matters will often provide employees with an opportunity to point to the existence of some understood practice, such as those habitual and customary practices relating to sick pay or holidays. For instance, if an employer states in the notice to the employee of the terms and conditions of the contract that there are no agreed terms relating to holidays, this is quite different from telling an employee that there are no holidays. The latter statement is quite categorical, while the former leaves the way open for the employee to point to customs, habits and practices which indicate that some sort of provision for holidays is to be made.

Furthermore the 1978 Act requires any such statement given to the employee to include a note

(a) specifying any disciplinary rules applicable to the employee, or referring to a document which is reasonably accessible to the employee and which specifies such rules;

(b) specifying, by description or otherwise—

(i) a person to whom the employee can apply if he is dissatisfied with any disciplinary decision relating to him; and

(ii) a person to whom the employee can apply for the purpose of seeking redress of any grievance relating to his employment,

and the manner in which any such applications should be made; and

(c) where there are further steps consequent upon any such applications, explaining those steps or referring to a document which is reasonably accessible to the employee and which explains them.

(d) stating whether a contracting-out certificate [under the Social Security Pensions Act 1975] is in force for the employment in respect of which the statement is given.

Since 1965 there has been a special procedure by means of which an employee may obtain a correct statement of terms and conditions. He may complain to an industrial tribunal if a question arises as to whether the correct particulars, and any changes in them, have been given. Since, however, the tribunal has no powers to enforce its determination of what the correct terms are, the employee who wants convincing evidence of his employment terms must first go to the tribunal and then, if he complains of a breach of those terms, to the ordinary courts in a breach of contract action.

Both employers and employees should take care to have an accurate statement, and the actual conduct of either in appearing by conduct to accept a change from the original agreed terms may prevent later denial of those terms in the event of legal proceedings on the contract. For instance, an employee who receives a written statement requiring him to give a minimum of four weeks' notice when the original agreement was for one week may, if his conduct indicates acceptance (at least, no rejection) of those terms, be precluded from raising the original agreed term in legal proceedings.

Health service employment conditions

The requirements in respect of written particulars of employees' remuneration and conditions of service which have just been outlined do not apply to the Crown. Certain sections of the Employment Protection (Consolidation) Act 1978 which relate to security in employment, and which are considered in a moment, are specifically stated to apply to the Crown, and that includes, for our purposes, employees of National Health Service authorities. The above provisions as to pay and conditions of service in the 1978 Act represent an expanded version of what had earlier been laid down by the Contracts of Employment Act 1972. And in 1974 the case of *Wood* v. *Leeds A.H.A.(T.)* decided that the 1972 Act did not apply to the contracts made by a health authority with its employees.

Health authorities under the National Health Service Act 1977 are governed by Part III of Schedule 5 together with regulations which are either made under its powers, or which are preserved from an earlier date, including principally regulations made by statutory instrument under powers given by the National Health Service Reorganisation Act 1973. It is desirable not only that all contracts be in writing (even though, as we have seen, this is a matter of procedural convenience rather than one of legal requirement), but also that they should make specific reference to such national conditions of employment as may be applicable to the particular group or groups of National Health Service employees in question, and to the fact that such conditions may from time to time be altered. The only circumstances in which any such alterations may validly be made to an agreement as to remuneration or conditions of employment, once concluded, are either by a recommencement of formal negotiating machinery, the results of which are subject to the approval of the Secretary of State for Social Services; or, in exceptional instances, by the direct intervention of the Secretary of State himself.

In certain circumstances where there is in existence a written contract, section 5 of the Employment Protection (Consolidation) Act 1978 provides that there is no need for the supply of written particulars in addition. While, as a matter of law, the terms of the contract are offered by the employing authority to the employee, as a matter of practice they are settled by the

Whitley Council's machinery. This standing negotiating machinery includes provision for consultation in respect of remuneration, and conditions of service with trade unions and other bodies representing the staff side. Regulations which have been made under, or at least which now owe their legal force to, section 10 of the National Health Service Act 1977 include principally the NHS (Remuneration and Conditions of Service) Regulations 1974; the NHS (Appointment of Consultants) Regulations 1974; the NHS (Professions Supplementary to Medicine) Regulations 1974; and the NHS (Speech Therapists) Regulations 1974. The legal effect of all these and similar regulations is, amongst other things, to prevent any health authority from paying any more or any less remuneration to any class of officer (meaning health authority employee) than may be laid down for that class of officer in nationally negotiated agreements approved by the Secretary of State.

Termination of the contract of employment

Either side to a contract of employment may legally terminate the contract by giving notice of the length required in the agreement upon which the employment relationship is based. Termination without notice is normally a breach of contract which will give grounds for an action for damages, in the absence of grounds which a court would regard as sufficient to justify termination without notice. Unjustifiable termination without notice by an employer or employing authority would amount to summary dismissal.

The agreements in respect of notice must be read subject to the statutory requirements now generally affecting contracts of employment, and subject to exception only in occasional cases specified in the Employment Protection (Consolidation) Act 1978. Section 49 of the Act provides as follows:

"(1) The notice required to be given by an employer to terminate the contract of employment of a person who has been continuously employed for four weeks or more—

 (a) shall be not less than one week's notice if his period of continuous employment is less than two years;

 (b) shall be not less than one week's notice for each year of continuous employment if his period of continuous employment is two years or more but less than twelve years; and

 (c) shall be not less than twelve weeks' notice if his period of continuous employment is twelve years or more.

(2) The notice required to be given by an employee who has been continuously employed for four weeks or more to terminate his contract of employment shall be not less than one week.

(3) Any provision for shorter notice in any contract of employment with a person who has been continuously employed for four weeks or more shall have effect subject to the foregoing subsections, but this section shall not be taken to prevent either party from waiving his right to notice on any occasion, or from accepting a payment in lieu of notice.

(4) Any contract of employment of a person who has been continuously employed for twelve weeks or more which is a contract for a term certain of four weeks or less shall have effect as if it were for an indefinite period and, accordingly, subsections (1) and (2) shall apply to the contract.

(5) It is hereby declared that this section does not affect any right of either party to treat the contract as terminable without notice by reason of such conduct by the other party as would have enabled him so to treat it before the passing of this Act."

While the Act provides that the excepted classes of employee include Crown employees, Schedule 5 states that employees of health authorities are not, for purposes of this Act, to be regarded as Crown employees. Thus health authority and health service employees, generally, are covered by these provisions in just the same way as those working in the private sector of health care.

It is not at all easy to specify the grounds upon which a contract might be held to have been justifiably terminated without notice. In the case of *Wilson* v. *Racher* (1974), Edmund Davies L.J. (who has since become a Law Lord) said:

> "Reported decisions provide useful, but only general guides, each case turning upon its own facts. Many of the decisions which are customarily cited date from the last century and may be wholly out of accord with current social conditions. What would today be regarded as almost an attitude of Czarserf, which is to be found in some of the older cases where a dismissed employee failed to recover damages, would, I venture to think, be decided differently today. We have by now come to realise that a contract of service imposes upon the parties a duty of mutual respect."

While hard and fast rules as to justifiability of summary dismissal are therefore impossible to give, a number of propositions may usefully be made by way of generalisation from judicial decisions on this matter. The modern test is basically whether the conduct complained of by the employee is a breach of an important term of the contract of employment. On the rela-

tive importance of such contractual terms the conduct of the
parties and the words of their employment agreement are the
best guides. However, certain terms and in particular implied
terms, will always be given a special prominence in judges'
deliberations. Such obligations as those not to steal the
employer's property, or to damage it deliberately, and to obey
reasonable and lawful instructions, are examples. Single acts of
misconduct are less likely to provide justification for summary
dismissal than a persistent pattern of misconduct. And misconduct inside the place of work is more likely to give rise to
breach of an employment obligation entitling the employer summarily to dismiss than misconduct outside the workplace or outside working hours. Whether misconduct is sufficient to justify
summary dismissal is not dependent on proof that the misconduct has in fact had serious consequences. The test adopted
by the courts in seeking a justification of the employer's action is
the nature of the misconduct itself.

II

Unfair dismissal: the concept

The concept of unfair dismissal is commonly and erroneously
thought to be an innovation of socialist legislation under a
Labour government. It was in fact introduced as a concept into
the employment law of this country by the eventually unpopular
Industrial Relations Act 1971, enacted under a Conservative
government. The concept later became embodied in the Trade
Union and Labour Relations Act 1974, later amended, and subsequently in the Employment Protection (Consolidation) Act
1978. Unfair dismissal is most recently governed by the Employment Act 1980.
    Already recognised to some extent by the law of many
advanced industrialised countries, the concept of unfair
dismissal restricts the hitherto largely unlimited authority of an
employer to dismiss his employees for whatever reason he thinks
fit. The concept is independent of, and separate from, the notion
of wrongful dismissal, the latter being based squarely on the
express or implied term of a contract of employment, and the
surrounding circumstances in which the employment and the
employment relationship are conducted. So a wrongful dismissal

may, in the event, turn out not to have been unfair; and, much
more likely, a dismissal justified according to the tenets and
principles of the common (non-statutory) law which were
examined under the foregoing heading, may be an unfair
dismissal, according to statutory rules and principles which will
now be discussed.

So far as the United Kingdom is concerned the germ of the
concept of unfair dismissal came from a recommendation of the
International Labour Organisation which was approved by the
International Labour Conference at Geneva in 1963, including
the British delegation which voted for it. The basic principle
which underlies this concept is that termination of employment
shall not take place unless there is a valid reason for termination
connected with either the capacity or the conduct of the
employee, or based on the operational requirements of the
particular enterprise. Certain reasons are always to be invalid
reasons for termination. These are: participation in union
activities or membership; the taking in good faith (that is, in the
absence of spite or ill-will as the principal motive) of legal
proceedings against an employer alleging a breach of some legal
obligation; race; colour; sex; marital status; religion; political
opinion; national extraction or social origin.

The recommendation goes on to state that even dismissal for
serious misconduct should take place only where the employer
could not reasonably be expected to take any other course in the
particular circumstances. Furthermore, in connection with
redundancy, which may be a fair reason for the dismissal of an
employee, proper rules should be laid down for the selection of
workers to be dismissed where economic necessity requires a
reduction in the labour force. The recommendation's preferred
solution in cases of unfair dismissal is that of reinstatement of
employees unfairly dismissed. In the absence of reinstatement,
for instance where this would not be a suitable or practical
course, compensation should be paid.

Unfair dismissal: rules and principles

Subject to certain important restrictions which will be set out
under a subsequent heading, every "employee" (as statutorily
defined) has the right not to be unfairly dismissed by his
employer. This right is not dependent on the contractual terms,
express and implied, of agreement between employer and
employee. Indeed, it really represents a right in job security,
according to which employees have a sort of proprietary right in

their jobs. The concept of unfair dismissal is certainly, for legal purposes, not just a "common sense" concept capable of being judged and operated according to what the man in the street thinks to be fair or unfair. Indeed, the law of this country on the matter of unfair dismissal does not yet go as far as the recommendation adopted by the International Labour Conference in 1963 would have it go.

In the leading case of *W. Devis and Sons Ltd.* v. *Atkins* (1976) the judge mentioned four principal matters involved in an inquiry into an allegedly unfair dismissal. First, was there a dismissal and, if so, when, and what was its nature? The burden of proving that there was a dismissal (and, for instance, that the employee did not suddenly and for no apparent reason walk out) lies on the employee. Second, what was the reason for the dismissal? The burden of proving the reason (or if there was more than one, the principal reason) for dismissal is on the employer. The reason must be one which falls within a number of specified categories, including capability or qualifications, conduct, redundancy, statutory requirements, or "some other substantial reason of a kind such as to justify dismissal of an employee holding the position which the employee held."

In so demonstrating the employer must show the existence of a set of facts, known to him, or of beliefs held by him, which caused him to dismiss the employee. The implication of this is that, in establishing the reason, or principal reason, for the dismissal, evidence of events which have occurred subsequent to the dismissal, or of events occurring before the dismissal of which the person taking the decision to dismiss was not aware at the time of dismissal, is neither relevant nor admissible as evidence in proceedings for an alleged unfair dismissal. So, for instance, if the employee of a health authority was for no reason regarded by officers of the employing authority or by superiors as untrustworthy, with no specific evidence to back up the suspicion; and if that person were dismissed, and it were only later shown that there was in fact evidence to link that person with thefts or dishonesty, the dismissal might nevertheless be held to have been unfair. The lesson for employers and employing authorities here is that the person effecting the dismissal must be sure of his ground before proceeding. Furthermore, in a claim in respect of unfair dismissal, the employer can rely only on the reason in fact for which he dismissed the employee, and not the label which he attached to those facts.

In the case of *W. Devis & Sons Ltd.* v. *Atkins* (1976), mentioned above, the House of Lords upheld the tribunal's ruling that fraud could not be taken into account in assessing contributory fault in the employee because it was not known to the employer at the time of the dismissal. Lord Diplock described the legislation which required the tribunal to ignore such misconduct as a "veritable rogue's charter", saying:

> "The tribunal would be bound to award a fraudulent employee, because he had successfully concealed his fraud, a basic compensation which might well amount to a substantial sum."

Now, section 9(4) of the Employment Act 1980 amends the earlier legislation, so that in future the tribunal may reduce the basic award where the complainant was guilty of misconduct before he was dismissed, or before he was given notice of dismissal, even though such misconduct only came to light after the employer had taken action to dismiss him. Furthermore, by section 9(5), in any case where the tribunal is empowered to reduce the basic award, it may now reduce it to a nil amount—nothing.

Thirdly, not just the particular event or events which led to the dismissal should be examined but also reasons why such event or events in fact led to the dismissal. And, fourthly and as a consequence of the third question, it must be asked: Did the employer act reasonably? Unless the dismissal was for one of the reasons, discussed shortly, which are automatically unfair, the employer's reaction by way of dismissal must be a reasonable reaction in the circumstances of the particular case. This further qualification for the justifiability of a dismissal requires some elaboration.

Constructive dismissal

An employee may prove that he was dismissed, for statutory purposes, if he terminated the contract "in such circumstances that he is entitled to terminate it without notice by reason of the employer's conduct: so section 55(2)(c) of the Employment Protection (Consolidation) Act 1978 provides. Decided cases indicate that the employee is presented with no less than four hurdles before he can be said to have satisfied this test:

(1) The nature of the employer's breach of contract must be such as to entitle him to terminate the contract without notice. He may in fact leave without giving notice or he may leave after giving notice and working out the period of notice, but in either event the nature of the breach must have justified summary termination.

(2) He must show that the employer's breach was the reason why he left.

(3) He must not have terminated the contract *before* the breach of contract has taken place.

(4) He must not have waived his right to terminate the contract by delaying for an unreasonable period *after* the breach.

The employee must establish a causal link between his termination of the contract and his employer's breach. Thus, if an employee told his employer that he intended to leave to go to a better job, and if the employer then behaved in such a way as to break the employment agreement, the employee could not *then* assert that he had been constructively dismissed.

Reasons for dismissal

The test of fairness, or otherwise, of dismissal in a particular case which arises in dispute is a highly circumstantial question. Decided cases, both by tribunals and by the Employment Appeals Tribunal, cannot therefore be expected to yield anything very definite in the way of precedents for future cases. The decision in each case is largely dependent on its own individual merits. Nevertheless, it can be said by way of generalisation that there should have been a reasonable investigation by the employer; that there must be an adequate factual basis for the employer's knowledge or beliefs; that a reasonable procedure was followed prior to the sanction of dismissal being imposed; and, very importantly, that the sanction of dismissal was in fact the better course in the particular circumstances.

The test of the reasonableness, in all the circumstances of a particular case, of the employer's reaction and decision to dismiss, is now further qualified and rendered somewhat less strenuous by the Employment Act 1980. Section 6 of the 1980 Act provides that, in deciding the fairness or unfairness of a dismissal, an individual tribunal is to take into account the size and the administrative resources of the employer's undertaking or enterprise. It also amends the requirement of the 1978 Act in relation to the standard of proof. In this way, more subjective reasons for the action taken by the employer or employing authority may properly be considered. These reasons are stated by the 1980 Act to include the size and the administrative resources of the employer's undertaking, but are not restricted to those factors alone. The eventual test is now whether, given these factors among all the other factors which an industrial tribunal considers relevant and material to the issue before it, the dismissal was "in accordance with equity [meaning, simply, fairness and justice] and the substantial merits of the case."

Potentially fair reasons for dismissal

It was indicated earlier that, despite the width of the recommendation adopted by the International Labour Conference in 1963, the law of this country relating to unfair dismissal contains a degree of job protection which in some respects is relatively narrow. While the potentially fair reasons for dismissal which will now be examined in more detail give considerable substance in law to employers' responses to allegations of unfair dismissal, it should be stressed that these reasons are only *potentially* fair reasons for dismissal. They are certainly not automatically fair in any circumstances.

As to capability and qualifications, an employer may fairly expect certain standards and degrees of suitability for the job to be done. Capability is to be assessed by reference to skill, aptitude, health, or any other physical or mental quality. Qualifications include any degree, diploma or other academic, technical or professional qualification relevant to the position which the employee held. For instance, a failure to pass aptitude tests reasonably imposed during the course and time of employment may relate both to capability and to qualifications. The most usual example of capability is the question of ill health. Nevertheless, all the relevant circumstances must be considered in deciding whether the dismissal (as distinct from the employer's reaction to the events and occurrences leading up to it) was reasonable.

In the case of a prolonged absence from work, the question must be asked whether the employer can be expected to wait any longer, and if so, how much longer. The nature of the illness, physical or mental, the likely and past length of the continual absence, and the employer's need to have the work done, must all be considered. However, before an ill employee is dismissed he should at least be given an opportunity to state his case. Indeed, this is a necessary reasonable step in order to ascertain the true medical position and to allow the employee to throw light on the problem. It will in most cases be appropriate for the employer to seek an independent medical opinion, with the employee's participation and co-operation, so as to clarify any doubt about the illness, its probable length and its probable and possible consequences in terms of job capability.

In cases of ineptitude, where the reason relates to the unsatisfactory work performance of the employee, questions to be asked will include, for instance, whether it might not have been partly the fault of management or superiors that things went wrong; whether or not a suitable warning and a suitable explanation of what was thought to be unsatisfactory had been given; whether or not the employee showed signs of improving, or at least could reasonably be thought to have the capability of improving, the standard of work; and, in the case of probationary employees, whether or not the employer took reasonable steps to keep up the appraisal of the employee's behaviour and job efficiency, giving guidance by advice and warning when this was likely to be useful and fair to the employee.

A second reason for a potentially fair dismissal is the conduct of the employee. Rules as to what is right and what is wrong should be carefully brought to the notice of employees, so that they can know what to expect. A common example of misconduct leading to dismissal is disobedience to disciplinary rules or orders. The fairness of such rules themselves may properly be questioned, for the mere imposition of a rule will not justify a dismissal on the basis of its existence alone; the rule may be arbitrary, oppressive or unjust, and may be even immoral. Here again, cases turn very much on their own facts, but it may generally be said that: first, the employer must show the genuineness of his belief that the offence, wrong or other misconduct had been committed; that, at the time of the dismissal, he had reasonable grounds upon which to base that belief; that he carried out as much investigation as was reasonable in all the circumstances; and, in the case of minor offences, whether warning should have been given to the employee. It is in practice harder to rely on such rules if they have not been incorporated into the contract.

A third reason for potentially fair dismissal is redundancy. Generally speaking, the normal tests of reasonableness will be applied to determine whether the dismissal in issue is fair or unfair. Among the circumstances which may render the selection of a particular employee for redundancy unfair are: failure to consult an employee or his trade union before selection; failure to give reasons for his selection for redundancy; and failure to find the employee suitable alternative employment in the undertaking or, if need be, with an alternative employer. If the selection of a particular employee is found by a tribunal to have been unfair, it is legally possible for the employee to be awarded both a redundancy payment and compensation for unfair dismissal; but some adjustment in the amount of the award will be made.

There are two situations in which dismissal by reason of redundancy will automatically be unfair. First, if the reason for selecting this particular employee for redundancy in preference to other employees, or the principal reason, was inadmissible. So, for instance, if the reason for the selection of the particular employee related to his trade union membership or activities, this will be automatically unfair. Otherwise redundancy could be used to effect ends which are legally excluded by the law relating to unfair dismissal. Second, if the employee was selected for redundancy in contravention of a customary arrangement or agreed procedure relating to redundancy, and that there were no special reasons justifying a departure from that arrangement or procedure in the particular case of the employee in question. Such a "customary arrangement" must, it appears from decided cases on the matter, be fairly specific. It is not sufficient that the aggrieved employee simply states what can often be taken to be the normal practice of "last in, first out". On the contrary, the custom must be established to be well-known, certain and clear in the undertaking in which the employee worked. Of course, if a definite "last in, first out" practice did indeed clearly and certainly exist, this would advance the employee's case. Reference may usefully be made in practice to the A.C.A.S. Codes, especially Disciplinary Practice and Procedures in Employment: see the 1975 Employment Protection Act, section 6, which provides for such reference.

Automatically unfair reasons for dismissal

The reasons for dismissal which have just been discussed are reasons which are all potentially fair. Whether or not they are actually fair in a particular case depends upon all the material circumstances of that case. In contradistinction, the reasons given by an employer for dismissal which will now be enumerated can never be fair under the test of "reasonableness." In other words, the test of reasonableness in all the circumstances of the particular case is totally inapplicable here. The only saving condition is, as we shall see in a moment, entirely dependent for existence on a specific and exceptional statutory provision, to which itself there is an exception which has been widened by the Employment Act 1980, and so back to the basic concept of unfairness.

First, the Rehabilitation of Offenders Act 1974 provides that a spent conviction shall not be a proper ground for dismissing a person from an office, profession, occupation or employment.

The 1974 Act does not actually specify what is to happen if an employee with a spent conviction is dismissed for that reason; but it appears that this would normally be an unfair dismissal. Most importantly, however, statutory instrument number 1023 of 1975 provides that none of the provisions of that Act in relation to questions which may be asked in order to assess suitability shall apply in relation to admission to the professions of medical practitioner, dentist, dental hygienist, dental auxiliary, nurse, midwife, opthalmic optician, dispensing optician, pharmaceutical chemist or any profession to which the Professions Supplementary to Medicines Act 1960 applies and which is undertaken following registration under that Act.

Furthermore the instrument provides that the Act shall not apply, in relation to any question asked in relation to suitability for employment, in respect of "any employment which is concerned with the provision of health services and which is of such a kind as to enable the holder [of the office or employment] to have access to persons in receipt of such services in the course of his normal duties."

Second, a female employee is to be treated as having been unfairly dismissed if the reason or the principal reason for her dismissal is that she is pregnant, or is any other reason connected with her pregnancy. Since the relevant provision of the Employment Protection (Consolidation) Act 1978 is not specifically limited to medical reasons, it might be that absence from work for social and family reasons connected with pregnancy are also included as unfair reasons. Certainly, however, if a female employee proves to be physically or mentally incapable of carrying on her employment properly, the dismissal might be fair. However, the employer must, again, act reasonably in the circumstances in dismissing the woman, and must in any event have taken the prior step of offering a new contract of employment if there is a suitable alternative vacancy. Failure to do so, even if the aggrieved employee did not actually ask for an alternative job if one were available, will automatically make the dismissal unfair. If the woman is dismissed in circumstances which are in fact fair she retains her right to maternity pay. If a woman is unfairly dismissed for reasons of pregnancy or confinement, she may include her loss of maternity pay in her claim for compensation.

A further situation in which dismissal may be an unfair consequence of a woman's pregnancy or confinement arises in respect of the woman's right to return after work. An employee who has been absent for reasons due wholly or partly to pregnancy or confinement may be entitled to return to work with her original employer or with the successor of that person. Altering the previous position, the Employment Act 1980 places limitations on the employee's right to return to work in certain cases, and it achieves these by introducing two new defences. Under certain circumstances specified in sections 11 and 12 the employer may avoid the obligation to facilitate return to work where such is not reasonably practicable and alternative employment has been offered and either accepted or unreasonably refused. The other defence is available in circumstances where a small concern of five or less employees cannot reasonably practicably re-employ or offer suitable alternative employment.

It cannot be fair to dismiss an employee for his membership of an independent trade union, or for participation in union activities, save in one specific situation. Where there is a union membership agreement (which, incidentally, no employer is legally bound to agree to if he does not want to), dismissal may be not automatically unfair. It should be stressed that no contractually binding agreement need be proved in order for dismissal for this specific reason to be considered fair; an "arrangement" or definite practice is enough. This is an exceptional case of the fairness of a dismissal for reasons connected with trade union membership and activities, and it can be seen that the workforce or general body of employees is, to say the least, no less advantaged by this legal exception than the employer.

In cases where a union membership agreement can, exceptionally, render a dismissal fair even though connected with union membership or activities, an exception to that very exception exists, and thus back to the rule that the dismissal is unfair. The Employment Protection (Consolidation) Act 1978 withheld the right fairly to dismiss an employee who remained a non-union member in the face of a union membership agreement if the employee genuinely objected, on grounds of religious belief, to being a member of any trade union whatsoever. This exception was regarded by many as either too narrow, far-fetched or simply unrealistic. The Employment Act 1980 now extends the immunity of non-members in these respects to cases in which there is a deeply held personal belief. Section 7 of the 1980 Act also amends the 1978 Act in other important respects relating to existing and future closed shops.

Status and unfair dismissal

It was indicated earlier that the concept of unfair dismissal takes the law of employment beyond the terms and conditions expressly or impliedly contained in an employment contract or agreement and into the area of status, from which rights flow in respect of job security. It is now necessary to state the rules according to which employees qualify for that status. It is not any and every employee who qualifies for the legal privileges implicit in the protection of employees against unfair dismissal.

To qualify, an employee shall have been continuously employed for a period of 52 weeks at the date of termination of the employment. In ascertaining the effective date of termination, the statutory minium period of notice, laid down by the Employment Protection (Consolidation) Act 1978 must be added to the employee's period of continuous employment. This is so, whether or not the employee actually receives this notice. This means in effect that the qualifying period of an employee not given one week's notice is 51 weeks. Section 8(2) of the 1980 Act provides that failure to renew a fixed term contract of more than one year (previously two years) will not amount to a dismissal.

The rules and principles of unfair dismissal do not apply in the case of an employee who has reached, on or before the date of termination of the employment, the normal retiring age fixed by his or her conditions of service. This is the age at which the employee should retire unless service is extended by mutual agreement. This age may be above or below pensionable age. The rules do not apply to persons employed by their husbands or wives. So, for instance, the wife of a general medical practitioner who is employed by her husband as a medical secretary cannot, if they have a difference, claim any remedy from her husband in respect of unfair dismissal.

A further restriction on eligibility for a remedy in respect of unfair dismissal was introduced by the Employment Act 1980. Section 8 exempts firms with 20 employees or less from the unfair dismissal provisions for any new employee who has been employed for less than two years. The exemption will cease if, at any time during the period of service of the employee in question, the employer's total workforce exceeds 20 employees. The exemption will not cover dismissal on account of trade union membership or on certain medical grounds.

It also reduces from two years to one year the minimum length of a fixed term contract in which employees may agree to waive their right to complain of unfair dismissal if they are not re-engaged on the expiry of the contract. The unfair dismissal provisions will still apply to dismissal before the contract expires. Those working less than 16 hours per week are excluded from the definition of "employee", and this remains unchanged under the 1980 Act.

Remedies for unfair dismissal

The Employment Protection (Consolidation) Act 1978 provides for three types of remedy following a finding of unfair dismissal. These are: reinstatement, re-engagement, and compensation. While reinstatement and re-engagement are the primary remedies, intended as they are to make for security and continuity in employment, the statistics show that these remedies are ordered in less than two per cent. of the disputes which go for a hearing to an industrial tribunal. This is not surprising since, despite their being the "primary" remedies, the dismissal and the dispute will normally have soured relations between employer and employee beyond the point at which they could reasonably be expected to continue to work together.

Reinstatement requires the employer to treat the employee in all respects as if he had not been dismissed. So the employee's pay, pension, and seniority rights must be restored to him, and he will also benefit from any improvement in terms and conditions which came into operation while he was dismissed. Re-engagement differs from reinstatement in that the employee may be re-engaged in a different job from the one which he formerly held, so long as the new job is comparable with the old or is otherwise suitable employment. Furthermore, re-engagement need not be by the same employer; it may instead be with the successor of an employer or an associated employer. An industrial tribunal should consider re-engagement only if reinstatement is not suitable.

If neither reinstatement nor re-engagement is suitable, the tribunal will award compensation for dismissal which has been shown to have been unfair. Such compensation can consist of a basic award together with a further compensatory award. There may be an additional award where an employer refuses to comply with the tribunal's order for reinstatement or re-engagement. Subject to a maximum of £3,600, the basic award is calculated in the same way as the amount of redundancy payment under Part VI of the Employment Protection (Consolidation) Act 1978 (discussed below). Based on a maximum of 20 years' service, the basic award is, for each year of continuous employment, from 18 to 22, half a week's pay; from 22 to 41 one week's pay; and from 41 to 65, one-and-a-half weeks' pay.

The additional, or compensatory, award will be either between 13 and 26 weeks' pay, or between 26 and 52 weeks' pay in the case of a "discriminatory" dismissal, that is, dismissal based on reasons of sex, race or trade union membership or activity. The actual amount of money awarded will be, in the words of section

74(1) of the 1978 Act, "such amount as the tribunal considers just and equitable in all the circumstances having regard to the loss sustained by the complainant in consequence of the dismissal in so far as that loss is attributable to action taken by the employer."

Both the basic award and the compensatory award are liable to be reduced for two reasons. Any redundancy payment must be deducted, and deduction may also be made on account of the contribution of the employee's conduct to the dismissal, albeit the latter was in the event unfair. Further, in the case of the compensatory award (but not the basic award) a reduction should be made equivalent to the earnings of the employee in new employment since his dismissal, or to the extent that he would have had such earnings had he taken reasonable steps to mitigate his loss (that is, by getting a job). Reduction may also be made in respect of the extent to which the employee has contributed to his own dismissal.

III

Redundancy

The relationship between unfair dismissal and redundancy has been briefly examined. A further examination, again brief, may now conveniently be made of the rules and principles relating to compensation and consultation in respect of redundancy itself. The Redundancy Payments Act 1965 is now consolidated in the Employment Protection (Consolidation) Act 1978. While Part V of the Act relating to unfair dismissal applies in the normal way to National Health Service employing authorities, Part VI relating to redundancy does not so apply. Employees outside the National Health Service are covered in the normal way by the statutory rules. These include employees in private hospitals, clinics and nursing homes, and those employed by general practitioners. However, under powers given by the National Health Service Act 1977 the Secretary of State may approve schemes for redundancy compensation which are proposed as the result of Whitley Council negotiations.

In the case of employees covered by the 1978 Act, a right to receive compensation is given to those who are dismissed, laid off or placed on short time by reason of redundancy. Compensation is assessed according to the length of continuous employment with the particular employer. The employer who makes a statutory redundancy payment is entitled to claim a rebate, currently fixed at 41 per cent. of the payment, from the Redundancy Fund to which all employers contribute as part of their national insurance contributions. Employees whose employers have failed or refused to pay after all reasonable steps have been taken, or whose employers are insolvent, may claim in full from the Redundancy Fund.

An employee who is dismissed is taken as having been dismissed for redundancy if the dismissal is attributable wholly or mainly to either: the fact that the employer has ceased, or intends to cease, to carry on the business for the purpose of which the employee was employed by him, or has ceased, or intends to cease, to carry on that business in the place where the employee was so employed; or to the fact that the requirements of that business for employees to carry out work of a particular kind, or for employers to carry out work of a particular kind in the place where he was so employed, have ceased or diminished, or are expected to cease or diminish. It is not necessary that the sole reason for dismissal be redundancy—but it must at least be the main reason.

A distinction has been drawn in the decided cases between redundancy, on the one hand, and on the other the need of an employee to adapt to new methods and techniques with developing technology. This situation is quite likely to arise in a number of health service contexts. While health services of all types are often understaffed, the dismissal of an employee for his failure to adapt himself to technological advances is not a dismissal for redundancy, whatever other reason it may be based upon.

Conditions for redundancy payment

If an employee is dismissed because of misconduct no entitlement to redundancy payment can arise, since such entitlement is dependent upon the dismissal being wholly or mainly attributable to redundancy. Furthermore, an employee dismissed for redundancy shall be disqualified from receiving redundancy payment if he unreasonably refuses an offer from his employer to renew the contract on the same terms as before, such renewal to take place no later than four weeks after the dismissal. And an employee loses his right to redundancy compensation if he unreasonably refuses an offer of re-engagement in suitable alternative employment, such re-engagement to take place no later than four weeks after the dismissal. The concepts of *suitability* of employment and *reasonableness* of refusal are separable, but they are frequently dealt with together by industrial tribunals. As in the case of decisions on unfair dismissal, each one tends to relate solely to its own particular facts.

Certain categories of employee are excluded from eligibility for redundancy payments. These categories generally follow those excluded in respect of remedies for unfair dismissal. Excluded categories include men aged 65 or more and women aged 60 or more; domestic servants who are close relatives working in a private household; the husband or wife of the employer; employees who are employed under a contract of employment for a fixed term of two years or more who have agreed in writing to exclude any right to a redundancy payment in the event of non-renewal of that contract. Also excluded is any employee who has been continuously employed for less than two years. In computing the number of weeks of continuous service for the purpose of eligibility for redundancy payments, reckonable weeks are those in which the employee has worked for 16 hours or more.

National Health Service employees

Employees in the National Health Service are specifically excluded from the provisions of the Employment Protection (Consolidation) Act 1978 in respect of redundancy compensation. However, special schemes exist independently of the 1978 Act for many excluded categories of employee, and indeed the conditions of service negotiated through the Whitley Councils for the Health Service contain provisions in respect of redundancy which are more beneficial than the scheme under the 1978 Act. One condition which may be less beneficial is that the qualifying period of two years' reckonable service (that is, the minimum 104 weeks which count for eligibility to receive redundancy compensation) is based on whole time or part time working weeks of not less than 21 hours per week, as distinct from the minimum of sixteen under the 1978 Act.

An exclusion from eligibility parallel to that provided for in the Employment Protection (Consolidation) Act 1978, in respect of unreasonable refusal of suitable alternative employment, is examined in some detail in the *Conditions of Service* published in 1975 by the Whitley Councils for the Health Services. For exclusion purposes, "suitable alternative employment" refers both to the place and to the capacity in which the employee would be employed. The following considerations shall be applied in deciding whether a post is suitable alternative employment and whether it was unreasonably refused:

(a) Place. A post is normally suitable in place if it involves no additional travelling expenses or is within 6 miles of the employee's home. If the new post is at a greater distance, the fact that assistance will be given with the extra travelling expenses will normally outweigh any added difficulties in travel, but exceptionally an employee's special personal circumstances will be considered in comparison with the travel undertaken by other employees in comparable grades. If the post is too far for daily travel, it will be reasonable, since removal expenses will be payable, to require staff (other than those who can be expected to seek employment in their neighbourhood) to move home unless they can adduce special circumstances such as age.

(b) Capacity. Suitable alternative employment may not necessarily be in the same grade; the employment should be judged in the light of the employee's qualifications and ability to perform the duties. Nor need it be at exactly the same pay. A post carrying salary protection for the employee should on that fact alone be treated as suitable in capacity.

For the purposes of this scheme any suitable alternative employment must be brought to the employee's notice before the date of termination of contract and with reasonable time for him to consider it, and the employment should be available not later than 4 weeks from that date. Where this is done, but he fails to make any necessary application, he shall be deemed to have refused suitable alternative employment.

The redundancy payment shall be paid by the employing authority subject to the employee submitting a claim which satisfies the conditions, before he ceases to be employed. Before payment is made he shall provide a certificate that he has not obtained or been offered or refused to apply for or accept suitable alternative Health Service employment and he understands that the payment is made only on this condition and undertakes to refund if this condition is not satisfied.

Compensation

The amount of compensation to be received by an employee who is eligible for it under the rules just stated is based on the same principles which underline the "basic" award in respect of unfair dismissal. Thus, for each year of continuous employment between the ages of 18 and 21 the employee is to receive half a week's pay; for each week of completed employment between 22 and 40, one week's pay; and for each year of employment between the ages of 41 and 64, one-and-a-half weeks' pay.

IV

Unfair discrimination

As long ago as 1958 the International Labour Organisation Convention concerning discrimination in respect of employment and occupation required those ratifying the Convention (which do not yet include the United Kingdom, though it has signed conventions to a similar effect) to take measures against "any distinction, exclusion or preference made on the basis of race, colour, sex, religion, political opinion, national extraction or social origin, which has the effect of nullifying or impairing equality of opportunity or treatment in employment or occupation." In recent years legislation has been enacted in this country which goes some way, but not all the way, towards meeting those objectives.

The Race Relations Act 1968 prohibited discrimination on racial grounds. The Equal Pay Act 1970 requires equal terms of employment between men and women workers. The Sex Discrimination Act 1975 prohibits discrimination on grounds of sex or marital status in the employment field which falls outside the scope of the Equal Pay Act. The model of the Sex Discrimination Act was used to frame a new Race Relations Act 1976, replacing the 1968 Act.

Varieties of discrimination

First, and most generally, discrimination may be either direct or indirect. Second, whether the discrimination is direct or indirect, it may be based on sex, or race, or marital status, or on a combination of such factors. Discrimination on racial grounds is defined in the 1976 Act as grounds of "colour, race, nationality or ethnic or national origin." Nationality was added by the 1976 Act to the list of factors contained in the Race Relations Act 1968. The law applies more widely than merely to employees, but it is employees who are our present concern. Direct discrimination is simply "less favourable" treatment on grounds of sex, marital status or race. A single act of discrimination is sufficient to establish a case of direct discrimination. The act must have been committed with a discriminatory motive, although the motive may be inferred from the employer's conduct. The concept of indirect, or "effects," discrimination is different. To make out a case of indirect discrimination an employee must establish these things.

First, that the person about whose conduct the complaint is made applied a "requirement or condition" which he applies, or which would equally apply, to persons of the other sex, or to single persons, or to persons of another racial group. Examples of the expression "requirement or condition" in decided cases include those relating to an age barrier to job entry, and a seniority rule. Second, that the proportion of the complainant's sex, or of married persons or of the complainant's racial group is considerably smaller than the proportion of persons of the other sex, or of single persons, or of persons not of that racial group, as the case may be, who can comply with it. An example of a discriminatory requirement would be a prohibition on the wearing of turbans or saris, or a beard, unless the employer could show this to be justifiable, for instance on grounds of safety or health.

Areas of unlawful discrimination

The Sex Discrimination Act 1975 and the Race Relations Act 1976 make it unlawful for a person, in relation to employment by him at an establishment in Great Britain, to discriminate on any of the above grounds against applicants in selection arrangements and job offers, and against those employed in access to promotion, training and any other benefits, facilities or services. The legislation also makes unlawful discrimination on the above grounds by partnerships of six or more parties, by organisations of workers or employers and by professional and trade associations, as well as by bodies which can confer an authorisation or qualification needed for or facilitating engagement in a particular trade or profession. Discrimination by vocational training bodies, employment agencies and the Manpower Services Commission is also made unlawful. Health services applications of these rules are plentiful, especially in respect of professional qualifications and organisation and society membership.

It is also unlawful to publish, or to cause to be published, an advertisement which indicates or which might reasonably be understood as indicating an intention to do an unlawful discriminatory act. This does not apply if the intended act would actually have been lawful after all. The use of a sexual connotation, for instance, "stewardess" or "waiter" is taken to indicate an intention to discriminate unless the advertisement contains an indication to the contrary. It is unlawful to instruct or to pressurise another to discriminate improperly.

Exceptions to unlawful discrimination

Any exception to anti-discrimination legislation tends to weaken the basic principles, but there are now relatively few exceptions to the unlawfulness of discrimination. One exception exists in the case of discrimination on grounds of sex or marital status (but not in respect of racial discrimination) by small employers where the number of employees of the employer and any associated employer do not exceed five. In health services contexts this exception is likely to apply only to small general practices, on account of the larger numbers necessarily involved in most other personal health service enterprises.

A number of circumstances are listed in section 7 of the Sex Discrimination Act 1975 in which being a man or a woman, as the case may be, is a "genuine occupational qualification" and is therefore not unlawful. Toilet attendants are an obvious inclusion. Personal welfare counsellors are also included. Importantly, those employed in single-sex health care institutions are also included. But not all employees in a single-sex hospital or clinic are within the scope of this exception to the unlawfulness of discrimination. The exception is restricted to single-sex provision in respect of special care, supervision or attention. So hospital kitchen staff, gardeners and cleaners would not come within the exception, and any discrimination against them would stand to be unlawful according to the normal principles.

Midwives are worth a specific brief mention. It is now possible for a man to qualify as a midwife. But midwives are expressly excluded by section 20 from protection against unlawful discrimination. This effectively means that male midwives can lawfully be discriminated against in respect of employment, promotion, transfer and training.

Nothing in the legislation requires positive or reverse discrimination in favour of women or non-whites. Indeed, such would be unfair discrimination on normal principles and thus unlawful. There are, however, certain exceptional situations in which special treatment may properly be given to members of a particular sex or racial group. Concentration on racial or ethnic qualifications in relation to health service activities will be examined in a moment.

Enforcement

Two principal methods of enforcement are used in the anti-discrimination legislation. The first method is by way of individual civil action before industrial tribunals (and, in cases other than those relating to employment, the county courts). The other method is by strategic enforcement in the public interest by the Equal Opportunities Commission and the Commission for Racial Equality. Under the first method an individual, who must normally make his complaint within three months, may receive one of three remedies if unlawful discrimination is proved: an order declaring the rights of the parties; compensation by way of money; or a recommendation that the person whose conduct is the subject of the complaint take steps to obviate or reduce the adverse effects of the discrimination. Unlike unfair dismissal, there is no power to award the remedies of reinstatement or re-engagement. If those are what a complainant wants he should frame his claim in unfair dismissal, based on grounds of race or sex. The maximum compensation awarded is from time to time prescribed by legislation, and at present stands at £6,240. Compensation may be reduced on account of the contributory fault of the complainant, or increased (up to a maximum of £6,240) if the person whose conduct is complained of refuses without lawful justification to comply with the recommended award.

Race and health services

In addition to its brief summary of the purposes and effects of the Race Relations Act 1978, Circular HC(78)36 is instructive in relation to the application of the letter and spirit of the law to health services. In relation to "genuine occupational qualifications" the Circular reads:

"Under the Act, an employer may offer a job to a member of a particular racial group if membership of that group is a genuine occupational qualification for the job. Membership of a racial group could be a genuine occupational qualification in cases where the job holder provided personal welfare services

for a racial group whose needs could most effectively be met by
a member of the same group. This provision could be used to
justify the recruitment of new staff only if the employer did not
already have a sufficient number of suitably qualified members of that racial group among his existing staff whom it
would be reasonable to employ on that work. Authorities may
wish to take advantage of this provision in some cases where
there are particular problems relating to the language or
cultural background of clients of the health services, for
example in the health education or health visiting field.

In discharging their general duties under the Act, Authorities
may wish to bear in mind the following points:

"(a) In recruiting staff, and in making decisions about
promotion and training opportunities, care should be taken to
ensure that the criteria employed are genuinely related to the
nature of the job concerned and, in particular, that any tests
which may be applied do not contain elements which are likely
to place members of minority groups at a disadvantage but
which cannot really be justified by reference to the requirements for the job itself. For example, a test of general
knowledge for a comparatively junior post should reflect the
standards required for that post so that artificially high
standards do not affect the chances of some racial groups.

(b) A review of staff structures may suggest that members
of minority groups are not enjoying full equality of
opportunity. Members of such groups may be unduly concentrated in jobs which carry lower pay or status, or may be
under-represented in supervisory posts. There may also be
informal patterns of segregation where members of minority
groups are concentrated in particular sections or departments
or on particular shifts.

(c) There may be evidence to suggest that members of
minority groups fail to apply for more senior posts in their field
because of fears of discrimination. It may be desirable to take
steps to encourage applications for promotion by members of
these groups who, it is felt, would be well qualified for it but
have been reluctant to put their names forward.

It should be emphasised that employment Authorities
should do more than seek to secure bare compliance with the
provisions of race relations legislation; and employment
policies and practices should therefore include effective positive procedures to ensure equality of opportunity for members
of minority groups. This can best be achieved by developing a
policy which is clearly stated, known to all employees, has,

and is seen to have the backing of senior management, is effectively supervised, provides a periodic feedback of information to senior management, and is seen to work in practice. Guidance on the formation and monitoring of such a policy is given in two booklets published by the Commission for Racial Equality. 'Equal Opportunity in Employment' and 'Monitoring an Equal Opportunity Policy.' "

Equal Pay

The matter of equal pay for "equal" work is governed principally by the Equal Pay Act 1970. This short but important statute sought to eliminate, by December 29, 1975, discriminatory treatment as between men and women in pay and other terms and conditions of employment. The Act represented the culmination of a long campaign for the equal treatment of men and women in employment, not only by feminist organisations but also by the TUC which first advocated the principle in 1888. While the objectives of the Act met with a considerable degree of success in changing the attitudes of employers and potential employers, a not unsubstantial amount of regret was voiced in many quarters that employers had five years to find ways of avoiding the spirit of the Act by altering, in time for the commencement date in December 1975, job descriptions and specifications so that the letter of the laws would be complied with. Though the Act applies also to men, it is women who are normally in practice affected, though complaints from men in respect of terms and conditions of work have also occasionally been made.

Indeed, the title of the Act is something of a misnomer since the statute aims to achieve equal treatment not only in respect of pay, but also in respect of other terms and conditions of employment such as holidays, hours, provision of clothing and sick-pay (but only where such terms are *contracted*). Pensions are probably excluded. Section 1 provides for equality of treatment regarding terms and conditions of employment as between men and women employed on like work or on work rated as equivalent as the result of a job evaluation exercise. The requirement of equal pay and equal treatment is, importantly, implied into individual contracts; the consequences of this for enforcement will be mentioned in a moment. Section 2 confers jurisdiction upon industrial tribunals to determine claims arising out of the contractually implied term just mentioned. The Sex Discrimination Act 1975 adds to section 2 a further power, that where a dispute arises in relation to the effect of an equality clause the employer may apply to an industrial tribunal for an order declaring the rights of the employer and employee in relation to the matter in question. Section 3 provides for the elimination of discrimination on grounds of sex in collective agreements and employers' pay structures.

A woman has a right to equal treatment when employed on work of the same or a broadly similar nature to that of men in the same employment. The tribunal should look at the respective contracts of the man and woman and see how they are carried out in practice. Mere job titles are of little importance but job specifications may be useful. The tribunal should consider whether the work done by each is of a broadly similar nature, or whether differences exist and, if there are differences, whether these are of any practical importance for the purposes of the issue of equal treatment.

The Act expressly extends to those in Crown employment and so National Health Service employees come within its ambit. The individual may enforce her right to equal treatment through a statutory term of the contract of employment, the so-called "equality clause." The claim will be due either for arrears of pay, if remuneration is the matter in issue, or for damages for breach of the duty to accord equal treatment.

There are certain circumstances in which only the Sex Discrimination Act, and not the Equal Pay Act, will apply. Such will be the case if the less favourable treatment relates to a matter which is not included in a contract, either expressly, or impliedly by way of the Equal Pay Act; or if the less favourable treatment relates to a matter (other than the payment of money) in a contract, and the comparison is with workers who are not doing the same or broadly similar work, or work which has been given an equal value under a job evaluation exercise by the employer; or if the complaint relates to a matter (other than the payment of money) which is regulated by an employee's contract of employment but is based on an allegation that an employee of the other sex *would* be treated more favourably in similar circumstances (that is, it does not relate to the actual treatment of an existing employee of the other sex).

It should be added that Article 119 of the Treaty of Rome, as interpreted by EEC Directive 75/117 (1975) acts as an aid to the interpretation of United Kingdom Equal Pay legislation in both the tribunals and the courts. Under the Directive it *may* be possible to claim, in a *High Court* case, for equal pay for work of equal value, even where no job evaluation scheme has been conducted.

Chapter 4

LIABILITY THROUGH OTHERS

I

Liability through others

Negligence, assault and battery are all torts, or civil wrongs, which may give rise to an action for damages on the part of the plaintiff, the person who brings the action or complaint, against the other party or body whom the law calls the defendant. These are wrongs which will occupy more of our attention in the following chapters, and they will be discussed in some detail in their own right. What concerns us at this point, since a basic groundwork of the effects and incidents of the employment relationship in health services is being given, is that these and other civil wrongs can bring liability to bear not only on the persons directly and personally responsible for their commission but also upon those persons or bodies by whom the wrongdoing employees are employed. This brings us to the principles and rules governing vicarious liability and allied grounds of legal liability.

Liability on account of the wrongful actions of employees occurs most frequently in the case of their negligent acts, largely because the tort of negligence (discussed later in a chapter of its own) is the most frequent ground upon which action or complaint is based. Negligence as a legal wrong is conduct falling below a standard of care which can reasonably be expected to be exercised by an ordinary careful person in the position of the person whose carelessness causes harm to another. There are certain actions which render employers vicariously liable in criminal law for criminal acts which are committed by their employees. But the rules and principles involved in that area do not concern us here, where our business is with the civil law relating to compensation as between individuals or bodies for harm caused.

Economic considerations

It may be asked why our law contains such rules which bring liability for the wrongs of an employee onto the shoulders of an employer. The reasons are in part moral reasons; but the principal reason appears to be economic. Employers might be thought to exercise a degree of control over the activities of their employees in such a way that, if things go wrong in the course of employment, normal ideas of justice and propriety enable the injured third party to bring an action for damages against the "controller." But in any but the simplest form of employment conditions the employer can be said to control the activities of employees only in the most tenuous of ways. Indeed the control test as to when an employee is to be considered to be acting within the course of his employment has long since been abandoned as any realistic approach to vicarious liability.

Economic considerations, on the other hand, can much more easily be seen to be playing the leading role in the additional burden of liability on employers. It is important to note, in passing, that the imposition of vicarious liability on an employer does not remove legal liability from the employee who has done the wrong which has caused the harm. Vicarious liability is additional, not substituted liability. Legal liability to pay damages to the injured third party victim remains also on the shoulders of the employee. Of course, the injured person cannot claim double the money merely because more than one defendant is involved. The point is that the person who has suffered the harm, or damage, has the opportunity of claiming compensation, or damages, from more than one source. And if the further source is an employer or employing authority with greater funds than any individual employee could expect to possess, and, more importantly, carrying insurance against the risk of third party injury (or "insuring itself," as the N.H.S. does), there is an economically better chance of compensation going to the deserving.

Accidents and policy

In the case of accidents and injuries caused by those engaged in the provision of personal health services in the National Health Service there has been a fairly recent tendency of the courts to avoid the intricacies of the law relating to vicarious liability by imposing liability directly on hospital or health

authorities for breach of their duty in respect of their failure
properly and adequately to provide personal health care in the
case of injured patients. This is an overtly policy-based reaction
of the law to the problem which an injured patient, say someone
whose operation goes wrong as the result of someone's
carelessness, however senior, would face in bringing an action in
respect of carelessness alleged to have been committed by senior
medical and surgical staff who could only in a strained sense be
described as employees.

II

Vicarious Liability

With regard to the liability of an employer to compensate third
parties injured by his employee's torts a legal system may adopt
a number of stances. On the one hand the third party's chances
might be made to depend on the terms of employment arranged
between the various controllers of the operations which injure
him, including under the term "controller" the person who
causes the injury himself. On the other hand a legal system
might impose an enterprise liability, strict in nature and
dependent not on the way in which injury came about but simply
on the fact of its having occurred. English law says that the legal
rights of a third party victim of employees' tort should not be
made to depend upon the terms of an agreement to which he is
not a party. However, the employment relationship appears not,
if linguistic implications are any guide to the substance of the
issue, to be entirely irrelevant. The test as to who is a servant (if
the socially divisive nomenclature of times past must be used) or
an employee is made to depend in some part upon a right to control; and the relationship is characterised by the notoriously fluid
concept of the scope or course of employment. It is this latter
doctrine, if such it can be called despite its vagueness, which the
law uses in order, apparently, to temper the strictness of an
employer's third-party liability. Like other legal concepts,
"scope of employment" is susceptible to difficulties of definition,
but recent cases indicate that it is extraordinarily elusive.

Who is a servant?

The doctrine of "scope of employment" is, as will be seen, most difficult to predict in its practical operation from case to case. But there is another difficulty present in this area of the law which must be faced before attention is given at all to "scope of employment." For it must first of all be decided whether the person, in respect of whose acts an employer is sought to be made vicariously liable, *is* a servant, or employee as non-lawyers would normally say. Here a vital distinction should be made between a contract of service and a contract for services. In the former type of contract, the person whose acts are sought to make out vicarious liability in the employer is engaged by the employer under and according to the terms of a service contract. Under that contract the employer may reserve the right to control all the activities of the employee which are connected with the job or jobs to be done. This is not to say that all employers actually control all the employment activities of all employees. To do so would be manifestly absurd and would defeat the object of delegating responsibility in the first place. However the *right* to control the employee's activities in this regard is an essential mark of a contract of service. With such a contract may be contrasted a contract for services, in which the services (thus stated deliberately specifically) to be rendered to the person who commissions them (for reasons both of accuracy and of clarity we shall not call that person an employer) are to be carried out according to the discretion and better judgment of someone else, be it the person taken on to do the job, or that person's employer.

There are other indications as to who is a servant other than the right to control operations, namely who is the paymaster, who can dismiss? But the concept of the right to control assumes a particular importance when the "lending" of servants is considered. In the leading case in this area of the law of tort, *Mersey Docks and Harbour Board* v. *Coggins and Griffith (Liverpool) Ltd.* (1947), A (to use abbreviations for the sake of clearer and shorter reference) employed B as the driver of a mobile crane, and let the crane together with B as driver to C. The contract between A and C provided that B should be the servant of C, but B was paid by A, and A alone had power to dismiss him. In the course of loading a ship X was injured by the negligent operation of the crane by B. At the time the accident happened C had the immediate direction and control of the operations to be carried out by B and his crane, for instance the picking up, carrying and setting down of the ship's cargo, but he had no power to direct *how* B should work the crane and manipulate its controls. In the event, after a thorough consideration of all the relevant aspects of the relationships between A and B, and C and B, respectively, the House of Lords held that A, as the general or permanent employer of the crane driver B, was liable in tort to the injured X. This decision was reached in spite of the somewhat unhelpful remark in the evidence of the crane driver, as quoted in the judgment of one of their Lordships, to the effect that "I take no orders from anyone!"

When is a servant acting within the "course of employment?"

Clearly, an employee is so acting when he is doing what an employer actually tells him to do. Similarly, taking the line of approach indicated above, an employee is also acting within the scope of his employment when doing something which the employer has a right to control. So, for instance, a petrol tanker driver's negligence in dropping a lighted match near petrol tanks consequently causing an explosion was held to impose vicarious liability on his employers in respect of the consequent financial loss caused by the damage, that is, the loss flowing from the actual damage and the bills in respect of it. It would be idle to object that the tanker driver was not employed to drop matches and cause explosions, for if such an objection to employers' liability were countenanced, the whole object of shifting the third party's loss onto the shoulders of someone (frequently an employer who carries general insurance in respect of his whole enterprise) who is better able financially to bear it would be confounded. There remains, however, the difficulty created by the fact that the concept of scope or course of employment is often by no means synonymous or coterminous with the terms and conditions of employment which are set out in, and implied into, the contract which forms a bond between employer and employee.

That an actual contract of service is no complete guide to whether an employee will be held by the courts to be vicariously liable for the torts of his employee can be seen from even the most cursory view of the cases. In the case of the careless petrol tanker driver, *Century Insurance Co. Ltd.* v. *Northern Ireland Road Transport Board* (1942), the wrongdoer was certainly not employed to drop matches, nor was he employed to act in a careless manner. But he was employed to deliver his tanker load of petrol and to supervise its discharge at destination. The case of a railway station porter who manhandled a passenger out of a carriage compartment in the belief, erroneous as it transpired, that the passenger had boarded the wrong train, established that the porter was acting within the scope of his employment despite the fact that his execution of that task was done in a rough and, indeed, mistaken manner. From the injured third party's point of view, as adjudged through the eyes of the law, the porter was doing his job (namely, of supervising the best interests of railway passengers) even though his mode of doing it left much to be desired.

In conclusion so far, it would be wrong to imagine that an employee is acting outside the scope of employment merely because he does something in an unauthorised way. An employer certainly does not employ people to act carelessly to the detriment of others. Indeed, any such agreement between employer and employee would in all probability be held void and unenforceable as being contrary to public policy or even illegal. Nor, on the other hand, can an employer evade the stipulations of the law of tort simply by providing in the contract of service that the employee shall not act in a careless or negligent manner, or by specifying a duty not to commit a tort. While such a contractual provision would undoubtedly affect the contractual rights of employer and employee as between each other, an injured third party's rights and remedies cannot in English law (except in special circumstances not immediately relevant to our present concerns) be defeated or in any way restricted by the terms of an agreement to which he is not privy, that is, to which he is not a party. In so saying, we encounter the very difficult problems created by the express prohibitions on conduct which may lawfully be provided in a contract of service, but the effect of which in regard to third party victims of employees' torts are severely restricted by the law.

Scope of employment and express prohibitions

The law relating to vicarious liability in tort reaches the apparently remarkable conclusion that an employee is acting within the scope of his employment even if he does something which is expressly and clearly forbidden by either a contractual obligation stipulated by the employer or by other means, provided that the employee can still be said to be doing "something to do with his job." That this admittedly vague and unsatisfactory way of putting the matter is not easy to improve on will become clear from the discussion of judicial decisions in this area which follows.

In the case of *Limpus* v. *London General Ominbus Company*, decided by the House of Lords in 1862, the question arose as to whether an omnibus company (in those days the buses were horsedrawn) should be vicariously liable in tort for injury caused by the wilful and reckless obstruction of other such horsedrawn buses, despite an express prohibition, in the driver's contract of employment with the company, on the racing with or obstruction of other buses belonging to competing companies. Opponents of nationalisation might take some solace from the change to the present tamer conditions. The House of Lords held that the employing company was so liable. In the *Century Insurance* case mentioned above the tanker driver was doing his job, but he was doing it negligently. In the *Limpus* case the attitude of the law was that the bus driver was doing his job, albeit in wilful disregard of an express and clear instruction. Though *Limpus* is the case most frequently cited for such a proposition of law, there are others like it. The early cases evidencing such a principle of vicarious liability make occasional reference to a *benefit* to the employer resulting from the employee's acts or conduct, and appear to set this down as the rationale or justification from the imposition of vicarious liability in these circumstances. It is paradoxical that wrongful and injurious actions of an employee should be held to be beneficial to his employer. But the reasoning of the law is clearly that, whenever a task is delegated to an employee, the delegation is at least *deemed* to benefit the employer. Any other view of the motives of employers would display a philosophy both pessimistic and uneconomical, and it would certainly frustrate the legitimate expectations of third party victims of harm or injury.

Against what may, without inaccuracy, be called the *Limpus* line of cases may be set cases such as *Twine* v. *Bean's Express Ltd.* which was decided much more recently in 1946. The Court of Appeal held that a van driver who was expressly instructed not to give lifts to strangers but who nevertheless did so was not acting within the scope of his employment when a gratuitous and (from the employers' point of view) unwelcome passenger was picked up and subsequently killed by the careless driving of the employee. This result was based squarely on the proposition that the van driver was not doing what he was employed to do, even in a careless or indeed wilfully wrong way. He was not employed to give lifts, nor was the giving of lifts anything to do with his job. In terms of a possible benefit to employers, the driver of the horsedrawn omnibus *might* have benefited his employers (that is, if he had driven properly and had not involved them in an action for damages), but the van driver *could not* have so benefited the employer since what he did was quite unconnected with the employer's enterprise. Or so it seems. A recently decided case indicates, however, that even the difficult distinctions so far drawn are not in themselves sufficient to decide all the problems of express prohibition and "scope of employment."

Getting the job done

In *Rose* v. *Plenty* (1976) the Court of Appeal held, by a majority decision, that Co-operative Retail Services Ltd. were vicariously liable for injuries sustained by a thirteen-year-old boy who used to help one of their milkmen, Mr. Christopher Plenty, in his deliveries, pickups and money collection; and this in spite of notices up at the depot making it quite clear that roundsmen were not allowed to take children on the vehicles. One notice said, indeed, that "Children and young persons must not in any circumstances be employed by you in the performance of your duties." Such notices would no doubt have been regarded by keen-eyed lawyers as less than comprehensive, but at least they were a clear indication of the "set-up" which existed at the depot. Thus two separable but potentially coincident courses of conduct were expressly singled out for the clear prohibitions: taking children on the vehicles, and letting them do the work. In the instant case they did coincide.

The line of cases characterised by *Limpus* v. *London General Omnibus Company* raises the question whether an employee is acting "in the course of employment" when acting in the face of an express prohibition relating to the job to be done, and answers it in the affirmative. Another set of authorities, of which *Twine* v. *Bean's Express Ltd.* is typical, puts the question whether an employee is so acting when giving lifts, again in the face of an express prohibition. Here the answer is in the negative. In *Rose* v. *Plenty* the Court of Appeal was faced with the nice question: Was the employee acting within the scope of his employment when doing his job (or at least, so as not to beg the question, getting it done), by a means which involved the prohibited carrying of a passenger, which *alone* would have been outside the scope of employment?

Though the Court of Appeal was presented with the fact of the roundsman's negligence, the circumstances of the plaintiff's coming to be owed a duty of care are not unremarkable. After going to one house, Leslie Rose jumped onto the milk float. He sat there with one foot dangling down so as to be able to jump off quickly. Mr. Plenty drove too close to the kerb, and as the milk float rounded the corner the wheel caught Leslie's leg and he was dragged out of the milk float and broke his foot. It may well be that the driver ought to have looked to the safety of his young passenger by getting him to keep his legs tucked in. But milk floats which keep to the nearside are seldom chastised, while those which drive in the middle of the carriageway are frequently an infernal nuisance and are, as statistics show, a frequent cause of accidents.

Emphasis was placed, in two of the judgments of the members of the Court of Appeal (Civil Division) on an observation of Lord Dunedin in the case of *Plumb* v. *Cobden Flour Mills Company Ltd.* decided in 1914. While it seems, in the light of the foregoing observations about terms of an employment contract and the notion of "scope of employment" to be pretty pointless to ask "What was the employee employed to do?" (since the answers given by the employer and, perhaps, the employee on the one hand apt to be greatly at variance with the objective assessment of a court of law in a vicarious liability case), nevertheless some connection still appears to be relevant as between terms of employment and scope of employment. Lord Dunedin indicated that "there are prohibitions which limit the sphere of employment, and prohibitions which only deal with conduct within the sphere of employment." Indeed, Scarman L.J. said in *Rose* v. *Plenty* that "those words are an echo of what has long been the law." Though in theory a distinction might be drawn between an employee's doing something which he was not employed to do, and his doing something which he was *employed not to do*, this difference of emphasis does not appear, as such, to have much bearing on the common law's attitude to scope of employment in vicarious liability. Be that as it may, the situation in *Rose* v. *Plenty* is arguably one of the illicit "delegation" of the very job itself, or at least part of it. To the extent that the milkman "delegated" his job of delivering the milk, collecting empties and obtaining payment to the boy he was not *doing* his job—either in a physical or in a temporal sense. Mr. Plenty was at most, at operative times of unauthorised delegation, getting the job done. To object that Leslie Rose was injured in his capacity as a passenger and not as a "delegate" (as by being injured by a crate or bottles which the milkman knew or ought to have known to be in a dangerous condition) would be to import even finer distinctions into the law relating to vicarious liability than those which are already there, to the chagrin of many including the dissenting Lawton L.J. If the words of Lord Dunedin, which "have long represented the law," are to have any application at all, then it is suggested that the facts of *Rose* v. *Plenty* surely qualify for the application of the expression "prohibitions which limit the sphere of employment." If not, it is difficult to conceive of a set of facts which would qualify for that formula but which would be substantially different from those in *Rose* v. *Plenty*.

In the course of argument Lawton L.J. asked counsel for the plaintiff whether if in *Twine's* case the driver had asked the passenger to do some map reading for him in order to get more quickly to the place where in the course of employment he wanted to go, that fact would have made the employers liable. Counsel replied that it would. Presumably the same result would follow from a pedestrian's offering to show the driver the way because "I'm going that way myself" and merely nodding or shaking his head in response to a query from the driver as to the correctness of his opinion about the best route. The employer would thereby be "benefited."

The way ahead

It is true that such as case as *Rose* v. *Plenty* is unlikely to arise so much in the future, since the Road Traffic Act 1972, s. 143 now provides that a vehicle is not to be used on a road unless there is in force an insurance policy covering, *inter alia*, injury to passengers. Nevertheless the general principle of *Rose* v. *Plenty* is apt to remain. The matter is always open to a different interpretation if an appeal ever reached the House of Lords. If "scope of employment" is to have any relation to what an employee is employed to do, then the last connection between employment and liability to third parties, namely who does the job, should surely be maintained. However "scope of employment" is a concept of the law and there is no magic in the name which a concept happens to bear. One may take leave to wonder whether if decisions like *Rose* v. *Plenty* are to recur, the time has not now come frankly to acknowledge an enterprise liability, strict in nature and characterised by attention to defences rather than to positive grounds for liability.

Criminal and fraudulent acts

It has been seen that even a wilful wrong committed by an employee, or servant, can bring vicarious liability to bear upon the employer or employing authority, and that this result can ensue even in cases where the wilful wrong of the employee is done deliberately contrary to an express prohibition on such acts and conduct by the employer. Lest any surprise be felt at this result, it may be recalled that the liability on the employer is strict, that is, it is liability imposed in the absence of fault. It may also usefully be recalled that not only is vicarious liability independent of fault but also that it is liability imposed by the law additional to, and not instead of, the personal liability of the employee. It must never be forgotten that the personal liability of the employee as the actual wrongdoer remains throughout. It is just that an employer is usually in a better economic position to pay damages especially if the acts of the employee which cause the third party injury are insured against.

In the light of these considerations it comes as somewhat less of a surprise when the law, as it does, imposes liability on an employer or employing authority even in some cases of theft or fraud on the part of the employee. It was at one time thought that if a servant stole goods his master, or employer, could not be vicariously liable to their owner on the ground that the act of stealing necessarily took the servant outside the course of his employment. Such a view, however, overlooks the important point that an employee to whom the goods, which he later steals, have been entrusted, is effectively doing what he is employed to do, namely keeping charge of the goods; but that he does it in a dishonest way. In *Morris* v. *C. W. Martin and Sons Ltd.* (1966), where some of the earlier decisions were overruled, the plaintiff had sent her fur coat to the cleaners, and the recipient of the coat at the cleaners, with the plaintiff's permission, sent it on to the defendants who were specialist cleaners. The defendants handed the coat to their employee for him to clean it, and he stole the coat. It was held by the Court of Appeal that in these circumstances the defendants were liable to pay damages by way of compensation to the plaintiff whose coat was stolen.

Even the fraud of an employee can cause his master, or employer, to be vicariously liable to a third party to whom the employee's fraud causes loss, provided that the employee's fraudulent conduct falls within the scope of what is called his "actual or ostensible authority." In other words, the employer is liable in respect of the employee's fraudulent wrong if the employee was doing things connected with what he was supposed to be doing, or at least if he was doing something which the injured third party reasonably took to be part of what the employee was meant to be doing.

The bailment of goods

The case of the stolen fur coat which was discussed a moment ago could have been decided on the short ground that, as in other

cases involving either careless or intentional acts committed
within the course or scope of employment, the employee was
doing what he was employed to do but was doing it in an unlawful or unauthorised manner. But the Court of Appeal in *Morris* v.
C. W. Martin and Sons Ltd. went to some lengths to indicate an
alternative basis for the defendants' liability. They placed a
great deal of relevance on the duty owed to the plaintiff by the
defendants themselves as *bailees* of the coat. A bailee, or person
subject to the duties incumbent on one who receives a bailment,
is a person who receives goods, either voluntarily or for a fee, and
undertakes safekeeping of them on another's behalf. A bailee of
goods is subject to what is sometimes called a "non-delegable"
duty; in other words, the duties involved in the safekeeping of
the goods are not discharged merely by passing responsibility for
them to someone else.

The Court of Appeal in the case of the fur coat decided that the
defendants had sought to delegate to another person their duty
in respect of the safekeeping of the coat, and this the law will not
permit. The coat had been bailed to them, and it was their duty
to look after it, or at least to see that it was properly looked after.
This they did not do; the facts spoke for themselves, the coat was
stolen.

This decision, and others to the same effect, have important
implications in the context of health service activities for those
who, either themselves or through their employees, undertake
the safekeeping of others' property and valuables. Such is the
case of a hospital or clinic whose staff supervise the preparation
of patients for hospitalisation or for treatment involving the
removal of clothing or temporary separation of property and
valuables from their owner. The case of theft by employees from
the hospital, clinic, health authority or other person or body
engaged in health care activities is different; for in the present
context attention is being directed solely to the complaints of a
third party to an employing authority in respect of the duties of
safekeeping of property owed by that employer or employing
authority to the third party either directly or through the agency
of its employee. Both matters will be given further attention in
Chapter 9 in which the subject of theft is itself examined in
detail.

The independent contractor

Vicarious liability attaches to an employer through the wrongful acts of an employee acting within the scope and course of

employment. While there are certain specific cases in which the engager or commissioner of services from an independent contractor, under a contract for services (as distinct from a contract of service) is liable for their wrongs, these are all instances in which liability is cast *directly* onto the shoulders of that person. Even though the person who gives some of the orders, or at least the initial instruction that such and such a job shall be done, is the person who in these specific cases shoulders legal responsibility if a third party is injured or harmed by the ensuing activities or state of affairs, this is most certainly not a case of the vicarious liability of an employer. Here again we encounter the idea of "non-delegable" duty, or a duty which the law casts upon one who commissions a job or who engages certain services, in circumstances in which care to avoid harm or injury is so important that responsibility for exercising that care cannot properly be passed on to someone else.

The circumstances in which the law does not allow the buck to be passed are, generally speaking, those in which the likelihood of harm is especially great; or, if not especially great, that any harm or injury which actually does ensure is likely to be severe. That is the general policy of the law, but we can be more specific. Circumstances in which one who engages an independent contractor actually authorises, instructs or ratifies the latter's wrongful conduct, and cases in which the person who engages the other's services is himself at fault, can be disposed of quickly. For in these situations there is no difficulty in the law's attaching personal liability directly to the engager. These cases are not cases of genuine exception to the general rule that a person is not normally liable for the wrongs of an independent contractor. They are only apparent exceptions.

The genuine exceptions are those in which the activities which the independent contractor is engaged to perform involve withdrawal of support from neighbouring land or from adjoining premises; operations affecting the highway other than normal use for the purpose of passage—such as felling a tree adjoining the highway or putting up an overhanging sign or notice; activities involving fire, or those involving a potential nuisance to other premises or to members of the public; and, generally, what are referred to as "extra-hazardous activities," such as those involving dangerous or volatile chemicals, explosives or potentially dangerous equipment. Furthermore, one who engages the services of an independent contractor cannot in law delegate to that person any duty imposed upon the former by the provision of a statute. The duty created by statutory provisions, and that includes regulations made pursuant to powers given by the statute, is a further example of a non-delegable duty, responsibility for the performance of which cannot properly be passed on to another or other people.

Finally, there is a well-recognised exception to these specific cases in which, exceptionally, a person is liable for the wrongful or careless acts of an independent contractor. There is no liability for what is called the "collateral" or "casual" negligence of an independent contractor, that is, negligence in some collateral respect, as distinct from negligence with regard to the very matter delegated to be done. As our illustration we may take the case of *Padbury* v. *Holliday and Greenwood Ltd.* (1912). The defendants engaged a subcontractor to put metallic casements into the windows of a house which the defendants were building. While one of these casements was being put in, an iron tool was placed by one of the subcontractor's employees on the window sill and when the casement was blown in by the wind the tool was dislodged and fell and injured the plaintiff who was walking along the street underneath. The court, after hearing evidence about the relevant facts, decided that the tool had not been placed on the window sill in the ordinary course of doing the work which the subcontractors were engaged to do. It was held that the plaintiff's injuries were caused by an act of collateral negligence and that the defendants were therefore not liable. It is clear that the decision would have been different, and that the plaintiff would have received damages by way of compensation, if the negligence had taken the form of careless handling of one of the casements themselves and if, consequently, a casement or part of one of them had fallen and injured the plaintiff.

Joint and several liability

Vicarious liability provides a special instance of joint liability. If two or more people acting, as the law says "in concert," in other words as part of a common plan or joint operation, combine to cause injury or harm to a third party, the latter can sue any or all of them for damages. Several liability occurs when the conduct or actions of two or more people in fact combine to cause injury to the third party, but not as a result of a common design. In cases of several liability, the injury just happens, as in the case of a collision between two carelessly-driven motor cars causing injury to a pedestrian.

It may usefully be mentioned here that the vicarious liability which is imposed on an employer for the wrongful acts of an employee causing injury, harm or loss to a third party provides a special instance of joint liability. Here joint liability is imposed by operation of law on an employer, not because the employer has acted as part of a common design in injuring the third party plaintiff, but simply because he is an employer whose employee has committed a wrong in the course of his employment. Just as in the case of joint liability imposed as a result of the factual combination of wrongful actions, so also here, the plaintiff can bring an action for damages against both employee and employer or employing authority. It is for this reason that, for instance, an action for damages for personal injury to a patient following alleged carelessness in medical treatment may be, and often is, commenced against both the staff involved and also the health authority, which employs or engages them.

General practitioners

The Family Practitioner Committee which is established by the appropriate health authority engages the services of general practitioners in its area on the basis of contracts. Those contracts are contracts for services and not contracts of service, so that in consequence general practitioners are not employees of the Family Practitioner Committee or of the establishing health authority, but are independent contractors engaged by way of contracts for services. It might, incidentally, be mentioned here that, contrary to apparently widespread belief, general practitioners within the National Health Service do not have a contractual relationship with their patients. It is thought by lawyers that the contractual relationship is confined to instances in which the practitioner has entered into a contract to provide treatment and services to a patient on a private basis, in other words as a private patient.

Furthermore, it is not permissible for a general practitioner to enter into a private agreement in respect of treatment and services with a patient in respect of whom the practitioner owes duties pursuant to Family Practitioner Committee arrangements, in other words who has such a patient on his NHS list. Any such treatment must be done by a general practitioner other than the one to whom the patient is attached under the National Health Service. This sort of obstacle does not, incidentally, apply in the relationship between a patient and a specialist consultant. It is possible that some activities which are carried on in general practice premises are done by people who are employed by a health service authority, in normal cases the area health authority. Such could be the case with nurses giving immunisation or rehabilitation clinics on the premises of a general medical practitioner. What is important to note here is not so much by whom specifically these people are employed, but that they are not carrying out their duties in the course of employment by the general practitioner.

In the case of other staff of general medical, dental, ophthalmic and pharmaceutical practices, including both medical secretaries and receptionists and also ancillary staff such as cleaners, the activities of those people will be regarded as pertaining to the ordinary course of employment by the general practitioner or partnership which has engaged their services. So the ordinary rules, outlined earlier, will apply to such personnel as much as to any employee.

Other applications

The same principles apply also to any staff of whatever kind who are engaged by way of a contract of service in health care institutions outside the National Health Service such as private hospitals, clinics and nursing homes.

In the case of an enterprise supplying temporary nurses to persons or institutions needing them, payment being made directly to the company or partnership which hires out their services, the nurse remains the employee of that company or partnership. The principle established in the case of the Mersey Docks and Harbour Board, discussed earlier, applies to this situation.

Vicarious liability and hospitals

Problems arising from the incidence of vicarious liability and its general absence in the case of injuries caused to third parties by independent contractors become most acute in the context of hospital activities. The problems arise partly from the assessment of the legal relationship between hospitals and their employed or engaged staff in relation to injury to third parties, and partly from an apparent concern of courts and judges to impose liability on hospitals and health authorities independently of legal niceties distinguishing between employees and contractors for the purposes of the incidence of third party liability.

It was once thought that the acid test of distinction between employees and independent contractors lay in the degree of control which an employer could expect, and be expected to, exercise over the activities and conduct of the employee, and the relative absence of such control in the case of independent contractors. While this test of control held sway the courts used to say that a hospital authority could not be liable in negligence in matters involving the exercise of professional skills. A leading case to this clear effect was *Hillyer* v. *St. Bartholomew's Hospital* (1909). However, since the decision of the Court of Appeal in *Gold* v. *Essex County Council* (1942) which involved the actions of a radiographer, it has been held by the courts that a variety of hospital medical staff are in law to be regarded as employees of the hospital or health authority for the purposes of vicarious liability for third party injuries. Such has been decided in the case of house-surgeons, full-time assistant medical officers and, apparently, staff anaesthetists, as well as radiographers. It has even been suggested in some judicial decisions that visiting consultants and surgeons under the National Health Service are to be regarded as employees for this purpose. This attitude is not welcomed by either senior medical staff themselves or their defence and protection organisations. As we shall see in a later chapter, liability in English law for accidents is still firmly based in most instances on the principle of fault. Any tendency which may be discerned in the judicial decisions on vicarious liability of employers to fix a health authority with liability at least partly on the ground that it can better pay the bill, is not welcomed by staff whose own fault might tend in such circumstances to be assumed rather than exhaustively proved. Plaintiffs may be more sure of getting their money as the result of a discernible tendency to fix health authorities with legal liability; but, on the other side, valued personal reputations may be at stake.

However, in many cases involving the alleged liability of a hospital or health authority, there has been a tendency to treat the liability not as vicarious liability but rather as the direct or primary liability of the hospital or health authority for breach of its own duty to treat the patient properly and with reasonable care. Their duty may thus be assimilated to the non-delegable duties which cast an unexceptionable burden on those who get contractors to engage in certain particularly risky activities on their behalf. If this avenue of approach is taken, problems as to the status of employed or engaged staff are avoided. The high-water mark of this approach is to be found in the judgment of Denning L.J. (as he then was, before becoming a Law Lord and then Master of the Rolls) in *Cassidy* v. *Ministry of Health* (1951):

"If the patient himself selects and employs the doctor or surgeon, as in *Hillyer's* case, the hospital authorities are of course not liable for his negligence, because he is not employed by them. But where the doctor or surgeon, be he a consultant or not is employed and paid, not by the patient himself but by the hospital authorities, I am of the opinion that the hospital authorities are liable for his negligence in treating the patient."

And Denning L.J. (which is spoken as Lord Justice Denning) went on to place the burden squarely on the shoulders of the hospital authority itself when he said:

"It does not depend on whether the contract under which he was employed was a contract of service or a contract for services. This is a fine distinction which is sometimes of importance; but not in cases such as the present, where the hospital authorities are themselves under a duty to use care in treating the patient."

This is effectively an example of the enterprise liability alluded to earlier; and, as will be seen in the context of negligence, an interesting contrast to the *Hincks* case (discussed in Chapter 2) is presented.

III

Who pays the bill?

It was noted in Chapter 2 that one of the consequences of the fact that National Health Service activities are carried out on behalf of the Crown is that the Service is self-insuring. In other words, no separate policies of insurance are taken out with an independent insuring or indemnity agency to cover mishaps and negligence. Health care institutions outside the National Health Service will carry such independent policies of insurance and will not be self-insuring. Individual staff both within and outside the National Health Service may carry liability insurance against claims for damages, usually in the form of negligence claims. In the case of medical staff this is effected by way of membership of either the Medical Defence Union, the Medical Protection Society or the Medical and Dental Defence Union of Scotland.

It may usefully be noted in passing that in the recent decision in *Medical Defence Union* v. *Department of Trade* (1979) the court held that the Medical Defence Union (and the same may be assumed to apply to the other societies) is not to be treated in law as an insurance company. The result is that this and the other defence societies do not have to conduct their business in such a way as to comply with statutes governing insurance companies, with all the necessary formal procedures which such business entails. A principal reason for the decision in that case was that the Medical Defence Union exercises a discretion as to whether or not to support its members in actions brought against them and, if they decide in the member's favour on that point, as to how much of the claim will be met.

It has been seen earlier in this chapter that legal proceedings may be commenced against both the member of the medical staff alleged to have been personally responsible for the wrongful harm and also the health authority which employs, or at least engages, that person. Since medical staff may have the backing of a defence society, and since authorities within the National Health Service are self-insuring, the third party victim who alleges wrongful harm or injury is assured of compensation in the event of the action's being successful. As to who pays what, in consequence of success of the plaintiff's action against the member of staff who was personally at fault, the 1954 Circular, HM (54) 32 is important. The scheme of compensation, which applies to dentists as well as to medical practitioners, is noted below.

The sharing arrangement

An employer or employing authority held liable by way of vicarious responsibility to pay damages to an injured third party has a legal right to make an indemnity claim against the person who has been personally careless or who has otherwise acted wrongfully. If any such claim, under an implied contractual term or by way of contribution between joint wrongdoers, was brought against a doctor who was a member of a defence society, a three-way process was instituted which was not economical of time or effort. Consequently in 1954 the procedure to be adopted thenceforth was modified. From then on, where any doctor who may be held liable is a member of a defence society, and that body accepts responsibility for him, any compensation paid to the plaintiff is to be apportioned between the doctor, or doctors, and the health authority as agreed privately between them or, in the absence of such an agreement, in equal shares.

The success of these arrangements clearly depends on mutual

confidence between the defendants and a fully co-operative attitude on the part of both parties from the beginning. The circular of 1954 states that there should be full consultation at the request of either party in the formulation of the defence.

Chapter 5

SAFETY IN EMPLOYMENT

I

Civil and criminal liability

The objectives and policies underlying the varied and diffuse areas of the law which affect health and safety in employment and which provide for remedies in the event of danger or actual injury are themselves varied. Some of the laws in question aim solely to compensate, others to impose a directive or prohibition, or even a fine; and some rules have the effect of bridging the gap between civil and criminal liability by having both individual and public objectives in view.

The distinction between civil liability and criminal liability has already been encountered and explained. Briefly to recap, the enforcement of the criminal law is concerned with the imposition of criminal sanctions in the form of fines or imprisonment, and the civil law is concerned in large part with the award of damages as part of its general concern with the adjustment of interests as between individuals. The distinction between criminal law and civil law is prominent in any discussion of the law relating to health and safety at work. To give an example of each, before going on to a more detailed review of this area: an injured employee can sue the appropriate employer or employing authority for damages; that employer may, in the same or similar circumstances, be subject to the provision of the Health and Safety at Work Act 1974, an Act which provides for no civil liability in damages, but the enforcement of which *could* lead to a fine being imposed on the employer or employing authority.

But the picture so far given is a crude one, and more detail is needed for it to become both comprehensible and representative of what actually goes on in practice. Let us therefore look in more detail, first at the civil liability of an employer to an employee injured at work. Here we are principally concerned with damages as a form of compensation (so far as mere money can hope to be) for damage or injury. This area of the law does not have the punishment of the employer as one of its objectives. Nor, indeed, does it have as one of its principal objectives a change of practice or system by an employer. However, a sensible employer will no doubt in practice see to it that such injuries will not be repeated on future occasions, so far as precautions against it are reasonably practicable.

Safe conditions of work

Any person, who, as a result of the breach of a legal duty of care owed to another person, injures or harms that person will be liable in negligence. A fuller description of the general considerations applicable to negligence liability will be given in the following chapter. In this respect an employer is no different from anyone else in that this duty to take reasonable care extends to all those who are foreseeable—and employees are some of the most foreseeable people around, so far as an employer is concerned. An employer—and this general term includes an employing authority such as a health authority—owes a duty to all employees to provide a safe system of work. This duty contains a number of separable aspects which all combine to produce the general duty.

Appointment and employment of staff

One is to provide personnel who are properly trained, or at least suitable, for the job of work which they are employed to do. There was recently a case (discussed in Chapter 1 in relation to the powers of the Health Service Commissioner) of a man who had always wanted to be a surgeon but who had never qualified as one, who posed as a qualified surgeon and actually participated in a number of surgical operations. Perhaps remarkably, there were apparently no adverse injurious consequences of what this person did. But had another member of staff been injured by the charlatan's failure to operate a piece of equipment in the proper manner, inquiries would have been put in hand as to whether the employing authority was negligent in appointing this person and whether the injury to the other employee occurred as a result of this negligence. The other elements of the overall duty of the employer are the obligation to provide adequate and safe machinery and materials (which can in relevant cases include clothing), and a duty to see to it that the general scheme or system in which people and machinery functions is a safe system. All these elements, then, can be subsumed under the general heading "safe system of work."

The duty is not only in respect of the original appointment of the staff. If by reasonable diligence the employer could have become aware of the subsequent incompetence of someone appointed, it would have been his duty to remove him. Further, the employer must not only employ a staff that is competent generally but must employ a sufficient number of staff of competent persons to deal with all the risks and dangers which the employer ought reasonably to expect might arise in the undertaking carried on by him.

In *Hudson* v. *Ridge Ltd.* (1957) an employee used to indulge in practical jokes on his fellow employees. The management knew this. One "prank" caused the plaintiff injury. The employer was held liable. He should have disciplined and if necessary dismissed the "joker."

Safe system

This involves the provision of suitable premises and the arrangement of the method of working so as to avoid injuries to the employees and a proper system of supervision where the nature of the undertaking reasonably requires it.

In *Parkes* v. *Smethwick Corporation* (1957) the plaintiff had been operated on for hernia in 1935, unkown to the defendants who had employed him as an ambulance driver since 1951. The plaintiff and his colleague carried a heavy patient from the second floor of a house to the ambulance. The plaintiff moved backwards up the steps of the ambulance and as he did so he suffered a hernia. He claimed that his injury was caused by the defendant's negligence by reason of their failure to provide a safe plant and equipment or a safe system of working. It was held that on the facts there was no failure of duty by the defendants in not ensuring that the plaintiff was physically equal to his duties nor was there any failure to provide safe plant and equipment; and that there was no duty on a local authority to give a detailed system of work to ambulance men as their work did not require that a detailed system should be prescribed since it involved an infinite variety of situations and that the exact way of carrying a patient from his room to an ambulance must be left to those on the spot. Accordingly, the defendants had not failed to provide a safe system of work.

The duty of an employer in negligence normally extends only to protecting employees against personal injury. So in many cases the property (including the clothing) of an employee would not be covered by the employer's liability. Such would be the case of oil leaking from a machine onto an employee's clothing. But negligence liability, producing a claim for damages by an employee against an employer, will certainly operate in the case of damaged clothing or property resulting from an accident in the course of which personal injury is also suffered. Such would be the case if a negligently maintained piece of machinery sprayed oil all over an employee, causing eye injury and damage to clothing. Such would also be the case in the event of fire or caustic substances producing simultaneous damage and injury, say, to an arm and shirtsleeve covering it.

If an employee suffers from a particular susceptibility, such as dermatitis as the result of frequent contact with grease or other irritants, and if the employee wants to continue his job in exactly the same conditions despite his knowledge of the health risks involved, the employer is certainly under no legal duty to refuse to employ him or to dismiss him from a job involving such conditions, provided that the employer sees to it that the employee fully understands the risks involved. The explanation of the particular risks involved must be as full and detailed, and at the same time as comprehensible, as all the circumstances of the particular case permit. It is not clear whether these principles of explanation and consent would apply in the case where really serious injury or death could result from a danger at work. It could well be that a court would decide that an employer is under a positive duty, in pursuance of his obligations to maintain a safe working system, to refuse to allow, say, an epileptic to work on scaffolding or a haemophiliac to work with sharp or abrasive materials or machinery.

The duty to protect the employee in the course of his employment is not confined to the actual performance of the work but also applies when he is doing something reasonably incidental to work. So where an employee slipped on a greasy duck-board while washing her tea cup after the recognised tea break, she was entitled to damages. The duty does not, however, apply in situations where the employee goes off to do something on his own, for himself, which is neither required nor expected. Employees may well be acting contrary to their rules of work in so doing. If, however, an employee does something at work which, although not part of the job he is employed to do, is nevertheless something which might reasonably be required of him, a duty of care will be owed by the employer. The place where the duty of care is owed will normally be on the premises of the employer or any outside place of employment. The latter will include health services staff whose employment includes home visiting (and in normal cases the obligation to make the place which is the subject of the home visit safe for that purpose will be augmented by the duty of the occupier of the premises to make those premises safe or at least to give warnings of known risks). Transport to and from the place of employment by the employer will also be covered by the duty of care.

Safe equipment and premises

The employer must take reasonable care to see that the equipment provided for the employee's use is safe, and to see that it is maintained in a safe condition. Regular inspection is therefore necessary. In one case, a nurse went into the changing room to change into her uniform. When she sat down on a chair it collapsed under her. Examination showed that it was riddled with woodworm. The employer's duty was to take reasonable care for the nurse's safety. For a chair to collapse from woodworm showed that it has been infested for a considerable time. During that time the chair had clearly not been properly inspected. The employer was therefore liable in negligence: *Baxter* v. *St. Helena Group H.M.C.* (1972).

The employer must provide the employee with equipment which is adequate to protect him against the risks involved in doing the job, for example masks, goggles, barrier cream and the like. This duty is owed to each individual employee, and his particular susceptibilities have to be borne in mind by the employer. In *Paris* v. *Stepney Borough Council* (1951) the plaintiff was employed in chipping rust off vehicles. No goggles were provided. He had only one eye and was injured in that eye as a result of his work. While there might not have been a duty to provide goggles for people with two sound eyes there was such a duty in respect of the plaintiff; for there was, for him, a risk of much more serious loss than for others.

Likewise, if the employer knew that the employee was susceptible to certain substances he would have to take appropriate action to protect him. In *Smith* v. *St. Helier Group H.M.C.* (1956) the plaintiff was employed as a theatre orderly. She alleged that owing to the negligence of the defendants she contracted dermatitis as a result of the constant use by her in her work of a solution of Dettol and soap and hot water. She was in fact more sensitive to Dettol than the great majority. Devlin J. said:

"It was not suggested that the defendants were aware that the plaintiff was one of those sensitive people—perhaps if they had been some duty might have been put on them in law. . . . It was impossible for the plaintiff to establish any case against the defendants based on negligence in the absence of any proof that they knew of particular sensitivity, nor could it be suggested that they ought to have taken any particular precautions as regards the use of Dettol by her."

The Medical Defence Union Report for 1975 refers to an incident in which a cleaner was injured by a needle in a waste paper basket. The M.D.U. advises that such hazards must be guarded against by a safe system for disposal of sharp or otherwise dangerous waste material.

Suppose that the employer has acquired the equipment (which has injured the employee) from a reputable supplier, and has made such inspection of it as was reasonable (which might have meant none at all where, say, the employer could not be expected to instal facilities to inspect and test it). In those circumstances the employer would not be liable, the House of Lords held, in *Davie* v. *New Merton Board Mills* (1959) because he had in fact taken reasonable care by buying from a reputable supplier and making reasonable inspection himself. It is true that in such a case the employee could sue the person who supplied his employer with the defective equipment, but he might be untraceable or difficult to sue (such as a foreign manufacturer).

To remedy this situation the Employers' Liability (Defective Equipment) Act 1969 was passed. This says that where an employee suffers personal injury in the course of his employment in consequence of a defect in equipment provided by his employer and the defect is attributable wholly or partly to the fault of a third party, then the injury shall be deemed to be also attributable to negligence on the part of the employer. This means that both the third party and the employer can be sued, or either of them. The third party remains liable for his negligence: the employer can be used as well as or instead of him. The Act binds the Crown.

Health Service applications

Before any further comment is made, let it be noted that the 1969 Employer's Liability (Defective Equipment) Act specifically binds the Crown. Section 1(4) reads:

"This section binds the Crown, and persons in the service of the Crown shall accordingly be treated for the purposes of this section as employees of the Crown if they would not be so treated apart from this subsection."

The final phrase was doubtless inserted on account of difficulties in the law relating to Crown proceedings as to who is an employee of the Crown. Let it also be remembered that statutes do not, as a general rule, bind the Crown unless such intention is specifically enacted. Hospitals administered under the National Health Service are to be regarded as employers for the purposes of the Act, and the apparently greater burden placed on health authorities will surely be seen as worthwhile in view of the more ready protection afforded to members of staff. The potential risks in the use of complex and often dangerous equipment, purchased by hospitals for use by employees in carrying out their duties in the hospital, put such employees in a position in which they ought not to have to bring an action proving negligence against the supplier or manufacturer. Needless to say, employers outside the National Health Service are bound in the normal way by the Act in just the same way as any other employers. Thus its provisions apply normally to private hospitals and clinics as well as to general medical, dental and ophthalmic practitioners operating under a contract for services from the Family Practitioner Committee but independently for the purpose of employing staff.

Injuries from violence

While instances of the duty of care owed by an employer to provide safe working conditions could be multiplied, a final word may for the present moment be given about a subject which concerns many health service staff and in particular nurses: that is, violence. It appears from cases which have come before the courts that an employer owes a duty of care to take reasonable precautions to protect employees from physical violence in the performance of their duties. In the case of health service staff carrying valuables, a duty will be owed to them by their employing authority to see that they are reasonably safe in so doing, according to the nature and value of the articles being carried and all the relevant circumstances of each particular case, including likely or known dangers. In one decided case, in which an employee who was sent to collect £1,500 wages was robbed, the employers had to pay the injured employee damages after they were found to be guilty of negligence in failing to employ a security firm to collect the wages. In the case of violent or potentially violent patients this principle will no doubt apply also: both mental wards and A and E departments present obvious dangers to staff in this respect.

Assaults by patients on employees

Where an employee is assaulted in the course of his employment by a patient, what remedies has he? He can of course claim
damages from him for the civil wrong of assault, and it would be
open to him to bring criminal proceedings as well. This is so,
even if the patient is a mental patient. Confining ourselves to the
civil liability of such a patient, there is no reason why he should
not compensate those he injures even if he is suffering from
mental illness. Another possibility is that the employee could sue
the employer (the health authority) for failing to take adequate
steps to safeguard him from assault. However such a claim would
not be certain to succeed: a person who goes to work in a mental
institution might be said to consent to the possibility of injuries
inflicted by violent patients, especially if the system could not be
proved to be faulty.

The third point concerns the Criminal Injuries Compensation
Board, set up in 1964. Under the scheme anyone who is the
victim of a crime of violence can claim compensation from the
Board. If the Board is satisfied with the claim it awards damages
on common law principles. It is not necessary for the assailant to
have been prosecuted—he may be unknown—but the matter
should be reported to the police at the earliest opportunity.
Under the scheme the fact that a claimant was an employee at
the time of the assault is neither here nor there. In one award a
doctor whose hand was injured when a patient attacked him with
a billhook in his surgery was awarded £1,066. In another, a nurse
at a factory no longer able to work after having been assaulted by
an employee she was treating was awarded £3,256. In a third
case, the husband of a woman who was being treated in a
casualty department attacked and bit off part of the ear of the
casualty officer: the husband was imprisoned and the doctor got
£150 from the Board.

*The management of violent, or potentially violent, hospital
patients*

In March 1976, the D.H.S.S. issued Health Circular (76)11
under the above title and the document, with an appendix by the
Royal College of Nursing, gives guidance on a difficult subject.
The circular points out that serious acts of violence by patients
in hospital are relatively infrequent, but arrangements in general
hospitals, as well as psychiatric, should be reviewed in the light

of this guidance. The Appendix to the circular shows that prevention of a violent incident is the first objective, and the need to ensure that a potentially violent patient is in the most appropriate place for care. Staff attitudes are important in both prevention and management of violent incidents, and nursing staff have a particular responsibility in this direction. The number of staff (suitably trained or instructed) allocated to a ward must take account of possible violence and the circular explains that there should not be other patients at risk with patients who may be violent. It is hoped that most patients who exhibit violence from time to time can be treated in a local hospital, and only in a few cases should it be appropriate to transfer to a regional secure unit, or similar accommodation. The problems arising in Accident and Emergency Departments are recognised, and staff should be aware of the difficulties that may be encountered and the occasional need for some form of physical restraint. In some circumstances patients suspected of having offensive weapons may be searched, and staff should have means of calling for assistance. Powers of search are briefly discussed in Chapter 9.

Advice is given on dealing with violent incidents which occur, although it is recognised that the action taken will be a matter for judgment in the recognised circumstances. A patient may be restrained with the degree of force which is necessary and reasonable in the circumstances, and staff acting in good faith and in accordance with training received should not be blamed as a result of an incident. However, authorities must not condone or defend actions which appear to be wrong or inappropriate. It is recognised that staff can be vulnerable to unfounded complaints in some situations, and membership of trade unions and professional organisations is in the interests of staff needing advice. Each hospital should have an adequate system of reporting incidents which involve violence, restraint, isolation or damage, and the report of an incident should be brought to the attention of the authority as well as the officers concerned. The action to be taken as a result of a report must be determined and, generally, relatives should be informed of any incident of violence. If staff are injured as a result of violence, they may have rights under the Criminal Injuries Compensation Scheme, as well as Industrial Injuries, but the incident must have been fully reported to the authority.

Circular HC (76)11 also explains the appropriate action to be taken when a mentally disordered patient not liable to detention attempts to leave hospital in circumstances which could lead to injury to himself or other persons. Junior staff should seek assistance from senior officers, but can take reasonable steps to restrain the patient in order that a decision may be taken on the need for detention under 29(1), or report under section 30(2) of the Mental Health Act 1959. If such a patient has already left hospital, an appropriate officer must decide if a report should be passed to the Police, Social Service Department and/or the patient's relatives, with recommendations that the patient should be returned under compulsory powers. The doctor in charge of a patient's treatment must always be kept fully informed of the circumstances, and junior nursing staff must report to their appropriate officers. Care must be taken to ensure that patients are not wrongfully detained, and that members of the public do not suffer from any neglect by the hospital.

The conditions for the exercise of formal, or "compulsory," powers of detention in respect of mentally disordered patients are discussed in Chapter 13.

II

Safeguards and statutory duties

Statutes impose many duties on employers which are intended to protect employees. If these duties are broken the employer may be prosecuted and fined. The outstanding example is the Factories Act 1961. One of the duties imposed by that Act is to see that every dangerous part of any machinery is securely fenced. Now suppose the employee is injured through the employer's failure to do this. The employer may be prosecuted. This will not be much consolation for the injured employee. However the courts have interpreted the Act imposing the duty on the employer as giving a right of action to the employee so that he can sue the employer for damages. Here, the duty was imposed on the employer not by the common law (as in the case of negligence) but by statute. So this action by the employee is called an action for breach of statutory duty.

An interesting example is *Wearing* v. *Pirelli*, a decision of the House of Lords in 1976. Employers appealed against a decision that they were liable for a breach of statutory duty under Factories Act 1961, s. 14(1), for an injury sustained by a machine operator. The employee had been injured when a tool he was using was caught in the revolving drum of an unfenced machine. The employers claimed that as the employee had not come into direct contact with the machine they were not in breach. It was held that the employee was injured by the drum itself whether the tool or he himself had come into contact with it. It would be a denial of justice to refuse the employee relief on such a narrow distinction. Other cases where employees had been ineligible for relief had arisen in different circumstances, and to follow them in this case was inappropriate.

Now the same facts may give rise to an action in negligence and in statutory duty, and the employee may win on both grounds or win on one and lose on the other. If he does win on both he does not get double damages. The situation is that the existence of both grounds of action gives him two possibilities of getting whatever damages he may be entitled to because of his injury.

A particular problem is that, while it is the function of the legislature to promulgate rules for the general guidance of the public at large, or of a certain section of it (seen from a legislative point of view as an identifiable class rather than as a group of individuals), it is the function of the courts to apply general rules in the solution of particular cases as they arise. Judges can certainly do something very much akin to legislating when they wish to implement some economic or social policy; but the differences between judges and legislators in this respect are twofold, namely that the "legislative" authority of judges lies very much behind them in the form of precedents, and that judges are themselves always subject to legislative contradiction. Even a decision of the House of Lords cannot stand as a precedent for future cases if a statute has intervened which effectively (though not usually by name) overrules it.

A natural conclusion from the fact that there is frequently scant guidance from certain paternalistic statutes (for instance, factory safety, transport rules) would be that Parliament intended the courts to legislate whenever the relationship between private individuals came into question; and that the legislature itself was content to provide guidance and sometimes impose criminal sanctions as part of the relationship between private individuals and the state. It is therefore justifiable to conclude that, paradoxically, judges do not really legislate in the area of non-statutory negligence, but that they are effectively compelled to do so in cases where it is the state itself (through Parliament) that has seen fit to impose further duties over and above those which enterprises would otherwise owe to their "neighbours," those affected by their acts and omissions.

The law at the crossroads

The elements of fault and risk can be seen in operation in the case of *Bux* v. *Slough Metals Ltd.*, decided in 1974. The plaintiff, a Pakistani steelworker in the defendant's works, was injured when a pan carrying molten metal knocked against another piece of machinery with the result that he sustained severe injuries to his eyes. A provision of the Non-Ferrous Metals (Melting and Founding) Regulations of 1962 requires the provision and maintenace of suitable protective equipment including "suitable goggles or other suitable eye protection for persons employed in ... work at a furnace where there is risk to the eyes from molten metal; or pouring or skimming; or work involving risk to the eyes from hot sand being thrown off." Suitable goggles—suitable, at least, for purposes of protection—were provided to relevant employees in 1969. However, the plaintiff ceased to wear his goggles when they inconveniently steamed up in a very short space of time. In awarding damages to Mr. Bux, reduced by 40 per cent. on account of his own contribution to the injuries which he had sustained, the Court of Appeal held that in every case it is a question of fact whether the statutory duty was co-extensive with, or more or less extensive than, the common law duty. The duty imposed on the defendant company by the relevant regulation in this case did not supersede the common law duty of the employer, for the regulation was silent as to the legal position where an employer knew that suitable goggles which he has provided were consistently not worn by his men when engaged in work involving risk to their eyes. That legal position was the same as it had been before the regulations came into force. The question whether instruction, persuasion or insistence with regard to the use of protective equipment should be resorted to, depended on the facts of a particular case, one of those being the nature and degree of the risk of serious harm liable to occur if the equipment were not worn. It was found as a fact that, in the circumstances of this particular case the plaintiff would have worn goggles if he had been instructed to do so in a reasonable and firm manner, such insistence being followed up by some sort of supervision. The defendants were therefore in breach of their common law duty to maintain a reasonably safe system of work by giving the necessary instructions and enforcing them by way of supervision.

The materialisation of a risk specifically envisaged and delineated by statute is apt to be only inelegantly expressed in terms of common law negligence. If the statute is to take precedence (which all statutes in our legal system must, subject to their "interpretation" by the courts) then it is high time that a legislative policy be adopted whereby at least general predictions may be made as to the availability of private damages resulting from the breach of a statutory policy.

Policy and insurance

It may be concluded that, while in some cases the ordinary common law relating to negligence (for instance, consisting in the failure to provide a reasonably safe system of work) appears merely to complement the general duty imposed by the statute in such a way as to open the way for an individual claim for damages, the real effect of the court's "construction" of a statute or regulation in such a way as to compensate injured individuals is to heighten the standard of care owed to them, or at least to make a breach of duty easier of commission. Inasmuch as a risk has been created by the establishment or pursuit of a particular enterprise involving hazard to individuals, the materialisation of that risk in the shape of an accident is prima facie deserving of compensation. One major factor in the final judicial decision as to the availability of damages is the availability and viability of insurance to cover the risk. In some areas of activity, insurance is compulsory, as under the Employers Liability (Compulsory Insurance) Act of 1969. In others it would be well nigh impossible to insure against all consequential loss.

Now it is all very well saying that if an employee is injured by the negligence of his employer he can sue him for damages. What if the employer has not got enough money to pay the sum awarded? Clearly the employee will not get anything. The Employers' Liability (Compulsory Insurance) Act 1969 deals with this situation. It says that every employer carrying on business in Great Britain must insure against liability for bodily injury or disease sustained by his employees and arising out of and in the course of their employment. It is a criminal offence to fail to do so. (Motorists are likewise required to take out insurance against liability to passengers and third parties). The Act does not bind the Crown (and hence health authorities) as the Crown carries its own insurance. But it does bind private clinics and similar institutions, as well as employment by general medical, dental and ophthalmic practitioners.

Other forms of compensation

A survey in any but the barest detail of the benefits available to injured or disabled workers is outside the scope of this book.

This is, however, a convenient point at which to indicate some of the principal sources of financial compensation which may in appropriate circumstances be available in addition to, or instead of, the payment of damages.

The Workmen's Compensation Act 1897 introduced the very important principle that where an employee was injured at work he was entitled to compensation without having to prove any default on the employer. This Act was superseded by the National Insurance (Industrial Injuries) Act 1946. This Act has in turn been amended from time to time, the latest statute being the Social Security Act 1975.

The assumption which underlies this legislation is that industrial accidents are to be regarded, not as instances of individual negligence, but as incidents which are inevitable in the course of employment. Accepting the modern doctrine that the State should be comprehensively interested in the welfare of its members, it clearly becomes desirable that the State should provide for the maintenance of those disabled by industrial accidents and of the dependants of persons killed in industrial accidents. Under the Acts the State is made the insurer against industrial accidents; insurance premiums, or contributions, are paid to the State and the benefits of the scheme are guaranteed by the State; and special machinery for adjudicating claims and for settling questions or disputes has been established outside the scope of the ordinary courts.

The scope of the insurance

The Act insures all persons employed in insurable employment against personal injury caused by accident arising out of, and in the course of, insurable employment and against incapacity caused by scheduled industrial disease. Personal injury includes disfigurement. The Act is very wide in its scope, no limit of income is imposed, and both sexes are insurable. In respect of non-fatal cases, the benefit provided by the Act is related either to incapacity for work or to a permanent or substantial loss of physical or mental faculty. "Accident" means any untoward or unlooked-for event. Thus if a nurse is attacked whilst in the course of her duties, this is an accident.

The expression "out of and in the course of employment" can raise problems. Successful claims include: a nurse injured while sleepwalking—she was at the time living in a nurses' home, which she was obliged to do; a member of a blood collection unit injured at an hotel where he was obliged to stay; and a nurse at a mental hospital injured while playing football with patients as part of their therapy. But an unsuccessful claim was made by a nurse at a mental hospital who was injured playing football for the hospital team; he was not required to play, though he had been given time off to do so.

The onus of proving personal injury lies on the injured person, though it is not necessary for him to establish his case beyond all reasonable doubt—the degree of certainty required only in criminal proceedings. It is sufficient if the balance of probability leans in his favour.

Difficulties arise where it has to be determined whether the claimant's condition is due to the alleged accident or to some previous accident or the process of pre-existing disease. A railway engine driver was awarded benefit in respect of hernia due to the continual operation of a stiff lever, it being held that each strain would cause widening of the tear; on the other hand, a railway worker who had heart disease and who suffered an attack of angina pectoris whilst lifting steel sleepers was held not to have suffered injury by accident.

Injury benefit is payable to an insured person who is rendered incapable of work as a result of injury by accident. Disablement benefit is payable after the injury benefit is over and may take the form either of a pension or of a gratuity. There are five variations of the benefit and these depend on the relationship of the beneficiary to the deceased, namely widows, widowers, children of the deceased's family, parents. Prescribed relatives may be entitled.

In addition, by section 76 of the 1975 Act a person so insured is insured also against any prescribed disease and against any prescribed personal injury not caused by such an accident. The Minister can prescribe a disease or injury in relation to any insured persons where he is satisfied that it ought to be treated, having regard to its causes and incidence, as a risk of their occupations and not as a risk common to all persons, and that it is such that the attribution of particular cases to the nature of the employment can be established or presumed with reasonable certainty. For example, anthrax has been prescribed in respect of those employed in handling wool, hair or skins or other animal products.

An example of particular significance in health services activities is that of tuberculosis. Tuberculosis has been prescribed in respect of those employed in one of the following occupations:

(a) in the medical treatment or nursing of one or more persons suffering from tuberculosis, or in a service ancillary to such treatment or nursing. It is not essential that the treatment or nursing should have been undertaken specifically because of the patient's tuberculosis, or even that the presence of TB was known or suspected at the time. Thus, for example, a nurse or ward made in a general ward of a hospital may be able to qualify for benefit, even though none of the patients was known to be suffering from TB;

(b) in attendance upon one or more persons suffering from tuberculosis where the attendance was needed because of some physical or mental infirmity. The attendance must consist in doing something to or for the patient himself which has physical or mental infirmity prevents him from doing for himself;

(c) as a research worker engaged in research in connection with tuberculosis; and

(d) as a laboratory worker, pathologist or a person taking part in or assisting at post-mortem examinations of human remains where the occupation involved working with material which was a source of tuberculosis infection.

Normally the hospital employees of a health authority will come, if at all, within categories (a) or (d). Within (b) might come welfare officers, health visitors and home helps.

III

Worker protection legislation

There is still in existence an enormous mass of legislation (statutes) applicable to particular areas of activity. Some of the broader-based statutes include the Factories Acts, the Offices, Shops and Railway Premises Act, and the Mines and Quarries Act. There existed until quite recently a variety of methods for enforcing the provisions of this mass of legislation. But as a result of the Robens Report of 1972, legislation was passed in 1974 streamlining and simplifying the enforcement procedure relevant to most of this legislation. The provisions and specific safety requirements and prohibitions of all this previously existing legislation remain in force, but enforcement procedures are unified and strengthened. The substance of the duties imposed on employers in respect of their employees' safety, and indeed often on the employees themselves for a variety of reasons, has been created by individual statutes such as those just mentioned. However, it was not until recently that a general procedure was available by which the substance of these duties could be most efficiently enforced. This latter was the function of the Health and Safety at Work Act 1974. Before discussing that Act it is convenient to give examples of some of the many duties imposed by two principal worker protection statutes, the Factories Act 1961 and the Offices, Shops and Railway Premises Act 1963.

The Factories Act 1961

Section 175 of this Act defines a factory as

"any premises in which or within the close or curtilage or precincts of which persons are employed in manual labour in any process for or incidental to (a) the making of any article or the part of any article, (b) the altering, repairing, cleaning, demolition, breaking up or washing of any article, (c) the adapting for sale of any article the work of which is carried on by way of trade or for the purposes of gain."

This general definition is extended to include the sorting of articles, the washing or filling of bottles, any laundry ancillary to another business or incidentally for the purposes of any public institution, printing and lithography, premises where mechanical power is used, premises where articles are made or prepared incidental to the carrying on of building operations or works of engineering construction.

Notwithstanding references to trade or gain the Act extends to premises in the occupation of the Crown or any municipal or other public authority which would otherwise be excluded because the work carried on thereat is not carried on by way of trade or for the purposes of gain (that is, N.H.S. hospitals and other premises not carried on for trade or gain, but thus brought within the Act).

Certain parts of the premises of hospitals (whether voluntary or public authority, including those set up under the N.H.S. Act 1946) are thus brought in and the Factories Acts apply to laundries, engineers' or clerks of works' departments, and in mental hospitals to the tailor's shop and the printers' shop for example. *Wood* v. *L.C.C.* (1940) decided that a hospital is not a factory. In this case the plaintiff was a kitchen maid. She was mincing corned beef in an electrically operated machine. The machine clogged, and she freed it by sticking a finger into a hole.

She succeeded in freeing the machine, but at the expense of part of her finger. The beef was not for sale, but for consumption by patients and staff. She argued that the machine should have been fenced so as to prevent her from putting her finger into the blades. But was the kitchen a factory? Only if it was could her action succeed. There was manual labour: hers. And there was, she said, a breaking up of an article: the corned beef. The court said that this sort of activity, and the washing of dishes, though strictly within the definition, could not make a hospital kitchen a factory when one looked at the whole nature of the premises, and at the nature of the work going on there. The action failed therefore.

This is, however, an area in which new situations can readily be distinguished from earlier precedents and *Wood* v. *L.C.C.* was indeed distinguished (that is, not followed because of what the court regarded as a material factual difference) in the recent case of *Bromwich* v. *National Ear, Nose and Throat Hospital* (1980).

The plaintiff was injured in the course of his employment as a plumber and fitter at the defendants' hospital, while working in a workshop containing two grinding machines, a lathe and a bench drill provided for the use of employees engaged in general maintenance and repair work. The workshop was only used from time to time for mechanical and electrical repairs and minor installation work for the hospital. The plaintiff was injured when he attempted to use one of the grinding machines to trim off a metal strap he was making for a piece of hospital equipment with the rest on the machine not properly adjusted. He brought an action against the defendants for damages for personal injuries, claiming that the defendants were in breach of their statutory duty under regulation 15(1) of the Abrasive Wheels Regulations 1970 in failing to ensure that the rest was properly adjusted. The regulations only applied to premises which were a factory within the meaning of section 175(1)(a) of the Factories Act 1961, which defined a factory as premises in which persons were employed in manual labour in the making of an article or part of an article, or the altering or repairing of an article. The defendants denied liability, contending that, even if the work done in the workshop did consist of such work as making and repairing articles, the workshop was not a place to which the 1961 Act could have been intended to apply because it was merely used in connection with the maintenance of the hospital and was purely incidental to the functions of the hospital which had to be inspected.

The court held that, in regard to the nature of the workshop and the work carried out there, it was prima facie a factory and there was nothing in the general provisions of the Factories Act

1961, looked at as a whole, to show that those provisions were clearly not applicable to it and the processes carried on there; nor would the application of the Act to the workshop produce a bizarre or ludicrous result. It could not, therefore, be inferred that Parliament had not intended the Act to apply to the workshop, and accordingly the 1979 regulations applied to it. It followed that, the defendants not having satisfied themselves that the plaintiff was competent to use the grinding machine, they were responsible in law for the accident and the plaintiff's claim succeeded in full.

By far the most important of these Acts from the point of view of hospitals is that relating to the fencing of machinery. Every part of the transmission machinery, and every dangerous part of other machinery, and all parts of electric generators, motors, rotary converters, and flywheels directly connected to them, must be securely fenced unless in such a position or of such construction as to be as safe to every person employed or working on the premises, as if securely fenced; and any part of a stock bar which projects beyond the headstock of a lathe must be securely fenced unless it is in such a position as to be as safe to every person as if securely fenced.

The Offices, Shops and Railway Premises Act 1963

The object of this Act is to set standards of health, welfare and safety for employees in office, shops and railway premises. The standards set follow closely in many respects those laid down for factories by the Factories Act 1961. No part of the 1963 Act applies to any premises which are a factory for the purpose of the 1961 Act. The Act applies to office premises, shop premises and railway premises "being premises in the case of which persons are employed to work."

Office premises means a building or part of a building, being a building or part, the sole principal use of which is as an office or for office purposes.

Office purposes includes the purposes of administration, clerical work, handling money and telephone and telegraph operating; and clerical work includes writing, book-keeping, sorting papers, filing, typing, duplicating, machine calculating, drawing and the editorial preparation of matter for publication.

The definition of office premises is intended to have a wide application. It includes offices forming part of a building mainly used for other purposes; for example, an office in a hospital, club or factory. Whatever the size of the office, it will be within the scope of the Act if its sole or principal use is for office purposes.

The Act also applies to premises occupied together with office premises for the purposes of the activities carried on there. For example, stairs, passages, landings, storerooms, entrance halls, and yards are covered if they are in the same occupation as the office, are physically adjacent to it and are used for purposes connected with the business of the office.

Shop premises includes shops in the ordinary sense of the word and also "A building or part of a building . . . which is not a shop but of which the sole or principal use is the carrying on there of retail trade or business." This includes a lending library operated for profit and places such as cafes and restaurants which serve food or drink for immediate consumption by members of the public. Thus a cafe is covered by the Act if it is principally used for serving the public, that is to say non-residents of the hospital. If used mainly by residents it is not within this Act.

The Act also covers staff canteens maintained in conjunction with office or shop premises for the purposes of the sale or supply for immediate consumption of food and drink wholly or mainly to people employed to work in the premises in question. Thus the majority of hospital canteens will be excluded because they do not cater wholly or mainly for office staff.

The Act and Crown premises

The Act does not, in general, bind the Crown though the Government has said that Crown premises will in practice conform to the standards required by the Act.

Apart from this, section 83 makes binding on the Crown certain provisions of the Act in so far as they impose duties, failure to comply with which might give rise to liability in tort. These provisions include all those mentioned under general requirements down to and including the fire items. Thus, if a person employed in premises managed by a hospital authority fell down a staircase which was not provided with an adequate handrail, it would be open to him to bring a civil action on the ground that there had been a breach of statutory duty imposed by the relevant section of the Act.

The Minister has made regulations concerning washing facilities, sanitary conveniences, and has prescribed certain machines as dangerous. These regulations fall within section 83 and bind the Crown. That concerning dangerous machines lists, for example, guillotine machines: the requirements concerning training and supervision must therefore be complied with by hospital and health service authorities.

The Minister has made regulations stating what information about the Act is to be given to employees. This does not bind the Crown, but hospital and health authorities have been asked to ensure that the regulations are complied with at hospital and Health Service offices.

There is, in its provisions, no power to enforce the Act against the Crown (apart from the civil liability mentioned), though the recently introduced Crown improvement notices effectively secure compliance. It has however been decided that the Inspectors should inspect premises managed by hospital authorities and that those authorities should comply with the administrative provisions of the Act as, for instance, in respect of the notification of accidents.

The Health and Safety at Work Act 1974

The Health and Safety at Work Act, which came into force at the beginning of 1975, created a Health and Safety Commission and Executive to oversee the whole area of health and safety at work. The enforcement powers are threefold. Health and Safety inspectors are empowered to issue improvement notices requiring the remedy of breaches of statutory safety provisions. And, where there is a risk of serious personal injury, inspectors may issue prohibition notices. This may be done immediately where the risk of serious personal injury is imminent. The ultimate instrument for securing compliance with the safety, health and welfare duties imposed by the Health and Safety at Work Act 1974 is the criminal law. Fines, or sometimes in very serious cases even imprisonment, are provided for in case of non-compliance with the duties envisaged by the Act when such breach leads to criminal conviction.

Under the 1974 Act it is not only the employing authority or employer who is subject to the duties and requirements imposed by the law. Employees also owe certain duties, and their activities, too, are subject to the enforcement procedures provided by the Act. In particular, an employee whose job includes a specific health and safety responsibility which his employment contract imposes on him or which he has otherwise agreed to take on, must fulfil the requirements of that duty as well as he reasonably can. Furthermore, employees generally are

under a statutory duty to assist the employer in the maintenance
and implementation of safety schemes and procedures. A recent
Health Circular, HC(78)30, sets out these employee duties
clearly and specifically:

> "An employee in the NHS, like any other employee has a duty
> under section 7 of the Act to take reasonable care for his own
> health and safety and that of any person who might be affected
> by his acts or omissions at work. This general duty applies also
> to an employee visiting a patient in the patient's own home.
> An employee also has a duty under Section 7 to cooperate with
> his employer in ensuring that the latter is able to discharge his
> duties under the Act. He has a similar duty to cooperate with
> any other person, apart from his employer, who has a
> responsibility imposed by the Act. This means, for example,
> that an RHA employee working on AHA premises would have
> a duty to cooperate with the AHA. If an employee fails to carry
> out any of these duties he is liable to be prosecuted.
>
> Where an employee has been given by his Authority a
> specific safety responsibility, either as an intrinsic part of his
> management function or as a specialist safety adviser or
> officer, failure to discharge this responsibility where it was
> reasonably practicable for him to have done so could result in
> liability under Section 7 of the Act."

The incidence of this duty under section 7 of the Act is frequently the subject of enquiry, but it is not as frightening as it
might appear. For inasmuch as health service employees are
under an obligation to do anything in relation to health, safety
and welfare at work, the requirements of the Act go no further
than what is already sensibly and properly done. It is the
procedures for enforcement that are generalised and strengthened. The Act certainly does not impose a legally greater
standard of care on health services staff. And even though the
ultimate enforcement of the Act takes the form of a fine or
imprisonment, the sort of conduct by an employee (under section
7) which would qualify for that penalty is conduct about which
we might in any case say "It would be criminal to let the person
get away with it!" In other words, for the act or omission of an
individual to give rise to liability in the form of a fine or even
imprisonment, it would have to be something of exceptional
recklessness or gross stupidity. But we live in an imperfect world,
and the 1974 Act provides even for rare and extreme cases of
imperfection.

The Health and Safety Executive has given an assurance that
no N.H.S. employee will be prosecuted in substitution for his

health authority, and that prosecutions would be brought only in cases where they would have been brought against employees of bodies not covered by Crown privilege.

The Department's attitude

The attitude of the Department of Health and Social Security to the objectives and effect of the Health and Safety at Work Act 1974 as it affects operations and activities within the National Health Service is summed up in Circular HC(78)30 thus:

"The general duties imposed by the Act have been in effect since 1 April 1975; and Authorities should by now have issued a statement of general policy with regard to health and safety. If any questions arise in relation to the interpretation of the Act or the general nature of the duties imposed, these should be addressed in the first instance to Personnel Officers.

The consultative document on *Priorities for Health and Personal Social Services in England* stated (paragraph 2.10) that 'the requirements of the Health and Safety at Work Act will need to be met.' It is important that Health Authorities should be fully aware of the duties imposed on them by the Act and of the need to ensure that these are properly discharged. In addition to the specific statutory duties arising from the Act, and the general responsibility of Health Authorities as employers for safeguarding the welfare of their employees, Authorities will appreciate that improvements in the standards of health, safety and welfare for employees will be reflected in greater efficiency and improved standards of service for patients."

Chapter 6

NEGLIGENCE LIABILITY

This chapter has a threefold purpose. First, the references which have of necessity been made in earlier chapters to "negligence" and "the tort of negligence" can now be explained in much greater depth than has so far been possible, and with specific reference to decided cases on the matter. Second, the opportunity now presents itself to examine the meaning of such concepts as "duty of care" and "standard of care" in a practical way with reference to a variety of activities, including the pursuit of specialist professions. And, finally, attention will be focussed on allegations of negligence in medical and health service contexts.

I

Liability for negligence

The law of negligence is one aspect, indeed a very major aspect, of the law of tort. One way in which a person can become legally liable to another is by breaking a contract. A contract is an agreement which the law is prepared to enforce, and this "enforcement" amounts at least to the consolation of getting damages—money—if the agreement is broken. The law of tort is concerned also with the award of damages; but here there has been no agreement between the people who find themselves legally entangled. Indeed, in the majority of tort cases there has been no relationship at all between the parties before the "wrong" is done (an accident, for instance). Instead, the law *creates* a legal relationship between the person who does something wrong and the other person who suffers from it. Many readers may have come across the expression "the nurse (or doctor) owes the patient a duty of care." In everyday terms, and in terms of the attitude which the nurse adopts towards his or her patients, such an expression seems to convey no more than the simple fact that nurses and doctors should do their job carefully, and in a caring way, as distinct from pursuing a perilous and slap-happy course through their daily lives—and that of their patients! But in law the expression "duty of care" means more than that. It means that a situation exists in which the law says that there is a relationship between two or more people, or groups of people, of such a type that if the carelessness of one causes harm, injury or damage to the other, the latter will be able to obtain damages by way of compensation. Note the terminology: *damage* is what is suffered; *damages* are paid in consequence to the person "damaged." One occasionally hears people saying that someone "has suffered damages." The only person who "suffers damages" is the careless person who becomes liable to pay them! But the law does not express it like that.

Breach of duty

There is no doubt that a duty of care in this legal sense exists as between doctors and nurses and their patients. If the law is to award damages to someone who is harmed, that harm must be proved to have resulted from a *breach* of that legal duty. So the three essential ingredients of the tort of negligence are: duty, breach, and damage. Let us examine these three elements in more detail, and in so doing put the question: what if our mistake happened when we were really tired, or feeling ill, or perhaps just daydreaming?

The law does not impose liability just because an accident happens. It makes allowances for what it calls "mere inadvertence." Thus, not everyone becomes legally liable just because they cause an accident. Events may simply have conspired against them; it is, as it were, their misadventure. Even if another person were to be harmed by an accident caused by mere inadvertence, it would be intolerable if the hapless person whose actions in fact led to the accident had to pay out damages on every such occasion. There has to be carelessness, and not just any carelessness but only that which the law will, in the event, brand as a "breach of duty," or a breach of the *legal* duty of care which it says was owed by the person who caused the injury or harm to the person who suffered it.

While it is a commonplace that nurses, doctors and all those engaged in medical care in the health services owe their patients a legal duty of care, it is by no means every act which causes someone harm which will amount to a breach of this duty. True, a duty of care exists; and, also true, harm or injury may occur to someone such as a patient or perhaps a fellow employee. But merely because someone gets harmed or injured does not mean that the harm or injury amounts to the breach of the legal duty of care. If, for instance, all practicable precautions had been taken against an accident, but the accident still occurred, the duty of care which certainly exists would not have been broken by the occurrence of the injury which, equally certainly, was caused. A leaking roof might have flooded a ward floor, and all the available nursing and ancillary staff might have worked very hard to mop up and prevent further water getting onto the floor. Nevertheless, if a patch of dried soap solution hitherto unnoticed became slippery as a result, a patient or indeed a nurse or auxiliary might slip and sustain injury. The ward staff in such a situation are under a legal duty of care. Injury has been sustained. But since all practicable precautions have been taken, no legal duty has been broken. The law, even with the wisdom of hindsight, does not expect perfection when acting under difficulties. The answer might be different if a nurse or auxiliary *knew* the soap solution was there, let it dry because they could not be bothered to clean it up, and if the staff also *knew* of the leaking roof. In those circumstances it would not be being too wise after the event to say that the precautions taken, or rather the lack of them, fell far short of what was reasonably practicable.

In emergencies also, the demands which are made by the law on the professional do not exceed what can reasonably be required of the good, sensible person in all the circumstances of each particular case. Acting under pressure, like acting under extreme fatigue or even just when feeling poorly, can produce errors and omissions. A balance must here be struck between the unfortunate individual who may suffer as a consequence of a mistake made in such circumstances, and the poor nurse (or whomever) who was doing her best and just let things go wrong. How is this balance of competing interests and claims to be struck? The specifically uninformative answer to the worried inquirer is that, within certain predictable limits, all depends on the nature of the emergency or pressure and on the circumstances which have caused it to happen. But we can be more specific than that.

If we were all permitted to fulfil whatever standard of care our physical state or our mood dictated, not only would everyone have a different standard of care applied to them from that which might be applicable to others, or to certain others; but, furthermore, each one of us might act from time to time with varying degrees of care, efficiency and foresight and still comply with the standards the law requires of us. But that could not be, since whatever "justice" we might do to ourselves we should certainly not be doing justice to those in our care or those who are otherwise affected by our acts and omissions (colleagues, perhaps). Therefore, the fact that a nurse, a doctor or other person engaged in health care activities was tired or "one degree under" (let alone one over the eight!) on a particular day would certainly not suffice in law to subject that person to a standard of care different in some degree from that required on occasions of fitness, good health and full efficiency. For the law to be otherwise would subject the patients to something of a lottery.

But what of the notoriously overworked junior house officer, or indeed any person engaged in health care activities whose very responsibilities or working conditions themselves produce the inefficiency in causing fatigue or stress? While each case would have to be carefully examined in the light of all the particular circumstances and considerations, it can be said with some confidence that the balance of interests between patient-care as a whole and the claims and expectations of an individual patient would not be well-served by the law's insistence that any and every error of judgment amounted to the tort of negligence and thus required the payment of damages to the injured patient. If, for instance, freak storms or snowfall produced an unprecedented spate of road accident casualties for an accident and emergency unit, the issue (mentioned earlier) of the practicability of precautions might well come into the picture. A further consideration of general application which affects the question of breach of duty of care is that of the importance of the object to be attained. Putting this issue together with the practicability of precautions in all the pressing circumstances of an emergency situation, it is unlikely that the wisdom of the law's hindsight would go anything like so far as to impose liability for damages for each and every error and omission.

Clearly distinguishable from such out-of-the-ordinary situations is the routine work of an Accident and Emergency department. True, there are emergencies—but these are normally emergencies just to the patient, and are emergencies which are (or should be) provided for by way of the routine system and organisation of the department. Also distinguishable is the situation of the nurse or doctor who is off-colour or tired through non-extraordinary causes (a bad cold, a few late nights). Here there is no situation of emergency and the law expects the same degree of care from all nursing and medical staff.

The cause of the damage

There is one final matter which must be included in this introductory account of the law relating to negligence if a full picture is to be given. We have looked at the notion of "duty of care," and we have dwelt at some length on the issue of what may or may not amount to a breach of that duty. But even if both these elements are present in a situation in which an individual suffers harm, it is not in every case a necessary conclusion that the tort of negligence will have been committed in relation to that individual. Let us take the decided case of *Barnett* v. *Chelsea and Kensington Hospital Management Committee* (1969) as an example.

At about 5.00 a.m. on January 1, 1966, three night watchmen drank some tea. Soon afterwards all three men started vomiting. At about 8.00 a.m. the men walked to the casualty department of the local hospital, which was open. One of the men (the one who later died) when he was in the waiting room, lay on some armless chairs. He appeared to be ill. Another of the men told the nurse that they had been vomiting after drinking tea. The nurse telephoned the casualty officer, a doctor, to tell him of the men's complaint. The casualty officer, who was himself unwell, did not see them but said that they should go home and call in their own doctors. The men went away, and the deceased died some hours later from what was found to be arsenical poisoning. It was not established how the arsenic got into the tea in the first place, but that was not the issue on trial in this case. Cases of arsenical poisoning are rare, and it was agreed when this tragedy came to court that even if the deceased had been examined and admitted to hospital and treated, there was little or no chance that the only effective antidote known at the time would have been administered to him before the time at which he died. His widow sued the hospital management committee (this was a case before the 1974 reorganisation) for damages in negligence, saying that the deceased's condition was not diagnosed or treated at the hospital and that this amounted to a breach of a duty of care on the part of those responsible and on that of the hospital authority which employed them.

When the matter came to court, and after lengthy argument by two Queen's Counsel, the judge decided the case like this: in failing to see and examine the deceased, the hospital's casualty officer was negligent and did not discharge the duty of care which in the circumstances was owed to the deceased by him (and therefore by his employer, the hospital authority). But the plaintiff (literally, the person bringing the action, the complaint—his widow) had not proved that her husband's death was caused by that negligence, that breach of duty.

The case is thus instructive in two respects: first, the damage, injury or harm of which a plaintiff complains must be proved to have been *caused* by the breach of duty of care; and, second, the mere fact that the casualty officer was himself unwell and was having a lie down elsewhere than in his department (so that the duty nurse had to telephone him) did not lead to the law's requiring any lesser standard of care from him than it would do if he was perfectly fit and well, and efficient.

II

Duty of care

There are many occasions on which someone carelessly causes loss, damage or injury to another, but the latter cannot recover damages. When a case is decided by a court of law (and note that for every case which comes to court there are literally hundreds which are settled between the parties) the court must first of all determine whether or not a duty of care exists in all the circumstances of the case.

Deciding on the existence of a duty of care is not just a factual investigation. It calls for the exercise of judicial discretion and policy.

The test used by the courts to determine the existence of a duty of care in negligence (*i.e.* a duty of care relating to the tort of negligence, and not, of course, a duty to be negligent!) is generally formulated in Lord Atkin's classic statement in the House of Lords' decision in *Donoghue* v. *Stevenson* (1932): the duty of care is owed to "persons who are so closely and directly affected by my acts that I ought reasonably to have them in contemplation as being so affected when I am directing my mind to the acts or omissions which are called in question."

Duty and omission

It is to be noted that, despite the inclusion of the term "omissions" in Lord Atkin's formulation, English law still does not impose any general duty to act. If you have negligently created a dangerous situation you are certainly under a duty to take care to avoid the consequences and if someone is injured as a result of your failure to avoid the materialisation of the risk, you can be liable in negligence. However, that situation is in law very different from, for instance, the case of someone who deliberately and callously walks past someone who has blacked out (say as a result of an illness) and who is in imminent danger of drowning in six inches of water. Assuming that poor person to be lying face downwards in the water, only a small amount of water is sufficient to cause asphyxia. There is no duty to rescue. The only circumstance in which the law imposes a positive duty to act to the benefit of another is in the case of pre-existing relationships, *e.g.* parents, guardians. In these cases the duty (of care) exists even before something goes wrong and endangers the victim.

To fail to act in a situation which is not of your making is not generally, therefore, a breach of the duty of care in negligence. This observation appears to require qualification in the context of vicarious liability in tort; but there the act of the employee becomes, in law, that of the employer: the situation is therefore, in law, "of the employer's making."

The modern judicial policy

Following a major decision by the House of Lords in 1977, it can now be said that the courts will, in a situation in which a defendant has caused damage, injury or loss to a plaintiff, presume the existence of a duty of care. This presumption can be rebutted (or defeated) by the defendant if he can show that sufficient reasons of policy or principle exist for the court to hold that no such duty of care exists in the particular circumstances: *Anns* v. *London Borough of Merton* (1977). It is no longer necessary, as lower courts have sometimes appeared to believe, to fit one's negligence claim into the facts of an earlier decided case in which the plaintiff was successful in his action.

It remains to be seen whether the courts take this statement of position, expressed briefly but very clearly in the judgment of Lord Wilberforce in *Anns* v. *London Borough of Merton*, as an opportunity to expand the existing restricted circumstances in which liability in the tort of negligence may arise as a result of an omission to act.

Duty and treatment

The line between commission (an act) and omission is not always an easy one to draw. While there are very clear cases on each side of a supposed line, the position of the line itself could give rise to problems. On the one hand, a member of the public who was present at a road accident in which a victim was severely injured has no legal duty to assist in order to prevent further injury, illness or even death. The fact that the member of the public was medically qualified would in law make no difference. Of course, there may be a compelling *moral* duty to assist in either or both of these cases, and more especially in the latter. But our present concern is specifically with legal liability and not with moral obloquy. The maxim that "Thou shalt not kill, but needest not strive officiously to keep alive" may have greatly varying moral claims according to circumstances, but in legal contexts its application is in no doubt.

What must be carefully distinguished from what lawyers frequently describe as a "mere omission" is a failure to act where there is a prior duty to do so. To take a clear case, a failure by a surgeon to check that he is operating on the correct limb is a negligent act and not a mere omission. It is the duty of the surgeon to act, and to act with reasonable care, the care expected of one who exercises his profession. Likewise, if an injured patient presented himself at an Accident and Emergency Department, a failure to give treatment would be in dereliction of a duty which the law would expect of specialists who put themselves in the position of being on the staff of such a department. So much for a failure to treat at all. But what about a very long delay in providing treatment? The law's concern is with what is *reasonably* to be expected of staff in all the particular circumstances. So, for instance, if there was a major accident of such enormous proportions that all the available departments within appropriate travelling distance from the scene were overloaded, a wait would be inevitable. Pain and suffering would have to be endured by some in order to effect life-saving measures in the case of others. A problematical point could be raised, however, in a situation in which the lack of facilities was in part caused by a past discontinuance of plans to build an extra and large accident and emergency department. It will be recalled from Chapter 2 that the Secretary of State is not in legal breach of his duty to provide services and facilities under sections 1 and 3 of the National Health Service Act 1977 by reason only of cutbacks in government expenditure, even anticipated cutbacks. In the judgment in the *Hincks* case some attention was drawn to the fact that the four plaintiffs were non-emergency cases. It is probable, however, that where such a matter as the major accident case were to be the subject of a civil action, the judicial decision would be the same. Perhaps the reasoning would not be quite as convincing in such circumstances.

Delay in treatment

If a patient is admitted to hospital as an in-patient in the normal way, the duty to treat seems beyond argument, save that the
time in which treatment can properly be expected may vary in
response to what is reasonable in particular circumstances. It
sometimes happens that cases of delay in receiving treatment
after admission is the subject of a complaint to the Health
Service Commissioner, whose functions and jurisdiction were
discussed in Chapter 1. More often the complaint is based on
allegedly protracted delay in admission in the first place, which
could sometimes result from inefficient administration as
distinct from lack of facilities sufficient to dispose quickly of an
extended waiting list. While such inefficiency, in the form of the
"maladministration" which is within the present jurisdiction of
the Health Service Commissioner to investigate, would not normally be the basis of a civil action in negligence, such an action is
not inconceivable. It might be difficult for the plaintiff to specify
a particular defendant or defendants, but that can often be a
problem. An action against the health authority could ease the
procedural difficulty provided that other issues of proof could be
properly satisfied. It is not easy to predict with any degree of
certainty the outcome of any such action if it were to be commenced. What can safely be said is that the climate of judicial
handling of the concept "duty of care," forming an initial link or
connection between the plaintiff and defendant, following the
House of Lords' decision in *Anns* v. *London Borough of Merton*
could turn out to be more conducive than earlier judicial opinion
to such an action's getting off the groud. Otherwise the procedure
would be that the complaint be "struck out, disclosing no reasonable cause of action."

In any event, in such a case, the health authority might itself
be the principal defendant, as distinct from being sought to be
held vicariously liable for the actions of its employees. The complaint would, in other words, be directed at the system as a whole
and not principally at specific individuals.

Duties, standards and special skills

A perennial question from students, and indeed from anyone
who gives this "reasonable man" the slightest attention, concerns his usefulness (if any) in the determination of the infinite

variety of factual issues and practical problems in which his standards, abilities and foresight are canvassed by courts of law. A "standard man" there may be, at least as the creature of the judges; but there is no such thing as a "standard" situation or chain of events giving rise to an action in tort for which damages are claimed for breach of a duty leading to damage. Moreover, the non-standard nature of a practical problem (if we may be permitted to use such an expression for the sake of emphatic contrast) is likely to affect plaintiffs and defendants alike, and often in the same case. For instance, one who professes a particular knowledge or exercises a particular skill may be held by a court to be in breach of a duty or care owed by him to the plaintiff unless he has put his special distinction into proper operation. Such is the legal relationship of doctors to their patients. The legal position in such cases may be represented in two ways: either the duty is "standard" but the opportunities of breach are increased to an extent proportionate to the special knowledge or skill; or the duty is "higher" than standard and therefore the skilful defendant must take positive steps to measure up to the demands of his profession.

Cases of medical negligence are infrequent when compared with the infinite varieties of carelessness which are forever occuping the attention of lawyers and the courts. Such cases, however, as do arise and are made the subject of a law report indicate that, despite the duty on the part of a skilled medical practitioner to put into effect his particular expertise, certain avenues are open to such a defendant to defend himself. The principal plea in such a case will not, of course, be the otherwise frequent plea that no duty of care was owed by plaintiff to defendant in the particular circumstances of the case, but rather that the requisite proper standard of care was maintained, or that general and approved practice was observed. This comprehensive term, employed by the courts in so many words, takes account of the dual risk which exists in the doctor and patient relationship. The patient is at risk because, of course, of the nature of his complaint; the doctor is in a sense legally at risk on account of the special duty incumbent on him. The principle of "general and approved practice" is one of the devices which is used by the law to balance the risks involved in order to produce a just result.

In *Roe* v. *Minister of Health* (1954) the plaintiffs entered hospital for minor surgery and emerged permanently paralysed from the waist down. The reason for this tragic paralysis was that the ampoules of the anaesthetic (Nupercaine) which was injected spinally, had tiny cracks in them, and some Phenol, the disinfectant in which they were kept, had percolated through those cracks and contaminated the anaesthetic. Both the judge at first instance and the Court of Appeal dismissed the plaintiffs' claim. Lord Justice Denning, as he then was, said: "We must insist on due care for the patient at every point, but we must not condemn as negligence that which is only misadventure."

The law of tort is concerned with loss allocation and distribution according to the established (though flexible) principles of English Common Law; it is not "Common Law insurance." It so happened that after this accident had occurred a textbook was published containing the following warning: "Never place ampoules of local anaesthetic solution in alcohol or spirit. This common practice is probably responsible for some of the cases of permanent paralysis reported after a spinal analgesia." To this, Lord Justice Denning added:

> "If hospitals were to continue the practice after this warning, they could not complain if they were found guilty of negligence. But the warning had not been given at the time of this accident. Indeed, it was the extraordinary accident to these two men which first disclosed the danger. Nowadays it would be negligence not to realise the danger, but it was not then."

It becomes clear on the examination of such a judicial decision that, despite the "averageness" and indeed the apparent mediocrity of the "reasonable man," his qualities should not be allowed by the Courts to produce results which will hamper the development of expertise which it is in the interest of everyone to have available. Again in the words of Lord Justice Denning:

> "These two men have suffered such terrible consequences that there is a natural feeling that they should be compensated. But we should be doing a disservice to the community at large if we were to impose liability on hospitals and doctors for everything that happens to go wrong. Doctors would be led to think more of their own safety than of the good of their patients. Initiative would be stifled and confidence shaken. A proper sense of precaution requires us to have regard to the conditions in which hospitals and doctors have to work."

It is not the occasion here to reflect on the long and uninterrupted hours worked by junior hospital staff, though one might at least take time to reflect on the *standard* of expertise which the law could reasonably expect of a drowsy expert.

Doing one's best

While compliance with what is agreed to have been general and approved practice is normally successful as a defence to an allegation of negligence, the courts nevertheless reserve the right to rule that such general practice, despite being "approved" in the medical profession, is not acceptable in law. But such an event will be exceptionally rare. The courts view the apparently similar response from a defendant that he was "doing his best" in a very different way. An illustrative example from a decided case concerns driving a car, a special skill despite its being a more common skill.

Late in 1967 a Mrs. Weston asked a Mr. Nettleship if he would give her driving lessons in her husband's car. Mr. Nettleship was asked as a friend and not as a professional driving instructor; indeed, he had no great experience even of amateur instruction. Following Mr. Nettleship's enquiry as to insurance Mrs. Weston assured him that there was fully comprehensive insurance cover (which there indeed was) and so he agreed. During the third lesson Mrs. Weston duly stopped at a junction and, Mr. Nettleship having engaged first gear for her, she obeyed his instructions to turn left slowly. Then, however, her implacable grip on the steering wheel resisted his instructions and efforts to straighten out and the car following, though slowly, a perfect curve, mounted the nearside pavement and struck a lamp post with an impact which fractured Mr. Nettleship's knee. Mr. Weston was insured by an ordinary Lloyd's policy by which the underwriters agreed to insure him and any person driving the car with his permission against liability at law for damages in respect of bodily injury to any person, including any passenger. Thus litigation arose as to the extent, if any, of such legal liability as was the subject of the insurance policy.

The unfortunate Mrs. Weston was convicted by magistrates of driving without due care and attention, was fined £10 and had her licence endorsed. Nevertheless the trial judge in this civil action dismissed the claim made against her, holding that the only duty owed by Mrs. Weston to Mr. Nettleship was that she should do her best, and that she had not failed in that duty. Mr. Nettleship's appeal to the Court of Appeal was allowed unanimously, though two of the three judges in that court were in favour of reducing the award of damages by half on account of Mr. Nettleship's contributory negligence. (It is to be noted that Megaw L.J.'s dissent with regard to this latter point was strong.)

The result of the Court of Appeal's allowing this appeal is that learner drivers have just the same duty of care towards other road users—and, indeed, to their passengers, as in the case under discussion—as experienced drivers, or at least those who have passed a driving test. It could be said that the same standard is expected from learners as from experienced drivers. However, in such a context the possible double reference of the term "standards" is evident. The degree of care to be exhibited by such a person as a learner driver is likely to be substantially greater than that required of an experienced driver to handle the vehicle to the same standard. This is not to say that greater experience engenders any less care, merely that the degree of concentration and application required of a learner driver to reach a given level of attainment (or "standard," to use one sense of that term) is likely to be greater than that which would be necessary in the case of someone with greater experience (assuming, of course, that experience brings with it improvement and increased skill).

To sum up, it is established by the case of *Nettleship* v. *Weston* that doing one's incompetent best is not enough, and that in taking on the responsibility of such a lethal weapon as a motor vehicle there is a duty to take requisite care. The duty incumbent on learner drivers is no less than that required of non-learners. The duty of care does not, therefore, differ in cases with different levels of actual attainment; and provided "standard" is used to describe the achievement of a certain level of attainment, neither does the standard differ. The difficulty of comprehension occurs when a standard of attainment (expressed as a statement of result) is described in terms of a "standard of care," an expression which looks on its face to be a suitable description of a means of reaching that result. Degrees of care, on the other hand, differ widely according to the effort, the application and the concentration required by individuals to measure up to a given level of attainment. Thus in one sense, so far from learner drivers being subject to a lower standard of care than those with greater experience, the opposite is in effect the case.

By the same token, a student nurse can be expected to occupy a similar position. That is, an error or omission which would, in a more senior nursing colleague, amount to a breach of duty and thus actionable negligence, will not be excused merely because it was a learner who made it. The law of tort, and the law relating to actionable negligence within it, aim not to punish wrongdoers but to protect, or at least to compensate, victims of harm or injury. If a student nurse were allowed to give treatment to a patient in circumstances where, one would have expected, the senior colleague should have had more sense than to let her go ahead, liability may be cast upon the senior. Moreover, as the employer of one or both, the health authority would itself be legally liable if the employees were "acting within the scope of their employment."

However, differences in circumstances as distinct from differences in skill can indeed have an important effect on liability, as the following case illustrates.

In *Wooldridge* v. *Sumner* (1963) the plaintiff was taking photographs at the National Horse Show, standing behind some potted shrubs which marked the boundary of the arena in which a competition for heavyweight hunters was taking place. A horse called Work of Art came down the far side of the course, rounded the bend at great speed, and then galloped furiously and apparently out of control down the line of shrubs to where the plaintiff was standing. In fright the plaintiff tried to pull another spectator out of the way, but fell back into the horse's path and was seriously hurt. The trial judge's award of £6,000 was reversed on appeal. Emphasising the horseman's "agony of the moment" Diplock L.J. (now Lord Diplock) held that an error of judgment in a fastmoving event such as this could not be classed as negligence. The fault may have been an error of horsemanship but was not such a fault as attracts liability in negligence. The judge concluded:

> "The most that can be said against [the defendant] is that in the course of and for the purposes of the competition he was guilty of an error or errors of judgment or lapse of skill. That is not enough to constitute a breach of the duty of reasonable care which a participant owes to a spectator. In such circumstances something in the nature of a reckless disregard of the spectator's safety must be proved, and of this there is no suggestion in the evidence."

Both the reasoning and the result of this case show that standards of care can vary. Indeed the very duty of care is at variance with that which would be owed to a plaintiff were he not in the position of a spectator and the defendant in the position of a sportsman. It would seem to follow that the *standard* of care required of the sportsman is also reduced in proportion to the particular exigencies of the duty owed.

Damages for nervous shock

The question of the recovery of damages in negligence can sometimes present some special problems in the case of one particular type of injury. Nowhere are the problems surrounding the related but separate issues of duty, breach and damage more difficult than in cases in which what the plaintiff seeks to recover is damages, not for personal injury in the sense that a broken leg or a lacerated finger is an "injury," but for what the law calls "nervous shock." The decided cases in this troublesome area of the law take a lot of explaining and even when fully explained are sometimes very difficult to reconcile with each other with any satisfactory degree of consistency.

If nervous shock is something essentially different from "ordinary" physical injury, then what is it? What is extraordinary about it? In the leading case of *Bourhill* v. *Young* decided by the House of Lords in 1942 it was said that cases of nervous shock "involve elements of greater subtlety than cases of ordinary physical injury" and that the principles relating to the recovery of damages in respect of nervous shock are in some way special or unusual. Nervous shock has been said to involve shock resulting from recognisable psychosomatic trauma. Manifestations of such shock can take a great variety of forms, including nervous rash, stuttering, onset of adverse heart and brain conditions, vomiting and general nausea, morbid depression and even, in rare cases, acute mental psychoses. Though the effects are physical, the medium through which they are experienced is mental. That is to say, the senses of the victim perceive what is, literally, shocking, and transmit the shock into the system thus producing visible or other detectable manifestations.

One important reservation must be emphasised. The law of tort will not award damages for mere grief or worry which is unaccompanied by outward "physical" manifestations of the type described, unless such is the result of "ordinary" physical injuries.

Let us consider the merits of the somewhat disparate array of judicial precedents in this area.

Decisions on nervous shock due to negligence

It is perfectly foreseeable that the relatives of the victim of an accident will be informed of his death or injury, and that they will suffer shock on hearing the bad news. It appears, however, to be regarded as self-evident that "a wife or mother who suffers nervous shock on being told of an accident to a loved one cannot recover damages from the negligent party on that account." Why should this be, and why should the judges appear so very harsh in apparently deserving cases?

One answer is that, if all those who suffered nervous shock at the sight or sound of a nasty accident could recover damages in respect of their nervous shock, then the negligent motorist who hit a pedestrian in the full light of day in a busy street would have a massive bill (or his insurance company would, if he was properly insured) as compared with the negligent motorist who caused an accident identical in all other respects save that it happened on a lonely road in the middle of the night. It is quite possible that the daytime motorist in our example might be liable to a number of passers-by; but what restrictions, tenable in the eyes of a respectable system of law, could be introduced so as to limit at least some of his liability to compensate.

In *Dulieu* v. *White* (1901) the alleged facts were that the plaintiff, who was a pregnant woman, was serving behind the bar of her husband's public house when the defendant's employee so negligently drove a horse-drawn van as to drive it into the public house. The plaintiff was not physically injured in the sense of having a limb broken or her face cut. But she did suffer shock, as a result of which she became seriously ill and gave birth prematurely to her child. It was held that she was entitled to damages, but on the rather narrow ground that the nervous shock must have been due to fear for her own personal safety. This so-called "area of impact" limitation would therefore include all those whose shock might just as well have been physically injury in the "ordinary" sense, for all the defendant was concerned; and it would exclude all others who, though suffering nervous shock and possibly becoming seriously physically ill, were nevertheless in no physical danger in the "ordinary" sense.

This test of recovery of damages for nervous shock was effectively that of fear of the occurrence of an event which, had it occurred, would have produced "ordinary" injury which does not attract the more "subtle" considerations of law and judicial policy referred to above. This test of recovery of damages was decisively rejected by a majority of the Court of Appeal in *Hambrook* v. *Stokes Bros.* (1925). As a result of the negligence of the defendant's employee, his unattended lorry began to run at alarming and increasing speed down a narrow street in Portsmouth. Mrs. Hambrook saw it coming and was terrified for the safety of her children from whom she had just parted around a bend and whom she could no longer see. Bystanders told her immediately afterwards that a child answering to the description of one of her own had been injured. Mrs. Hambrook suffered

severe shock and tragically died in consequence. In finding convincing reasons for rejecting the earlier "area of impact" view of
recovery for nervous shock, Bankes L.J. argued as follows:

> "Assume two mothers crossing this street at the same time
> when this lorry comes thundering down, each holding a small
> child by the hand. One mother is courageous and devoted to
> her child. She is terrified, but thinks only of the danger to her
> child, and not at all about herself. The other woman is timid
> and lacking in the motherly instinct. She is also terrified, but
> thinks only of the danger to herself and not at all about her
> child. The health of both mothers is seriously affected by the
> mental shock occasioned by the fright. Can any real distinc-
> tion be drawn between the two cases? Will the law recognise a
> cause of action in the case of the less deserving mother and
> none in the case of the more deserving one? Does the law say
> that the defendant ought reasonably to have anticipated the
> non-natural feeling of the timid mother, and not the natural
> feeling of the courageous mother? I think not."

This approach is certainly a convincing one from the moral
point of view, but it may not stand up to medical examination.
From a medical point of view the most likely cause of illness
through shock is fear for one's own safety. One reason for this is
that the very excessive discharge through the autonomatic
nervous system which it initiates is directed principally, if not in
a great many cases solely, towards protecting the person who
suffers the shock, in consequence of this reaction, from
immediate danger to his own personal safety. Be that as it may,
the test which the Court of Appeal in *Hambrook* v. *Stokes Bros.*
substituted for the "area of impact" or "fear for one's own
personal safety" approach is not without attraction—indeed,
subject to one decision which will shortly be argued to be out of
line with general authority, it can be said still to be a good
representation of the law. It ruled that a defendant would be
liable to compensate the plaintiff in respect of the latter's
nervous shock only if that shock resulted from what the plaintiff
either saw or realised by his (or, in the instant case, her) own
unaided senses, and not from something which someone told the
plaintiff. In the instant case there was, it is true, a piece of bad
news given to Mrs. Hambrook by a passer-by who had actually
seen the accident to Mrs. Hambrook's child, but the court was
clearly of the opinion that this formed but a part, albeit an
important part, of the terrifying situation which resulted in the
nervous shock.

This brings us to an important stage in the development of the law. In 1942 the House of Lords was faced with the case of the Glasgow fishwife (*Bourhill* v. *Young*). A fishwife was alighting from a tramcar and was being helped off with her basket by the conductor. A motorcyclist passed the tram and immediately afterwards collided with a motor car. The accident, caused by the negligence of the motorcyclist, caused his death. The fishwife, the plaintiff in this case, did not see the accident, which occurred about 15 yards off, her view being obstructed by the tram, but she heard the sound of the crash and, after the body of the motorcyclist had been removed, saw blood left on the road, having in the meantime walked to the spot where the accident had happened. In consequence of her experience she sustained a nervous shock and gave birth to a stillborn child of which she was eight months pregnant. She sued the personal representatives of the negligent deceased motorcyclist, but the House of Lords held in the subsequent appeal that she could not recover on the grounds that the motorcyclist owed her no duty of care. After having cited the celebrated dictum of Lord Atkin in *Donoghue* v. *Stevenson* which propounds the so-called "neighbour principle," Lord Russell of Killowen said that a duty of care "only arises towards those individuals of whom it may reasonably be anticipated that they will be affected by the act which con- stitutes the alleged breach." It is abundantly clear that a strong element of judicial discretion enters into this area of the law, as was the case in *Bourhill* v. *Young*; it was held that a duty of care did not exist *vis-à-vis* the plaintiff, though of course it existed *vis-à-vis* the driver of the motor car which was involved in the collision.

Some successful claims

There have, of course, been a good many other judicial deci- sions in this vexed area of the law. Lest it be thought that the courts might, by way of their restrictive attitude to those entitled to recover damages for nervous shock, be inclined to favour only the relatives of accident victims, the case of *Dooley* v. *Cammell Laird* (1951) may be cited. Owing to the defendants' negligence the rope of a crane broke so that its load fell into the hold of a ship in which men, the workmates of the plaintiff were working. The plaintiff, who knew they were down there, was the driver of the crane and, though himself in no personal danger, he suffered shock through witnessing the danger to the men in the hold. It was held that there had been a breach of a duty owed to the plaintiff because the defendants should have had him in contemplation as likely to be shocked if the rope broke. In the more recent case of *Chadwick* v. *British Transport Commission* (1967) the plaintiff's husband had acted as a volunteer rescue worker at the scene of the major rail disaster at Lewisham. As a result of the horror of his experiences he became ill with an anxiety neurosis. The defendants were liable in respect of his injuries.

An apparent exception to the well-established rule of the requirement of the shock having been suffered through the plaintiff's own unaided senses in the decision in *Schneider* v. *Eisovitch* (1960). An injured wife was told on recovering consciousness after a road accident that her husband had been killed in that accident. She suffered nervous shock in consequence, in addition to her existing "physical" injuries, and recovered damages in respect of both. This decision may be explained, if not also justified, on the grounds that some physical injury had already befallen her so that it would have been unconscionable to refuse her damages in respect of her further shock. It must be emphasised that, in the light of earlier authorities, this decision should not be taken as entitling all those relatives—even close ones—who merely hear of an accident rather than actually witness it, are entitled to damages for nervous shock; for that is certainly not the law, for all the judicial talk about a duty of care being owed to all those likely to be affected by the negligence of the defendant.

Injuries to unborn children

The statement that it has never been judicially decided in this country that a duty of care in negligence is owed to an unborn child still holds true. However, two points should be noted here. The first is a case in which there was, shortly before the trial of the issue of liability was about to take place, an admission of liability to a child who was, at the time of the motor accident in question, as yet unborn. The second is a recent statute in which a limited right in tort is given to children injured before their birth.

In *Williams and another* v. *Luff* (1978), a six-year-old boy who suffered from injuries sustained before birth had judgment entered for him for damages against a motorist who had caused the injuries by his negligent driving, but who had admitted that the boy had a cause of action against him at common law (that is, in the absence of statutory provision—for which see below). Counsel (*i.e.* the barrister) for the boy said that, so far as he was aware, it was the first action to reach an English court in which any such admission had been made.

For some time before this action came to court (the accident happened in January 1972) the defendant had admitted that the injuries were caused by the collision. What had, until just a week before the date set down for the trial, been denied was that the defendant owed any duty of care to the infant plaintiff. The court was, in effect, denied the opportunity for the first time in the history of English law of deciding whether or not a duty of care in negligence could be owed to an unborn child.

The Congenital Disabilities (Civil Liability) Act 1976

Certain provisions extending the protection (or at least the compensation) of the law to unborn children have been made by this recent statute. An action may lie against a person whose breach of duty to a parent results in a child's being born disabled, abnormal or unhealthy. It is to be noted that the duty shall have been owed to the parent (either parent) though it is not necessary that the parent suffer any actionable injury—the injury may be solely to the unborn child. In general no claim will lie on behalf of a child if the person responsible for its disabilities is its mother. But a woman driving a motor vehicle when she knows (or ought reasonably to know) herself to be pregnant is to be regarded "as under the same duty to take care for the safety of her unborn child as the law imposes on her with respect to the safety of other people." This means that if her child is born disabled or otherwise abnormal as the result of her negligent driving of a motor car, she will be liable in damages to the child, when born, in just the same way as some other negligent motorist who might collide with her.

Except, therefore, in the specific case of injury to the unborn child by the negligent driving of its mother, the unborn child itself cannot be said to be owed a duty of care *directly* by any defendant. The Act is a strange one.

III

Medical negligence

It is clear that a car driver owes a duty to other car drivers using the same piece of road as himself to exercise care towards them. Also in *Donoghue* v. *Stevenson* (1932) it was held that a manufacturer of products, which he sells in such a form as to show that he intends them to reach the ultimate consumer in the form in which they left him with no reasonable possibility of intermediate examination, and with the knowledge that the absence of reasonable care in the preparation of the products will result in an injury to the consumer, owes a duty to the consumer to take that reasonable care. Likewise, it is obvious that a surgeon owes a duty of care to the patient on the operating table in front of him, and the doctor owes such a duty to the patient whom he examines in his surgery.

What may not be so clear, except when a decision has been reached by a judge in a particular case, is the actual standard of care which is to be legally expected of medical men and other specialised staff. It has been indicated earlier that the issue of duty is heavily conditioned by policy considerations, and the same is true of issues affecting the *standard* of care within an already established duty. In medical cases one may be forgiven for thinking that the courts frequently display an attitude which is pro-practitioner and not pro-patient. Indeed, occasional unfortunate remarks of some judges are hard to distinguish from evidence of an anti-patient attitude.

Readers may be aware of the recent period in the United States of the so-called "medical malpractice crisis." If a crisis it be, then it has been brought about by an apparent over-willingness on the part of the courts to fix liability on medical and associated specialists in a manner almost unheard of on this side of the Atlantic. Various devices have been used in order to do this, including some rules of evidence which we encounter in a moment.

General and approved practice

The standard expected by the law is that of the reasonable man, or if the defendant has some special skill, for instance, a surgeon, that of the reasonably skilled surgeon in the speciality in question. We do not judge the doctor by the ability of the most skilled man in his field, but by the reasonably skilled man. This naturally leaves a good deal of room for argument and only the cases can show how things work out in practice. A very important point in deciding whether a professional person has been negligent is the view of his peers.

In *Chapman* v. *Rix* (1959) Romer L.J. said in the Court of Appeal that he knew of no case in which a medical man had been guilty of negligence when eminent members of his own profession had expressed on oath their approval of what he had done.

To say, by way of defence, that one has followed the standard practice will be a helpful line to take, but not necessarily conclusive, as the court may find that the standard was itself not satisfactory. However, in normal circumstances it will be sufficient.

The point of the allegation of negligence may, on the other hand, be the doctor's failure to observe the standard practice in the matter in issue. On this the observations of Lord Clyde in *Hunter* v. *Hanley* (1955) should be noted. (This is a Scottish case.) He said:

> "In regard to allegations of deviation from ordinary professional practice . . . such a deviation is not necessarily evidence of negligence. Indeed it would be disastrous if this were so, for all inducement to progress in medical science would then be destroyed. Even a substantial deviation from normal practice may be warranted by the particular circumstances. To establish liability by a doctor where deviation from normal practice is alleged, three facts require to be established. First of all it must be proved that there is a normal and usual practice; secondly, it must be proved that the defendant has not adopted that practice; and thirdly (and this is of crucial importance) it must be established that the course the doctor adopted is one which no professional man of ordinary skill would have taken if he had been acting with ordinary care. There is clearly a heavy onus on a plaintiff to establish these three facts, and without all three his case will fail."

In *Bolam* v. *Friern H.M.C.* (1957), the plaintiff, who was mentally ill, was advised by a consultant to undergo E.C.T. He signed a consent form, but was not warned of the risk of fracture involved (which is slight). The issue of consent to treatment is discussed in Chapter 11. A bone was fractured during the second treatment. No relaxant drugs or manual control were used except for support of the lower jaw, but male nurses stood on each side of the couch during treatment.

Evidence was given of opposing medical opinions as to the correct procedure. One opinion favoured the use of drugs or manual control generally; the other would confine the use of drugs, because of the mortality risk, to cases where there was particular need for them. B's was not such a case. There were also opposing opinions as to whether, if drugs were not used, manual control should be, and as to whether the patient should be expressly warned of the risk of fracture or left to ask of the danger.

The plaintiff sued for negligence in failure to use drugs or manual control, as well as for failure to warn him of the risks involved.

The jury were directed that a doctor is not negligent if he is acting in accordance with a practice accepted as proper by a responsible body of men skilled in that art, merely because there is a body which takes a contrary view. The jury found the defendant not negligent in all the circumstances of the case.

The time of the law's judgment

The next important point is that in deciding whether the defendant was negligent we must apply the standard which prevailed at the time when he did the act in question. Suppose the alleged negligent act was done in 1975, and the action comes on for trial in 1981. This point was made in *Roe* v. *Ministry of Health* (1954), discussed earlier. Roe was given a spinal anaesthetic. Nupercaine was used. It had been supplied in glass ampoules. Phenol had percolated into the ampoules from a solution in which the ampoules had been immersed. As a result of this contamination Roe was permanently paralysed from the waist down. The events took place in 1947, the trial in 1953. The court found that Phenol could find its way into an ampoule of Nupercaine stored in a solution of Phenol through cracks which were not detectable by ordinary visual or tactile examination. The anaesthetist did not appreciate this danger. Was this negligence on his part? The court held that on the standard of medical knowledge to be imputed to competent anaesthetists in 1947, the doctor was not negligent in failing to appreciate the risk.

Denning L.J. made this important general point: "We must not condemn as negligence that which is only a misadventure." Or we may say that the court's sympathy for the plaintiff must not lead it to find against the defendant in the absence of negligence. Finnemore J. put it this way in *Edler* v. *Greenwich H.M.C.* (1953):

> "There is a considerable onus on the court to see that people do not easily obtain damages merely because some medical or surgical mistake has been made, but if the court found that the doctor had failed to give a case the proper skill and care which patients had a right to expect, the court must not shirk facing the issue."

Medical literature

One aspect of professional competence is the need to keep up to date with new developments in one's specialism. To fail to do so may constitute negligence.

The issue arose in *Crawford* v. *Charing Cross Hospital* (1953). In this case the plaintiff was admitted to the hospital for a bladder operation which required the plaintiff's being placed on an operating table in a position whereby the table was so inclined that the plaintiff's head and shoulders were placed in a position lower than his pelvis. His left arm was extended at right angles to his body and secured in that position so that a blood transfusion could be given during the operation. After the operation it was found that the arm which had been so extended was partially paralysed. Gerrard J. held that the anaesthetist who had administered the blood transfusion had been negligent in the particular circumstances of the case in not avoiding the extension of the plaintiff's arm, at any rate to the degree he permitted, for longer than was necessary and that that negligence had contributed to the very severe degree of brachial paralysis from which the plaintiff suffered. The decision of Gerrard J. was reversed by the Court of Appeal who held that as the only evidence of negligence in the case was that the doctor concerned had not read an article in a recent medical journal drawing attention to the danger of extending a patient's arm in the position that this patient's arm was extended, it was placing an impossible burden on medical men if they were to be found guilty of negligence in not having read in a recent article of dangers of practice which had previously not been known.

Inadequate examination

A failure to subject a patient to a proper and appropriate medical examination may amount to a fall below the requisite standard of care and thus to a breach of duty constituting negligence.

In *Wood* v. *Thurston* (1951), W was brought in intoxicated to hospital, walking, by friends. He had some story of having been under a moving lorry. He was examined, given a dressing for his face and then allowed to travel 11 miles home by taxi. He died a few hours later. The post mortem revealed a fractured collarbone, 18 fractured ribs and badly congested lungs. The defendant doctor said he was not negligent in view of W's intoxication, which dulled his reaction to pain and prevented him from giving an accurate account of what had happened. However, it was held that, while intoxication might deceive the doctor as to the true condition, when an intoxicated person arrived at hospital with such a story, the doctor's examination should have been more careful. Use of stethoscope alone would almost inevitably have revealed his true condition. £3,550 damages were awarded to the deceased's dependants.

In *Payne* v. *St. Helier H.M.C. and Another* (1952), a man who had been kicked in the abdomen by a horse was sent by his doctor for examination to the Sutton and Cheam Hospital. The man was seen there by a house officer who had been qualified for two years. He noted a bruise and sent the man to bed and told him to call in his own doctor if he had any pain. Two and a half weeks later the man became very ill, was admitted to hospital and operated upon but died of general peritonitis. The widow, in her action brought under the Fatal Accidents Act, alleged negligence against the H.M.C. for operating a system which permitted a case of abdominal injury to be sent away without being seen by a consultant, and against the house officer that he had not paid attention to the fact that the bruising indicated a very severe blow, that as the general practitioner had sent the case to hospital a more experienced opinion was required and that the hospital failed to keep the patient in for observation or to have him examined by a surgeon of consultant rank. Donovan J. held that the H.M.C. was not negligent in respect of its system of working although he said he hoped that it had now been changed; but found the casualty officer had not exercised reasonable care and attention in his diagnosis and treatment of the patient and in his failure to keep him in hospital. Damages were allowed against the casualty officer and the H.M.C. as his employers but they received an indemnity of 100 per cent. in respect of the damages against the doctor and two-thirds of the costs.

Communication between doctor and patient

It was seen in Chapter 1 that problems in health care frequently resolve themselves into problems of communication and the transfer of information. The Health Service Commissioner has from the outset had jurisdiction to investigate and report on problems of maladministration consisting in communication breakdown. While the Commissioner has, at the time of going to press, no jurisdiction to investigate matters consisting solely in the exercise of clinical judgment, an individual patient who complains of pain, suffering or injury due to problems of communication can of course commence civil proceedings by way of an action in negligence.

Where a patient is being given treatment which requires his collaboration and demands a warning of danger, the warning must be adequate. In *Clarke* v. *Adams* (1950), the patient was subjected to heat treatment. The machine was dangerous. The operator of the machine said, "When I turn on the machine I want you to experience a comfortable warmth and nothing more. If you do I want you to tell me." The patient was badly burned and had to have a leg amputated. Was the warning adequate? The warning, said the court, must be such as to make it absolutely clear that it was a warning of danger. Did this form of words tell the patient that his safety was at stake? It did not and, therefore, the defendant was liable. This was so even though he had used the form of words he had been taught in his training to give. The standard practice was unsatisfactory, and therefore the defence of general and approved practice was unsuccessful.

Another problem that arises is where a patient is prescribed certain drugs, and it is dangerous to take certain foods whilst on these drugs. In *Buckle* v. *de Launay* (1970) a man alleged that a doctor had failed to warn his wife not to eat cheese whilst taking the anti-depressant drug Paruate. She had done so and had died. The question for the court was simply whether the doctor had given the warning. The court was satisfied that he had. The legal correspondent of the British Medical Journal has commented that in such cases it is a wise precaution to give the patient a written as well as an oral warning. Where the manufacturers provide cards with a list of forbidden foods this should be handed over to the patient and at the same time a note made that the card was given to the patient.

Communication between medical staff

The M.D.U. has said many times in its Annual Report that failure in communication is a frequent cause of litigation. A most common instance, they say, is the doctor's failure to see the radiologist's or pathologist's report. For example, a man fell from a ladder, injuring his wrist. At the casualty department of the hospital an X-ray was ordered. The casualty officer examined the film but could detect no injury. The patient was discharged and told to see his own doctor if the pain persisted. Two days later a radiologist examined the film and found a fracture. The report was entered on the casualty card by a member of the nursing staff, but neither the family doctor nor the casualty officer was told of the report. The former did not learn about the report for ten months. A claim for damages had to be settled by the Union.

A point of some importance is the legal liability of, say, a junior hospital doctor who gives a patient treatment on the instructions of a more senior doctor, and the treatment is inadequate, so that the patient is injured. In *Junor* v. *McNichol* (1959) it was held that a house officer must display the skill and care required of such a person but he must also carry out the instructions of the consultant in charge of the case. Where as here, the junior officer carried out those instructions, and the patient was injured, he was held not liable in negligence. However, there is no duty to carry out instructions which are manifestly wrong and if the junior thinks that something may be amiss he should check the instructions.

Questions of medical negligence may arise when a patient is being passed from one doctor to another. *Coles* v. *Reading H.M.C. and Monk* (1953) is an interesting example. C's left index finger was crushed by a lump of coal. He was given first aid, and went to the nearby cottage hospital. At no time was he given an anti-tetanus injection, nor was a test made to find whether he was unfit for such. He was told at that hospital that he must go immediately to another hospital for further examination. C's friend who was with him told the sister he would take C there. C at no time went to that other hospital, but he did see his own doctor later that day. C died from the wound. The court said that when transferring a patient from one hospital to another there ought to be proper communication, *i.e.* that which is reasonably necessary for safeguarding a patient's interests. This might be by a written or telephone message to the next person or, in the case of a suitable patient, direct to the patient. The responsibility of ensuring that a proper system of communication existed rested on the person in charge of the hospital: it ought not to be left to the sisters or nurses without any guidance. The court found that C was not given to understand either the importance of going to the second hospital or that there was any risk involved in not going. The hospital authorities were, therefore, negligent. What of C's own doctor? He, too, was found negligent. The court thought that he had taken the case too lightly. He had probably assumed that, as C had come from a hospital, everything necessary had been done. He should have made some inquiries. Had he done so he would have been put on the right track.

Errors in operations

It is clear that to operate on the wrong patient must almost inevitably amount to negligence and such a claim also would be impossible to defend. The same is true of carrying out the wrong operation on the right patient (*e.g.* taking off the right instead of the left leg). The M.D.U. has to settle many such claims.

Another type of case where a claim for damages is difficult to resist is where a swab or other object is left inside a patient. The M.D.U. and Royal College of Nursing have published a joint memorandum on the safeguards to be taken against such an occurrence. Despite this, says the M.D.U., it continues to receive not infrequent reports of swabs being found at operation sites even though the operation has been superficial. It would be negligent not to institute the most stringent procedures to prevent this happening; and, if they were introduced, it would be negligent not to follow them.

Patients presenting special risks

A hospital, clinic, nursing home and indeed any other relevant health care institution is under a duty to take precautions to avoid the possibility of injury, whether self-inflicted or otherwise, occurring to patients which it knows or ought to know have a history of disturbance or mental disorder, or whose complaint could foreseeably cause such a state. A case in point is *Selfe* v. *Ilford & District H.M.C.* (1970). In a ward of 27 patients were four suicide risks, including S. There were three nurses on duty. Each knew that S had to be under constant supervision. One went to the lavatory, another to the kitchen, leaving the charge nurse alone. He answered a call for assistance by another patient. S then got out of a window behind his bed (the ward was on the ground floor), walked along a path and up some steps onto a roof, from which he threw himself. He became a paraplegic. The court found the H.M.C. liable. To leave S unobserved and with an open window behind his bed was asking for trouble. Damages of £19,500 were awarded.

Children, too, may be expected to take less care and to behave less responsibly than sane adults, and so they too may present special risks. Greater care is obviously necessary to protect them from injury than adults. Thus, in *Newham* v. *Rochester Hospital Board* (1936) a boy of 7 was left unattended near an open window. He fell out and was injured. The hospital was liable to him. In *White* v. *Tilbury & South East Essex H.M.C.* (1964) W, when three months old, was sent to hospital with acute bronchitis. He was put in a steam tent where he was scalded by boiling water from a steam kettle. The defendants admitted negligence; the only thing in issue was the amount of damages. The defendants' offer of £1,500 was rejected by W, and the jury awarded him £3,400, in respect of the permanent bald patch on the right side of his scalp and a slightly deformed ear. In *Cox* v. *Carshalton H.M.C.* (1955) a child in bed suffering from a certain degree of disablement had been left to manage a jug of hot inhalant on a tray which she had done quite successfully before. Unfortunately, whilst the nurse was out of the room attending another patient the jug tipped over and the patient suffered injury. It was held that there had been no failure of supervision and regard was also given to the fact that it was in the child's own interest to have encouraged her to do things for herself.

Res ipsa loquitur

There are, however, certain circumstances in which the plaintiff receives assistance in fastening liability on the defendant for a negligent act. This is when the rule *res ipsa loquitur* applies. That means "the thing speaks for itself."

An example is *Cassidy* v. *Minister of Health* (1951). There the patient went into hospital with two stiff fingers. Having been treated for that, he came out of hospital with four stiff fingers, and a useless hand. That in itself suggested negligence. He might not be able to show exactly who was negligent or how he was negligent, but the whole operation was under the control of the defendant, and the misfortune he suffered was not the kind of thing which happened without negligence somewhere. In such circumstances the plaintiff is entitled to say, in the words of Denning L.J., "Explain it if you can." That is, the burden is then thrown on the defendants to show how the accident could have happened without negligence on his part. If he can offer a convincing explanation, the burden is then thrown back on to the plaintiff of positively proving negligence. In *Cassidy* the defendant was not able to rebut the presumption of negligence which arose in that case.

The rule of *res ipsa loquitur* may be expressed in this way: where the thing is shown to be under the management of the defendant or his servants, and the accident is such as in the ordinary course of things does not happen if those who have the management use proper care, it affords reasonable evidence, in the absence of explanation by the defendant, that the accident arose from want of care.

The law's view of the applicability of this maxim, the maxim which when broadly interpreted has helped to create the "malpractice crisis" in the United States, can change with the times. In *Mahon* v. *Osborne* (1939) a swab was left inside the patient, and the surgeon was sued. The court said that the doctrine did not apply in the case of a complicated operation, but the case should be regarded as discredited. The dissenting views of Goddard L.J. are now preferred. He said:

> "The surgeon is in command of the operation, it is for him to decide what instruments, swabs and the like are to be used, and it is he who uses them. The patient, or if he dies, his representatives, can know nothing about this matter. There can be no possible question but that neither swabs nor instruments are ordinarily left in the patient's body. . . . If, therefore, a swab is left in the patient's body, it seems clear that the surgeon is called upon for an explanation. That is, he is called upon to show, not necessarily why he missed it, but that he exercised due care to prevent its being left there."

He does not discharge the duty by merely asking, and being told whether the count is right.

Goddard L.J.'s view is supported by more recent cases and was specifically approved by the Court of Appeal in the unreported case of *Urry* v. *Bierer* (1955). In this case the facts were that a pack was left in a patient's abdomen after an operation in a private nursing home. It was admitted that there was an error in the counting of the swabs on the part of the theatre sister. It was admitted that the surgeon was entitled to rely on the sister's count of the swabs but Pearson J. found that it was not in accordance with any proved practice. He held that they were both equally responsible for the pack being left in the body. The Court of Appeal held that although on the evidence of other surgeons it could not be said that a surgeon who did not make use of tapes was thereby negligent yet the evidence did not disclose any convincing reason why tapes should not generally be used because, as everyone seemed to agree they were an additional precaution. A surgeon who discarded or disregarded that safeguard could be said to place an additional burden on himself.

Goddard L.J.'s views in *Mahon* v. *Osborne* were approved: "It is the task of the surgeon to put swabs in, it is his task to take them out, and, if on the evidence he did not use a reasonable standard of care, he cannot absolve himself by saying 'I relied on the nurse.' " The patient was entitled to expect that the surgeon would do what was reasonable to ensure that packs were removed from the body before he asked the sister if the count was correct. The one was independent of the other; the sister's count was an additional check for the protection both of the patient and of the surgeon. That it failed occasionally only emphasised the need for diligence on the part of the surgeon in that respect. The surgeon was, therefore, found equally liable with the sister.

Harm threatened by staff disability

What should a member of staff do if a colleague appears to be incapacitated and thus a danger to patients, as well as to other staff, whether through drink, drugs or any other cause? Circular HM (60) 45 is instructive: "It is recognised that when members of hospital medical or dental staff are aware of these circumstances it is their clear duty to do what they can to see that the safety and care of patients is not threatened in this way."

This is certainly a moral duty. Is it not also a legal duty? It continues: "Boards and Committees are asked to invite Medical Staff Committees to consider this memorandum and devise specific arrangements based on the following proposals which represent the agreed views of the Minister and Joint Consultants Committee."

The circular goes on to suggest that for each hospital or group there should be a small sub-committee of the Medical Staff Committee who would receive and take appropriate action on any report of incapacity or failure of responsibility, including addiction. Information would normally be given orally in the first instance to the sub-committee or whichever member of the sub-committee is most readily available. Hospital staff other than medical or dental staff who have information which in their opinion should be brought to notice, should first approach the head of their department.

The sub-committee should make such confidential inquiries as are necessary to verify the accuracy of any reports. Unless they are satisfied that the possibility of harm to patients can be excluded by the exercise of their influence with the individual concerned they should bring the circumstances to the notice of the appropriate health authority. It would then be their responsibility to decide what to do.

In case the worry of libel or slander should arise the Circular explains that the defence of qualified privilege would exist in such circumstances. This defence will, as will be seen in Chapter

10, be defeated only by evidence of malice, spite or ill-will on the part of the person making the allegation of incompetence or, perhaps, by an over-broad communication of the information of a quite disproportionate nature.

Error of judgment or negligence?

The substantive law of negligence is quite clear. What is not so clear, and what leads to the disputes some of which lead to litigation, is the evaluation to be given by judges to certain reactions and conduct of medical staff in the particular circumstances of cases which cause dispute. While each of the many judicial decisions which have just been canvassed sheds some light on the issue, the outcome of future cases still remains unclear. A particular problem facing the judges is that a finding of negligence necessitates proof of fault. The central role of fault in the award of damages for negligence can cause hardship to a plaintiff who fails to produce evidence, on the balance of probabilities, that the medical staff were at fault; but, if proved, a finding of fault can easily be seen as a condemnation of the medical or associated specialist and as such a slur on a good professional name. Taking the broad view of all concerned, there are many more losers than winners in medical cases.

The issue as to what, in general terms, will amount to medical negligence and what will not, being ascribed to a "mere error of judgment" recently came to the fore in the case of *Whitehouse* v. *Jordan*. The defendant, a senior hospital registrar, was in charge of the delivery of the plaintiff as a baby following a high risk pregnancy. After the mother had been in labour for 22 hours the defendant decided to carry out a test to see whether forceps could be used to assist the delivery. In doing so the defendant followed a suggestion by his head of department, a consultant professor of obstetrics, in his case notes on the mother. The defendant pulled on the baby with forceps five or six times and then fearing for the safety of the mother and child he carried out a Caesarean section quickly and competently. The plaintiff was born with severe brain damage and, acting through his mother, brought an action in negligence against the defendant alleging want of professional skill and care by pulling too hard and too long on the forceps and so causing the brain damage. At the trial there was evidence by a junior registrar who was present at the delivery that the defendant's use of the forceps was not violent or untoward. There was also eminent medical opinion that it was a matter of clinical judgment based on experience as to how hard and how many times a doctor should pull on obstetric forceps. The mother gave evidence and although her description of what had happened was not, in the court's opinion, physically possible, the judge interpreted it as meaning that the forceps were applied with such force that she was pulled to the bottom of the delivery bed. There was also in evidence a report prepared by the consultant professor shortly after the birth and after discussion with the defendant, in which the professor stated that the defendant had "disimpacted" the baby's head prior to the Caesarean section. Although the professor gave evidence that he had used the term "disimpacted" to denote that only slight force was needed to free the head before delivery, the trial judge interpreted the term in its medical sense, namely that the baby's head had become wedged or stuck in the birth canal because of the use of the forceps and force was required to move it. Because of his interpretation of the professor's report and the mother's evidence the judge found that the defendant had pulled too hard and too long on the forceps causing the foetus to become wedged in the birth canal, that in unwedging the foetus he had caused asphyxia which in turn had caused cerebral palsy and that in so using the forceps he fell below the high standard of professional competence required by law, and was therefore negligent. The defendant appealed.

By a majority of two to one the Court of Appeal decided that the doctor's conduct amounted to an error of judgment and not to actional negligence. But in a strong dissenting judgment Donaldson L.J. said that what distinguished this particular error of judgment from other errors was that on this occasion damage resulted.

The House of Lords' decision

The Court of Appeal had, exceptionally interfered with the trial judge's finding of fact. It would have been sufficient for the Court of Appeal to say that Mr. Jordan had not in fact been negligent. But Lord Denning went further and said that there was a difference between error of judgment and negligence, with the implication (he had been taken to mean) that an error of judgment was a category of its own and *could not* be negligence.

In the event, the Law Lords agreed that on a proper view all the evidence pointed to competent judgment and indeed to first class medical care. But they severely criticised the reasoning of the majority of the Court of Appeal. In particular they stressed their strong disagreement with any suggestion that the concept of "error of judgment" was a separate category which could not amount to negligence. The test for an error of judgment, said the Law Lords, is the standard of the ordinarily skilled medical person exercising, and professing to have, a particular skill. On this view it is clear that an "error of judgment" may or may not be negligent.

Chapter 7

PREMISES LIABILITY

I

The legal context

The ownership and occupation of premises carries with it a variety of legal duties and potential causes of legal liability. We have already met, in Chapter 5, certain situations in which the state of premises may bring about the possibility of legal proceedings by an employee against an employer or employing authority, or against the employer by way of criminal proceedings for breach of a duty imposed by statute in pursuance of a policy of worker safety and protection. Those duties also extend to a variety of activities which are carried on in the employer's premises, including especially the use of machinery.

In this chapter attention is turned from the situation of employees, discussed in Chapter 5, and directed to the legal duties of an occupier of premises to lawful visitors to those premises. The term "lawful visitors" is used specifically in the principal statute in this area, the Occupiers' Liability Act 1957. It clearly covers patients in premises concerned with the provision of health services and also, literally, the visitors to in-patients. Even in the apparently obvious application of the term "lawful visitor" to an in-patient's visitors, however, a reservation has to be made on account of the ability of an occupier of premises to restrict or even to exclude liability. So we shall later have to consider the legal situation of visitors out of hours, or those who go off on an unauthorised tour of inspection when visiting hours are over, as well as any exemption clauses put up in premises.

Occupiers' liability is not without connection with duties in respect of health and safety at work. Indeed section 3(1) of the Health and Safety at Work Act 1974 provides as follows: "It shall be the duty of every employer to conduct his undertaking in such a way as to ensure, as far as is reasonably practicable, that persons not in his employment who may be affected thereby are

156

not thereby exposed to risks to their health and safety." This provision clearly extends to members of the public who can be expected by the employer to be properly in the vicinity of the source of danger, or whatever the "undertaking" happens to be. The duty probably does not apply in respect of trespassers, though if premises are known by an employer or employing authority to be frequented by trespassers (which happens in many large hospitals and similar premises) it is conceivable that precautions even in such cases might be considered in law to be "reasonably practicable," given the circumstances.

Finally, the legal liability of an occupier of premises has close connections with the general principles of liability for negligence which were discussed in the foregoing chapter. It would not misrepresent the situation to say that the "common duty of care" which, says the Occupiers Liability Act 1957, is owed to all lawful visitors is a duty to take reasonable care, pointed up in a variety of specific contexts arising from the occupation of premises.

The common duty of care

Before the passing of the Occupiers' Liability Act 1957 the duty of an occupier towards persons entering his premises varied according to the different types of person who entered. The highest degree of care was owed to an invitee, less to a licensee and practically none at all to a trespasser. The Act abolished the categories of invitee and licensee, and created the new concept of "visitor." This includes those who were previously either invitees or licensees. Thus, hospital patients and also their visitors are "visitors" for the purposes of this Act.

An occupier of premises is, since the Act of 1957, said to owe a common duty of care to all lawful visitors, no distinction being any longer made in law between those who have actually been requested to go onto the premises and those who, while no such request has been made, are nevertheless lawfully on the premises otherwise than as trespassers, for instance postmen, milkmen, meter-readers, and in some cases the police. The introductory sections of the Occupiers' Liability Act sets out details of the meaning of the common duty of care in relation to practical circumstances. For instance, people who are lawfully on the premises for the purpose of exercising a particular profession, trade or calling are expected to show the degree of care for their own safety and well being as would normally be expected from such a person in such a situation. What is in each case "normal" or reasonable is ultimately up to a court to decide, assuming any such dispute were to go to the stage of litigation (which most do not—people usually settle their disputes out of court on the basis of informed predictions of what a court of law would be likely to decide in the circumstances of the case in point). Furthermore, children are not expected to show the same degree of care for their own wellbeing as grown-ups, though the old or infirm would once again be considered differently from younger able-bodied adults.

Section 2(2) of the 1957 Act defines common duty of care as "a duty to take such care as in all the circumstances of the case is reasonable to see that the visitor will be reasonably safe in using the premises for the purposes for which he is invited or permitted by the occupier to be there."

The visitor must also act with reasonable care on his part. For example, he must use the premises in a proper manner, he must look where he is going and he must not go to places where he is forbidden to go. In deciding whether an occupier has discharged his duty of common care towards a visitor regard must be had to all the circumstances. For example, it is reasonable to expect that children will generally be less careful than adults, and that a person acting in the course of his job, such as a fitter going onto the premises in question, should guard against any particular risks which are normally incidental to his job. A warning given by an occupier of premises to a visitor will not of itself absolve the occupier from liability; the occupier must go on to prove that the visitor also had an adequate opportunity and adequate means to avoid the danger. In the case, for instance, of injured or semi-ambulant patients or their visitors, or visitors to an out-patients clinic, it would clearly be intolerable if the law permitted liability for the wellbeing and safety of such people merely by means of a warning notice if the "visitor," once in the situation of risk or danger, had no reasonable means of avoiding it or getting out of it.

If a visitor is injured by a danger due to faulty work by an independent contractor, did the occupier employ a competent contractor and did he satisfy himself that the work had been properly carried out? If he did both these things the occupier will not be liable.

Thus it can be seen that the common duty of care is owed by an occupier to all lawful visitors to the premises occupied, and that a balance is to be struck between reasonable demands to be placed on an occupier and reasonable expectations to be made of a normally prudent visitor, depending on the age and calling of the visitor, and the purpose for which the premises are being visited.

Who is an occupier?

The answer to the question, Who is the occupier? can in many cases be obvious. But in others it can even lead to judicial proceedings in order to determine who is the occupier of premises, and thus who pays in bill in the event of a successful claim by an injured visitor to the premises. There can be many people present in a building, such as owners, tenants, contractors working on the premises, factory guards and others. All of these people can be brought within the ambit of the expression "occupier of premises" in appropriate circumstances, depending upon the degree of control exercised or expected to be exercised in relation to the premises or part of the premises on which injury, damage or loss occurs. Indeed, there have been cases in which, contrary to earlier prognostications, more than one person or body of persons has been held liable as an "occupier." All depends on their relationship to the premises and the correlative degree of control to be expected to be exercised on the basis of the relation of that person to the premises in all the circumstances of the case. In the event of more than one person or body of persons being liable as occupiers, joint or several liability may be imposed according to the normal principles of liability or joint tortfeasors. According to this principle, all or any of the persons sought to be made liable as occupiers may be named in the action brought by the plaintiff.

The test of liability is not so much based on occupation as on control, and liability is thus imposed on the person or persons who are expected by the law, sometimes after litigation has determined the issue, to have exercised this control. An owner in possession is no doubt an occupier, while a landlord who has let premises and has parted with possession with no right of entry on the premises is not an occupier. An absentee owner may "occupy" through the occupancy of an employee acting on his behalf, and may be subject to the common duty of care also when he has contracted to allow a third party to use the premises. Occupational control may thus be shared between two or more people, or authorities; but it does not follow that, where this is so, the actual duty required of each is necessarily the same, even though both are subject to *some* duty, namely the demands in all the circumstances of the common duty of care.

Application to the National Health Service

The demands of the Occupiers' Liability Act 1957 apply in the normal way to premises occupied by hospitals, clinics and nursing homes operating outside the National Health Service. They also apply in the normal way to premises occupied by general medical, dental and ophthalmic practices operating within the National Health Service. A certain reservation has, however, to be made in the case of all premises occupied by and for the purpose of the National Health Service. This includes all N.H.S. hospitals, clinics and nursing homes as well as all premises occupied by health authorites. It was noted in Chapter 2 that certain special legal considerations may apply to Crown activities, and we must now note the particular applications of Crown liability in the context of occupiers' liability.

Section 6 of the Occupiers' Liability Act 1957 provides as follows:

"This Act shall bind the Crown, but as regards the Crown's liability in tort shall not bind the Crown further than the Crown is made liable in tort by the Crown Proceedings Act 1947, and that Act and in particular section two of it shall apply in relation to duties under sections two to four of this Act as statutory duties."

In the case of tortious liability, the position of the Crown is dependent on the Crown Proceedings Act 1947. Section 2 of that Act renders the Crown subject to liability in tort in a number of circumstances as if it were a private person of full age and capacity. The two provisions relevant to the present discussion are that the Crown is liable

"in respect of any breach of the duties attaching at common law to the owernship, occupation, possession or control of property,"

and that

"where the Crown is bound by a statutory duty which is binding also upon persons other than the Crown and its officers, then, subject to the provisions of this Act, the Crown shall, in respect of a failure to comply with that duty, be subject to all those liabilities in tort (if any) to which it would be so subjected if it were a private person of full age and capacity."

Although the obligations of an occupier would seem to relate to duties attaching to ownership, occupation or control of property, section 6 of the Occupiers' Liability Act 1957 makes it quite clear that the obligations of the Crown under sections 2 to 4 of the 1957 Act fall within section 2(2) of the Crown Proceedings Act 1947 as "statutory duties," and not within section 2(1) of the 1947 Act. One consequence of this is that the obligations of the Crown under the 1957 Act are, as statutory duties, subject to the provisions of the 1947 Act.

We saw in Chapter 2 that one of the special rules relating to the legal position of the Crown, and this includes for the present purpose National Health Service activities, contains the principle that no Act binds the Crown in the absence of express words or necessary implication. An example of the effect of this rule on the liability of the Crown as occupier might be provided by the case of liability under section 4 of the 1957 Act. This governs the liability of a landlord out of occupation and the landlord's liability is dependent on his being under an obligation to repair. Whilst an ordinary landlord might be under such an obligation by reason of implied terms contained in the Housing Acts of 1957 and 1961, neither of these Acts applies to the Crown. This has the effect that because the Crown as landlord is not under an implied obligation to repair under these Acts, the Crown will not be liable under section 4 of the Occupiers Liability Act 1957 for injuries consequent upon any such failure to repair.

While health authorities could thus legitimately escape from liability under the Occupiers' Liability Act 1957 in respect of occupancy duties which they would otherwise owe to lawful visitors if they were not acting in pursuit of Crown activities, many authorities in fact make a practice of inspecting even premises let out at a rent to employees of the authorities, as well as in practice regarding such premises as being subject to health and safety provisions and regulations. While section 4 of the Occupiers' Liability Act has now been replaced by section 4 of the Defective Premises Act 1972, imposing a wider liability on a landlord having an obligation to repair (and explained below), the position of the Crown and thus of the National Health Service as an occupier remains unchanged in the respect just discussed. This is because the same formula in respect of the *extent* to which the Crown is bound by the Defective Premises Act 1972 is repeated, meaning that the landlord's obligation to repair is similarly unaffected by implied terms imposed by other statutes which are themselves not binding on the Crown.

It may be noted, incidentally, that the term "premises" in the 1957 Act is wide enough to cover temporary as well as permanent buildings, an important practical point when it is remembered

how many temporary buildings, staircases and passage ways are
used in connection with the extension or modernisation of out-
dated or inadequate health service premises. It can also cover
mobile accommodation such as caravans, and also vehicles such
as blood transfusion units.

Occupiers, contracts and tenancies

Section 3 deals with the duty of the occupier towards third
parties who come upon the premises in pursuance of a contract
between the occupier and another party; for example, contractors' workmen on building jobs for the hospital and
suppliers' deliverymen. The occupier owes to such third parties a
common duty of care as his visitors and this duty *cannot* be
excluded or restricted by contract. Further, the common duty of
care shall include the duty to perform his obligation under the
contract unless there is a provision in the contract to the contrary. If a third party is injured by a danger due to faulty work of
an independent contractor, provided he has taken reasonable
care, the occupier shall not be answerable unless the contract
expressly says so.

This section also applies to tenancies as if the tenancy were a
contract between the landlord and the tenant.

Section 4 of the Act, dealing with a landlord's duty towards a
visitor to the premises, has been replaced by section 4 of the
Defective Premises Act 1972. This says that where premises are
let under a tenancy which puts on the landlord an obligation to
the tenant for the maintenance or repair of the premises, the
landlord owes to all persons who might reasonably be expected to
be affected by defects in the state of the premises a duty to take
such care as is reasonable in all the circumstances to see that
they are reasonably safe from personal injury or from damage to
their property caused by a relevant defect. This duty is owed if
the landlord knows or if he ought in all the circumstances to have
known of the relevant defect. These rules also apply to a right of
occupation given by contract as if it were a tenancy, as where an
employee occupies premises by virtue of his employment. Note
that the landlord's duty under this section is not just to the
tenant but to "all persons who might reasonably be expected to
be affected by defects."

Section 5 says that where an occupier of premises confers on
another party to the contract the right to enter or use, or bring or
send goods to, the premises, the duty of the occupier implied by

the contract will be the common duty of care. This duty of care *can* generally be restricted or disclaimed by agreement, as we have seen. The occupier is prevented from contracting out of the Act only in the case of the person entering under a right conferred by law (discussed above) or in the case of a stranger to a contract under section 3 (also mentioned above). It may be that there are circumstances where a hospital authority might impose some restrictions on liability with regard to a paying patient received under section 5 of the National Health Service Act who is allotted a room of his own, in contrast to the non-paying patient or the section 4 patient; but there is little reason to suppose that such a distinction will ever be drawn. Certainly no distinction is made between section 5 patients and the other classes of patients with regard to the bailment of their belongings, that is, the legal process by which property is handed over for safe keeping. Bailment and the care of patients' property is discussed in Chapter 9.

Exclusion of liability

Section 2(1) of the Occupiers Liability Act states that "an occupier of premises owes the same duty, the common duty of care, to all his visitors, except in so far as he is free to and does extend, restrict, modify or exclude his duty to any visitor or visitors by agreement or otherwise." This provision does not specifically mention the circumstances in which liability may be so affected, but some circumstances are excluded from the application of this power on the part of an occupier. These situations include those affecting third parties to a contract, discussed above and referring to such people as maintenance men employed by outside contractors. They also include situations in which "visitors" enter by operation of law. This category of entrant onto premises includes policemen and bailiffs.

The normal case in which the power of excluding liability to lawful visitors will apply in any health services contexts in which it may be used will occur not by way of an exclusion by agreement, a contractual exclusion, but by way of a notice prominently displayed in such a position as clearly to apply to the premises or section of the premises to which its contents refer. Such notices may frequently refer to the occupier's exclusion from liability in respect of loss or damage to patients' property. However, an important distinction must be drawn in this respect between liability for property damage or loss and liability for injury.

Notices and fair exclusions

The Occupier's Liability Act imposes the common duty of care except to the extent to which the occupier of premises is lawfully able, by way of contract or otherwise, to restrict this liability or avoid it altogether. The provision of the Act to this effect does not specifically mention the circumstances in which the person seeking to alter, restrict or avoid his liability is so lawfully able. That question is dependent on further principles of both common law and statute. Soon after the passing of the Occupiers' Liability Act it was judicially decided that an occupier was at liberty lawfully to avoid the liability he would otherwise be under to a lawful visitor by the placing of a notice at the boundaries of the premises in question saying that persons entering the premises did so at their own risk. This judicial decision aroused a great deal of hostile criticism and was even hailed by some as a kind of charter for careless occupiers. However, the decision was legally correct within the bounds of the common law principle of consent, or the voluntary acceptance of risk.

In 1977, however, the full force of that decision was reduced very considerably by statute, namely the Unfair Contract Terms Act. This statute renders null and void any contract terms, or any "notice" (a term which is clearly meant to include the sign which was in issue in the earlier decision) purporting to restrict or avoid personal liability for personal injury or death to another resulting from negligence. Thus, while the earlier decision is still authority for the proposition that damage to property may be lawfully avoided by an appropriately displayed notice at the edge of the property or premises, the more important and more usual complaint of personal injuries caused to a lawful visitor will not be hindered by an alleged consent to risk; the law no longer allows it.

In the case of loss or damage other than personal injury or death a person cannot, since the 1977 Act, exclude or restrict this liability for negligence except in so far as the term or notice satisfies the requirement of *reasonableness*. The definition of negligence expressly includes the breach of the common duty of care imposed by the Occupiers Liability Act, but the prohibition of the 1977 Act on exclusion of liability applies only where the duty arises from things done in the course of a business or from the occupation of premises used for business purposes of the occupier. By section 14 "business" includes a profession and also the activities of any government department or local or public authority. The 1977 Act applies generally, therefore, to health services premises both within and outside the public sector.

It is to be noted by way of conclusion that the Unfair Contract Terms Act 1977 does not abolish the defence of consent to risk, but provides that a person's agreement to or awareness of an exempting condition or notice is not of itself to be taken as indicating his voluntary acceptance of the risk. All depends, in the final analysis, on the construction put by a court of law on the contractual condition or the notice in question, and in particular on the general point as to whether, in all the circumstances, it can be considered fair. The concept of fairness may depend not only on the circumstances of an individual case but also on legal rules from other quarters. For instance, as will be explained in a moment, even a trespasser on premises is now owed a "duty of common humanity." The particular incidents of such a duty will be explained but it may be noted at this point that it would be odd if an occupier could lawfully contract out of such a duty, albeit a low level of duty, to a lawful visitor, when that is the very duty which would be owed to the same person if a trespasser.

Risk and personal injury

The duty of an occupier to take reasonable care for the safety of lawful visitors extends to both activities which are carried on upon the premises, and also the condition of the premises themselves. As far as activities are concerned, examples are hardly necessary to illustrate the point, since the use of equipment, sometimes very sophisticated and often potentially hazardous, is a normal incident of the modern provision of personal health services. The misuse or careless use of any such equipment, and especially electrical or heavy mechanical equipment, presents obvious dangers for the lawful visitors—obvious, at least, in the sense that they can clearly occur, but by no means necessarily in the sense that they are so obvious to staff that an unwitting "visitor" may be expected to be aware of the risk.

A more frequent type of complaint against an occupier is that the physical condition of the premises, or something directly applied to or affecting those premises, is the cause of the danger. Examples include a staircase in a state of disrepair, a loose guard rail or handrail on a landing or balcony and decaying or faulty masonry which may cause injury in the event of collapse. These all create risks which may materialise into the breach by an occupier of the common duty of care.

It can happen that an activity on premises causes them to be

in a dangerous condition for visitors. In *Slade* v. *Battersea and
Putney Group H.M.C.* (1955) the wife of a patient, who was visiting him in hospital as a result of a message from the hospital that
he was dangerously ill, slipped after visiting him and fell on a
part of the floor of the ward where polish had recently been
spread. The polish had not been polished off at the time of the
accident and its presence rendered that part of the floor slippery
and dangerous to walk on. It was a rule of the hospital that a warning should be given if polishing were in progress but no warning
was given on previous occasions. She did not know that polish
was spread on the floor and she claimed damages for her fall. It
was held that the H.M.C. through its servants did not act with
reasonable care.

Poisons and drugs

While it is but one further example of a potentially hazardous
pursuit, mention may here be made of the need to attend to careful storage of poisons, drugs and radioactive substances. For
instance, the storage of poisons is provided for in some detail in
the Poisons Act 1972 and amplified in the Poisons Rules which
are statutory instruments made under powers provided in the
principal and enabling Act. If an institution has its own
dispensary or pharmaceutical department, all poisons except
those which have been issued for use within the institution must
be stored in that department. Furthermore, in the case of certain
poisons specified in Schedule 1 of the Poisons Act 1972, every
substance which has been issued to wards must be stored in a
cupboard which is reserved solely for the storage of poisons and
poisonous substances.

Another example of duties in respect of safekeeping which are
specifically laid down in statutory form is found in the Misuse of
Drugs (Safe Custody) Regulations 1973, which require
"controlled" drugs, with certain exceptions, to be kept either in a
locked safe or a locked receptacle. While the breach of such
duties is not expressed in the relevant statutes to involve civil
liability for damages, it is to be expected that breach of the duty
imposed in respect of safety by the statute will often, if not
always, lead to the occupier or occupying authority having committed a breach of the common duty of care if a visitor is harmed
or injured by a reasonably foreseeable materialisation of a risk
created in this area. While the occupier can properly expect lawful visitors to take reasonable care of themselves, bottles and jars

and objects which resemble sweets may act as a positive allurement to an inquisitive child. The general position of children on premises will be considered separately in a moment.

Damage to property

The scope of the common duty of care owed by an occupier of premises extends both to seeing that personal injuries are avoided and also that the property of patients, their visitors and indeed of all "lawful visitors" is safe from risk. Section 1(3)(*b*) of the Occupiers' Liability Act 1957 provides that the rules which it enacts shall apply.

"in the like manner and to the like extent as the principles applicable at common law to an occupier of premises to regulate ... the obligations of a person occupying or having control over any premises or structure in respect of damage to property, including the property of persons who are not themselves his visitors."

Therefore where property lawfully on the premises is damaged by a structural defect of the premises, whether it actually belongs to a visitor or not, the question in each case is whether or not the occupier has discharged the common duty of care.

The Occupiers' Liability Act does not, however, affect the common law rules applicable to the relationship between bailor and bailee. The subject of bailment will be discussed in rather greater detail in Chapter 9; but briefly, a bailment occurs where one person hands property or belongings over to another for safekeeping, whether for a fee or not. Furthermore, the Act has no effect on the common law rule (that is, the rule applicable before the Act came into operation) that an occupier has no duty to protect the goods of his visitor from the risk of theft by third parties.

In the case of *Edwards* v. *West Herts Group Hospital Management Committee* (1957) the plaintiff was employed by the defendants as a house physician at a hospital on the terms that he had to live there in a staff hostel adjoining the hospital, and that a certain sum should be deducted from his salary for board and lodging. After a number of his belongings had been stolen from his room, the plaintiff brought an action alleging that the defendants had failed to take reasonable care of his room and effects. The county court dismissed the action. On appeal, the Court of Appeal held that the relationship between the parties was not that of a boarding house keeper and a boarder (where such a duty is owed) but of master and servant, and that a master was under no duty to take reasonable care to prevent the theft of his servant's (employee's) effects.

The matter of patients' property, and especially the possible variation in liability in the case of private institutions, is examined further in Chapter 9.

Liability to Children

While children certainly do not constitute any special legal category for the purposes of the liability of an occupier of premises, the law cannot fail to take account of the fact that children are more vulnerable than adults and do not always behave as reasonable adults can be expected to behave. In *Glasgow Corporation* v. *Taylor* (1922) it was alleged that a child aged seven had died from eating poisonous berries which he had picked from a shrub in some public gardens under the control of the corporation. The berries looked like cherries or large blackcurrants and looked very tempting to children. They amounted therefore to an "allurement" to the child. The corporation knew that the berries were poisonous but neither fenced the shrub off nor gave any warning of the deadly berries. The House of Lords (on a preliminary point of law, to establish whether or not the factual issues were worth pursuing) held that these facts disclosed a good cause of action.

Some dangers do not, however, amount in law to "allurements." Thus a heap of rubble or a piece of water present obvious dangers and do not create liability if properly protected or fenced according to the circumstances. But to very young children practically anything can be dangerous, depending on the circumstances in which the child comes into contact with whatever then "causes" injury. Is it fair to expect the occupier to protect against risks which would be obvious even to slightly older, but nevertheless quite young, children? In the case of *Phipps* v. *Rochester Corporation* (1955) Devlin J. decided that in measuring the duty of the occupier, the habits of prudent parents in relation to little children should be taken into account. The case concerned a five-year-old boy who went blackberrying with his sister, aged seven, and who fell into a trench dug across an open space. On the particular facts it was not prudent for a parent to have allowed two small children to go alone on the open space in question; or, at least, a prudent parent would have satisfied himself that the place held no dangers for the children, and if he had done so he would have seen the trench and taken steps to prevent his children going there while it was still open.

Trespassers

Certain parts of most, if not all, health services premises are marked "Private," "No Admittance," or in some similar way, denoting that here are the limits to the lawfulness of the otherwise lawful visitor's visit. Disobedience to such a notice would normally render the inquisitive or disobedient visitor, or patient, a trespasser. It would be a nonsense if even storerooms containing potentially hazardous equipment, for instance, had in law to be made safe for entry by the curious and the meddlesome. But while the common duty of care is owed only to lawful visitors to those parts of premises into which they are expressly or impliedly permitted to go, certain duties are owed by an occupier of premises even in respect of trespassers.

The term "trespasser," it has been said, covers both the wicked and the innocent. Both the burglar and the straying hiker are equally trespassers in the eyes of the law. Until the case of *British Railways Board* v. *Herrington* in 1972 the position in English law (though not in Scotland) was that an occupier owed no duty of care to trespassers but merely a duty to refrain from reckless or intentional conduct. Intentional and reckless harm apart, the trespasser entered at his peril. The Act of 1957 did not make any alteration to this principle. In the case of children the common law had created certain exceptions in the interests of justice; in particular, the courts were more willing in the case of child trespassers (their age and experience being numbered among the deciding factors) to infer a licence from the occupier for them to be on the premises on which they had no other legal right to be. An unsupervised gap in a fence could create a situation in which, in the absence of any proper warnings or reprimands, a licence might be implied. Furthermore a line of decisions established that circumstances or conditions of premises which could be said to constitute "traps" or "allurements" to the young and inexperienced could also give rise to a duty to take care. The Occupiers' Liability Act appears to do no more than re-enact the common law on this point for it provides in section 2(3) that in assessing the common duty of care an occupier must be prepared for children to be less careful than adults.

The decision in the *Herrington* case substantially amended the law relating to occupiers' liability to trespassers as a whole.

Though they reached the conclusion with some hesitation the Law Lords held that the continued failure of the Railways Board to maintain properly or at all a boundary fence between a public place and an electrified railway line onto which a six-year-old boy had strayed and been injured was to him a breach of duty. The particularity of this "halfway house" duty attracted a new terminology from their Lordships. Accounts of this duty are expressed variously as the duty to act with ordinary humanity, or in accordance with ordinary common sense and civilised behaviour.

The duty to trespassers is thus affected and conditioned by factors which, in an ordinary negligence action, go to establish breach of duty. Such factors include the magnitude and nature of the risk, the practicability of precautions in all the surrounding circumstances, and the financial resources of the occupier. Each case will therefore turn very much indeed upon its own particular facts, and the outcome of cases of injury to trespassers is in the nature of things very difficult to predict even with a merely moderate degree of certainty.

II

Varieties of nuisance

A variety of legal wrongs, each bearing the name "nuisance," is examined in this section. Both public and private nuisance involve unreasonable interference with the interested group receiving relevant protection from the law, though the nature of the damage suffered differs as between these varieties of nuisance. A third variety of nuisance is the so-called "statutory nuisance" as provided against specifically by statute and taking some such form as noise, pollution or insanitary buildings. The case of statutory nuisance is based on public policies of health, cleanliness and sanitation enforceable at the instance of public authorities, for example, the appropriate local government authority.

By contrast, the nuisances known respectively as public nuisance and private nuisance can both attract remedies in tort, either by way of damages or by way of an injunction, or sometimes both. While a public nuisance is also a criminal offence punishable with a fine, the interest of the private individual, body or authority in public nuisance lies in the opportunity which, in appropriate circumstances, arises to obtain a civil remedy in respect of the nuisance. Private nuisance concerns the rights and remedies available in respect of the occupation of property and the reasonably quiet and undisturbed enjoyment of that property by the occupier or occupying authority.

While a nuisance can be committed as a result of negligence, there are many instances in which its commission does not depend on fault. Such is the case with statutory nuisances, for the section of the public which is adversely affected by noise, smoke or whatever is little interested in whether the nuisance could have been avoided with reasonable care. Such is also the case with public nuisance in respect of which an individual sues for damages, having received some special injury or loss over and above that experienced by the public at large, or at least the affected section of it. In the case of private nuisance affecting premises or their ordinary enjoyment, fault must be proved in some cases but not in others. The varieties of nuisance will now be examined in further detail.

Statutory nuisance

Where property or premises in question are not occupied by the Crown, no special problem arises and the provisions and prohibitions of the statute are applicable in the normal way. But the Crown, as was explained in Chapter 2, is in a special legal position. As a result of Crown privilege, no notice to abate a statutory nuisance served on a health authority need be complied with, no order to repair or demolish insanitary property served on an authority need be carried out, and no tenant of a hospital house can claim the protection of the Rent Acts in resisting a claim for possession brought against him by an authority on behalf of the Minister. It is, however, the policy of the Crown so far as possible to comply with the general law, as for example, if a property would have been condemned as unfit for human habitation by a local authority under the Housing Acts but for the fact that it is Crown property, such property will normally by agreement with the local authority be demolished by the Crown.

Certain nuisances are statutory nuisances under the Public Health Acts, but as the Crown is not bound by such Acts, the local sanitary authority cannot bring proceedings against the Crown for any such nuisance arising on hospital property. *Nottingham No. 1 H.M.C.* v. *Owen* (1957) is an interesting case. The Magistrates were asked to order the H.M.C. to abate a nuisance caused by smoke from the chimney of its general hospital. Despite the contention made by the solicitor for the H.M.C. that the hospital was owned by the Crown and could not, therefore, be summoned under the Public Health Acts the magistrates ordered the H.M.C. to abate the nuisance within four months. The H.M.C. appealed against the decision in the Queen's Bench Divisional Court and the appeal was allowed. The Lord Chief Justice said the question was whether the hospital now vested in the Minister of Health was in fact premises occupied for the public services of the Crown. Once a hospital is transferred to the Minister of Health it seems that he holds it in trust for the Crown. Therefore, the Justices did not have jurisdiction to make the order.

While the Noise Abatement Act 1960 does not apply to property occupied by the Crown, section 22 of the Clean Air Act requires that the local authority reports to the appropriate Minister where Crown Property is emitting smoke, and the Minister must enquire into the circumstances and, if there is just cause for complaint, take all practical steps to prevent or minimise the emission.

Public nuisance

A "public nuisance" is an infringement of the rights of the public at large; for example, the obstruction of the highway interfering with their right to pass to and fro. The remedy is either criminal proceedings or restraint by injunction at the suit of the Attorney-General. A public nuisance may also be a private nuisance where it affects a person in his individual capacity over and above that of the public. For example, the highway may be obstructed by the erection of a stand from which spectators can watch a procession. This is a public nuisance. If, in addition, one of the supports of the stand completely blocks the entrance to a shop and so precludes the shopkeeper from carrying on his business this will be a private nuisance insofar as the shopkeeper is concerned and he may take civil action.

Private nuisance

While an individual, or private, injury caused as a result of a public nuisance is sometimes referred to as a private nuisance, a private nuisance properly so-called consists in an unlawful and unreasonable interference with a person's use or enjoyment of land, or of some right over or in connection with the land. A private nuisance may consist in a commission or an omission, as a result of which interference is caused to another's health, comfort, or convenience in the occupation of his land. No fault, negligence or lack of care need be established for the plaintiff to be able to make out a case against the defendant who has allegedly committed a private nuisance against him. But if the defendant accused of nuisance has taken over the property from which the nuisance is alleged to emanate, he is said in law to have continued the nuisance, and then only if the fault can be proved. There is, in other words, no strict liability in nuisance otherwise than for its creation. If a nuisance is continued, a plaintiff does not have to go to the lengths of establishing all the elements of the tort of negligence itself; though, as in the case of negligence, and unlike the case of trespass, damage (here in the sense of the unreasonable interference with the use of the property of the plaintiff) is of the essence of a claim made in private nuisance. It is important to note that the right of action in private nuisance to premises is reserved to the occupier. The occupier's visitors will, if injured as a consequence of nuisance, be obliged to bring an action under some other head of liability, for instance in negligence.

The element of damage in private nuisance

Actual damage must be proved except where the enjoyment of an easement or natural right, such as a right of support, is affected. The remedy for a private nuisance is a civil action for damages or an injunction. Self-help is also permitted by law; in other words, a person may "abate" the nuisance, for example, by cutting off the overhanging branches of his neighbour's tree.

Where the interference takes the form of material damage to property as by the blighting of vegetation, it is easier for the plaintiff to make out a case than where the nuisance takes the form of interference to property by noises, smells, vibrations, overhanging trees. With regard to noise, smell and the more intangible infringements to enjoyment of property caused by depressing sights and sounds, regard is paid to the standard prevailing in the locality. The "damage" in the sense of an interference with normal enjoyment may be entirely relative to circumstances. It was said in one case that "What would be considered a nuisance in Belgrave Square would be tolerated in Bermondsey."

Instances in which a nuisance to the occupiers of surrounding property against health service activities include, conceivably, the depressing sight of a mortuary, the noise of plant or machinery such as a boiler house or hospital workshop, grit or smoke from a chimney, and maybe cooking smells and fumes from a hospital kitchen. A rather more probable instance would be the noise of crying babies from a maternity block situated too close to residential property. In the case of *Metropolitan Asylums Board* v. *Hill* (1881) it was held that even the possible danger of "germs" (viruses) blowing from a fever hospital might constitute a private nuisance to neighbouring property, though the decision would be unlikely to be followed in modern conditions of the protection of health and safety.

The balance of interests

This particular tort requires great nicety of judgment on the part of judges in balancing the conflicting interests of parties; for example, the desire of one neighbour to practise on his trumpet in the evening and of the other not to have his infant's sleep disturbed. The balance of interest in nuisance must inevitably be influenced by public needs. Thus, many cases embody a conflict between a private person's need, for instance, for quiet, fresh air, and adequate light, and the public need, for instance, for industrial undertakings.

The achievement of such a balance cannot be reduced to a mechanical formula since it is very much subject to the facts of each individual case. Consequently, the law of nuisance contains a number of general legal guides which are quite equivocal in character. They give the judge assistance rather than direction. Thus, the fact that an interference results from activitiy of a reasonable kind (running a theatre); or of a useful kind (fish and chip shop); or is only temporary (discharge from electric cable); or is an isolated act (hitting a cricket ball out of a ground where this has occurred); or existed before the plaintiff came to reside in the district (old established tannery); all tend to show that the interference is not an actionable nuisance, but no more. The interference may be actionable despite the existence of all or any of these factors.

The defendant's position

Control over premises will generally make a defendant liable if the nuisance should have been known to him, as in the blocked stream causing flooding to neighbouring land in *Sedleigh-Denfield* v. *O'Callaghan* (1940). This means that the person who has, or ought to have, control over premises from which the nuisance comes will be liable even for a nuisance created by a trespasser if it is reasonably practicable to abate the nuisance. It is no defence that the nuisance was caused by the acts or omissions of independent contractors engaged by the defendant to do something which may well cause a nuisance. Nuisance created or negligently continued by the defendant's employee leads to the possibility of the defendant's becoming vicariously liable for the wrongful act, according to the normal principles of vicarious liability discussed in Chapter 4.

Prescriptive rights

Twenty years' continuance legalises a private, but not a public, nuisance. One is said to acquire the right to do the act by prescription. Even so, someone who comes to the nuisance may have a valid action. Thus, in *Sturges* v. *Bridgman*, Bridgman carried on a business of confectioner for many years. He used a pestle and mortar, which created an irritating noise. The plaintiff, Sturges, bought a house next door, and had a consulting room there. He succeeded because, although the defendant might have acquired a prescriptive right by long usage, he had not acquired such a right against the plaintiff, in particular, who had not been in a position to do anything about the nuisance (even if he knew about it) until he bought the adjoining house.

The rule in Rylands v. Fletcher

Finally, in relation to the liability of a person, body or health authority in respect of premises it is worth noting the so-called rules in *Rylands* v. *Fletcher* (1868).

Whenever a person collects on his land anything which is not naturally there and which is likely to do harm if it escapes, he is liable for all damage that is caused, if the thing does escape. This rule was enunciated in the case of *Rylands* v. *Fletcher* (1868). He is liable whether he was negligent or not. This is strict liability. In other torts there is a mental element—some act of malice, or negligence or intention—but in this tort, he is liable even if the escape be purely accidental, unless, it seems, that escape is caused by an "Act of God," act or default of the plaintiff, with the consent of the plaintiff, by a third party or under statutory authority.

In the original case, it was water artificially accumulated on the defendant's land which escaped. A man-made reservoir is not naturally there; it is a "non-natural user" of land. The rule has been extended enormously beyond artifically gathered waters, to cover noxious fumes, vibrations, poisonous vegetation and even a flagpole.

Liability has been established under this rule in respect of both property damage and personal injury, though the original intention was to provide specifically for the former. Few cases now fall to be decided according to the rule in *Rylands* v. *Fletcher* alone, and many cases in which the rule could conceivably be invoked tend in practice to be settled according to the principles of negligence. The principles of negligence will be decisive, in particular, in any case where the "escape" complained of is alleged to have been caused by the act of a third party, for instance by mischievous children or by vandals.

Chapter 8

LIMITATIONS ON LIABILITY

A variety of liabilities has emerged so far in the discussion of the topics covered in earlier chapters. Liability in negligence, in trespass, in nuisance, in defamation, and the liability of an occupier of premises for the safety of visitors have all been mentioned as well as the possible civil liability for personal injuries as a result of the breach of a duty imposed for safety reasons by statute. What has principally been discussed in relation to all these opportunities for imposing liability in tort is the principle upon which liability is in each case based, as well as an indication of the sort of compensation which may be awarded once liability has been established.

But what of a plaintiff who waits many years before commencing legal proceedings? And what of a totally unforeseeable consequence of an injury, even if there is no argument about liability? And what of a plaintiff who contributes to his own injuries by carelessness or stupidity? All these issues can now conveniently be dealt with in one relatively brief chapter, for they all bear on limitations upon liability, given that the latter has already been clearly established in the first place.

I

Limitation in point of time

There are at least two reasons why a time limit should be set on a plaintiff's commencing legal proceedings. One is that a certain security in human dealings is desirable, so that people are not left for a wholly unreasonable or indeed unbearable time without knowing where they stand. The other has to do with the fallibility of the human memory which can produce unreliable results even after a short time, let alone a long period. The loss or destruction of documents can also add to the trouble. The principal statute governing the area of limitation of actions today is the Limitation Act 1939 as amended by more recent legislation which has been passed to meet particular demands not specially envisaged or provided for in the earlier legislation.

The 1939 Act, as amended, provides that actions founded on simple contract (that is, on an enforceable agreement made otherwise than by deed) or on tort shall not be brought after the expiration of six years from the date on which the cause of action accrued. We cannot say that the period runs from the date the wrong was done, or from the date on which the injury was caused, for those may be two separate dates. As will be explained, the time at which the cause of action "accrues" can differ in varying types of case. In the case of personal injuries, however, the period of limitation is three years running from the date on which the cause of action accrued or, in certain circumstances recently provided for by an amending statute, from the date on which the plaintiff first knew he had a cause of action. A court will not of its own motion come to the assistance of a defendant to say that the action is being brought "out of time"; the defendant must himself say so.

Commencement of the period

The 1939 Act states that the period of limitation runs "from the date on which the cause of action accrued." But no further explanation is given as to when and in what circumstances a cause of action does "accrue" and so reference to decided cases must be made by way of explanation. The cases show that the period begins to run from the earliest time at which an action could be brought. This means in practice that a cause of action arises at the moment when a state of facts occurs which gives a would-be plaintiff a right to succeed against a would-be defendant. The fact that the potential plaintiff could not at that first possible moment actually identify the person who, it transpires, is the potential defendant does not prevent a cause of action accruing. But a cause of action must arise, and it is not sufficient for the would-be plaintiff to say baldly that he has been injured or otherwise suffered harm or loss; for the mere occurrence of such misfortune may not involve another person in legal liability at all.

Differing heads of liability

Owing to the fact that the idea of "accrual" of a cause of action does not admit of a single explanatory formula, its practical incidence varies accordingly to the type of liability which is sought to be imposed and even, in certain special circumstances, according to the type of harm which the injury causes.

Some torts, including trespass in its varying forms of assault, battery and false imprisonment, and including libel and some forms of slander, are actionable without having to prove specific loss or damage. A court will award damages to a successful plaintiff without proof by that plaintiff that he has actually incurred any loss or injury, save that which the law presumes from the very fact of the libel or the trespass having been committed. In these cases the limitation period begins in general to run from the moment the wrongful act was committed, whether the injured party knows of it or not. This applies even though any resulting damage which may actually occur is not discovered until a later date; for such damage is not a new cause of action but an incident of the original cause of action.

On the other hand, in the case of torts which are actionable only on proof of actual damage, such as negligence and nuisance, the limitation period runs from the damage. So, for instance, the period of limitation for negligently caused personal injuries begins at the time the injury is caused. If the consumer of a defective product were injured more than three years after the date of negligent manufacture, the period would run from the date of the injury and it would be no defence for the manufacturer to say that the defect in the product should have manifested itself within three years of manufacture. In *Dutton* v. *Bognor Regis U.D.C.* (1972), a case which involved damage to a building owing to faulty inspection, but no personal injuries, the Court of Appeal stated that in such a case the period of limitation (six years in that instance) did not begin to run until the plaintiff could, with reasonable diligence, have discovered the defective state of his property. Such discovery might be outside the normal six year period. This somewhat controversial decision has yet to be tested in future cases, and is of course open either to confirmation or rejection on appeal to the House of Lords.

The Limitation Act 1975

In some cases difficulty can be caused by the fact that damage, harm or injury does not become apparent for some time after it has been inflicted. For example, exposure to dust may damage the plaintiff's lungs in an irreversible way, but the resultant physical condition may not become severe enough to make the plaintiff distinctly aware of it for some years. The same applies to many other forms of personal injury which may well arise in connection with the plaintiff's particular work. Those exposed in the course of their job to radiation or to drugs and substances which can have a cumulatively harmful effect may find themselves in this position.

The general rule under the Limitation Act 1939 was that in such a case time began to run (the period started from) when the injury was suffered, not when it was discovered. A right of action might therefore be barred before the plaintiff even knew he had it. The harshness of this rule in cases of personal injury has led to its alteration by statute. The period of limitation in personal injury actions is now in the alternative: either the date on which the cause of action accrued, or the date (if later) of the plaintiff's knowledge of it. A person has such "knowledge" when he knows all the following facts: that the injury in question was significant; that the injury was wholly or partly attributable to the allegedly wrongful conduct of the defendant, be that negligence nuisance or other breach of duty (an expression which naturally extends to civil action arising from the breach of a statutory duty); and the identity of the defendant.

An even more important provision of the 1975 Act gives a court of law the power to override statutory time limits altogether if it appears to the court to be equitable (that is, fair and just) having regard to the degree to which the ordinary limitation rules prejudice the plaintiff but also to the extent to which any exercise of this special power would prejudice the defendant. The power is exercised in the all too common situation where the plaintiff's advisers, as a result of some procedural slip, have allowed the normal three year period to expire.

II

Remoteness of damage

This chapter has so far considered a reason for imposing limits on the plaintiff's right to recover damages for a legal wrong based on the time which has elapsed since that wrong could, or should, have been followed by legal proceedings. The subject matter of the present section concerns damage or harm which is too "remote," not in point of time but in point of its very nature. The question was asked at the beginning of this chapter whether absolutely all the allegedly harmful consequences of a legal wrong are compensated by way of damages. The answer is no, and the reason for that answer will now be briefly examined.

While the breach of a contractual duty will lead to compensation for the legal and physical damage which is foreseeably caused, the development of the concept of "remoteness of damage" in the law of tort has been rather more complex. The concept "remoteness of damage" in tort actions must first be clearly distinguished from the notion of factual causation. This latter idea was encountered earlier in Chapter 6, in connection with the case of *Barnett* v. *Chelsea and Kensington H.M.C.* (1969). The casualty officer in that case was negligent, in the sense of careless and professionally less than responsible; but the tort of negligence was not in fact committed because the night watchman whose tea had contained arsenic would have died anyway from his advanced poisoning. In contradistinction to the idea of causation in fact, causation in law (or remoteness of damage) is a matter of policy, expressed in the form of judicial pronouncements of rule and principle, in seeking to limit the redressable consequences of a legal wrong to proportions which people in general might be expected to consider fair and reasonable to both plaintiff and defendant.

Directness and foreseeability

In arriving at this proper compromise the law has over the years used two principal "tests" of remoteness of damage, that is to say two policies by which to limit recovery of damages to certain roughly definable types of consequences. The two attitudes have been a test of directness of cause, and a test of foreseeability. While the law before 1921 was somewhat unclear, the Court of Appeal in that year in the case of *Re Polemis* came down firmly in favour of a test of directness of causation. The case concerned a ship which was being unloaded by stevedores. Owing to the fault of one stevedore a plank was dropped into a hold containing inflammable vapour from an unloaded cargo. The friction of the plank against the ship's hull caused a spark which ignited the vapour and the whole ship was gutted. The damage was in excess of a quarter of a million pounds—a lot of money in 1921! The Court of Appeal held that all the directly caused consequences should be compensated by way of damages.

In 1961, however, the Judicial Committee of the Privy Council, in another shipping accident case which came on appeal from Australia, favoured a test of foreseeability in preference to a test of directness. According to the rules and conventions of judicial precedent decisions of the Privy Council are not binding on other courts. They are, however, of great persuasive authority, not surprisingly since the bulk of the Judicial Committee's membership consists of Law Lords who, if sitting as the House of Lords, would certainly create binding precedents. While the nature of the respective tests of directness and foreseeability is different, their effect might in many cases be precisely the same, since direct consequences are very often foreseeable, and vice versa.

Reasonably foreseeable consequences

The test of foresight is that of the reasonable person in possession of all the relevant facts of the situation and in the circumstances of the defendant; it is not the foresight of the most prescient and prudent, nor is it only that which is screamingly obvious even to the most simple mind. Reasonable foresight is an attempt by the law at a middle way, a compromise. Thus it will be foreseeable that an injured pedestrian will suffer pain and discomfort; that his clothes may be damaged; that expenses may be incurred in the treatment of his injuries; that his expectation of life may be shortened; and that he may have to take time off work and may even be disabled. But it is not normally foreseeable that the pedestrian suffers economic consequences such as the loss of a lucrative business deal of which the defendant could not be reasonably expected to have had any knowledge immediately before the accident. This is not by any means a surprising result, and little difficulty is in practice experienced by the courts in relation to foreseeability of the actual consequence. What does cause difficulty, and can sometimes produce decisions with which it can be difficult to agree, is not the foreseeability of the consequences themselves but rather the foreseeability, or otherwise, of the manner in which those consequences have been caused to occur.

Foreseeability of causation

Following the decision of the House of Lords in the case of *Hughes* v. *Lord Advocate* (1963), an appeal from Scotland, the courts require the damage complained of to have been reasonably foreseeable in general outline only; in other words, that the defendant need not be proved by the plaintiff to have been able to foresee the precise combination and sequence of events which led up to the damage of which the plaintiff complains. In that case, employees of the Post Office had opened a manhole in the street and in the evening left the open manhole covered by a canvas shelter, unattended but surrounded by paraffin warning lamps. The plaintiff, a boy aged eight, took one of the lamps into the shelter and was playing with it there when he stumbled over it and it fell into the manhole. A violent explosion followed and the plaintiff himself fell into the hole, sustaining terrible injuries from burns. It was quite unpredictable that a lamp might explode, but the Post Office employees were in breach of their duty of care in leaving the manhole unattended because they should have appreciated that boys might take a lamp into the shelter and that, if the lamp fell and broke, they might suffer serious injury from burning. So the lamp, a known source of danger, caused injury through an unforeseeable sequence of events. The defendants were nevertheless held liable to compensate the boy for his injuries. The difference between flame burns and flash burns was not such as to render the latter unforeseeable when the former were foreseeable. It is interesting, incidentally, to note that the courts in the event elected to find no substantial distinction between two causes of burning, when fire insurance policies do not normally seek to draw the distinction in the first place.

The application of the principle, that damage need be foreseeable in general outline only, to the first instance (not an appeal) decision in *Tremain* v. *Pike* (1969) is not entirely clear. The rat population on the defendant's farm was allowed to become unduly large and the plaintiff, a herdsman on the farm, contracted leptospirosis, or Weil's disease, in consequence. Weil's disease is uncommon and is contracted through contact with rats' urine. The judge said that this disease was unforeseeable and "entirely different in kind" from such foreseeable consequences as the effects of a rat bite or food poisoning from contaminated food. The plaintiff, said the judge, could not simply say that rat-induced disease was foreseeable and that rat-induced disease occurred. This is only a first instance decision and seems wholly out of line with *Hughes* v. *Lord Advocate* which is likely to be followed in future cases.

The eggshell skull rule

It is a general rule of the recovery of damages in tort that a defendant takes the plaintiff, or victim, as he finds him. This means that the defendant cannot escape liability for consequences resulting from the peculiar or extra susceptibilities of the plaintiff by saying that they are unforeseeable. Before the decision of the Judicial Committee of the Privy Council in the *Wagon Mound* (1961) there was no need to state the distinct existence of any such special rule, since the direct physical consequences of a wrongful act were compensated by damages in the normal way. Only after a test of foreseeability gained general acceptance by the courts did it become necessary to state any special rule.

It was said in the case of *Dulieu* v. *White* (1901) that "if a man is negligently run over or otherwise negligently injured in his body, it is no answer to the sufferer's claim for damages that he would have suffered less injury, or no injury at all, if he had not had an unusually thin skull or an unusually weak heart." The same, or at least a similar, principle operates when the plaintiff's injury is exacerbated by a combination of his abnormality and some external force which foreseeably and naturally intervenes after the accident, such as medical treatment to which he is allergic: *Robinson* v. *Post Office* (1974).

The consequences of an intentional act, whether the victim is normal or abnormally sensitive, are never too remote.

III

Contributory negligence

A failure to commence legal proceedings in respect of an injury or wrong within the limitation period laid down by the various Limitation Acts can be as a result of the plaintiff's own fault as well as that of the plaintiff's advisers, legal or otherwise. But the principal instance in which a plaintiff's claim is adversely affected by his own fault is in a case of contributory negligence. If a plaintiff contributes, by his careless or even wrongful conduct, to the injurious consequences of an accident or other misfortune wrongfully caused by the defendant, the plaintiff is said to be contributorily negligent. This does not mean that the plaintiff has been "in breach of legal duty owed to himself"; for we do not sue ourselves, we sue others. It simply means that the plaintiff has shown want of proper care for his own safety and wellbeing in the circumstances in which injury or harm is wrongfully caused by another.

Indeed "negligence" is a most inapt term in many situations; for the wrong which is committed against the plaintiff may be negligence, but it may also be many other torts such as nuisance or breach of statutory duty. And while it will usually be carelessness on the part of a plaintiff which leads a defendant to say that the plaintiff has been contributorily negligent, it could even be an intentional act or indeed any act showing want of care for himself, additional to the defendant's wrong.

Reduction in damages

Provided the plaintiff is in some way at fault a court may, at the instance of the defendant, reduce the damages which would otherwise have been awarded to the plaintiff had no such fault or want of care been shown. Just as in the case of a plea that the plaintiff's action is time-barred, the limitation period having expired, so also in contributory negligence the allegation must be specifically raised by the defendant: the court will not do it for him. Whatever his complaint, if the plaintiff has by his own fault contributed to the cause of the injury or harm of which he complains, his damages will be reduced by such a percentage as, in the court's opinion, fairly reflects his contributory cause.

Thus both fault and factual causation are taken into account in settling on a final figure which will do justice to the plaintiff while not doing injustice to the defendant. It is very unusual, though not unknown, for a court to reduce damage by less than 10 per cent. or by more than 90 per cent. Beyond those limits the injury has normally been caused by the fault of one or other party to the exclusion of the other.

Factors for consideration

Despite the power which the courts have under the Law Reform (Contributory Negligence) Act 1945 to reduce damages in accordance with what is just and equitable having regard to the plaintiff's share in the damage, it can happen that a clear line can be drawn between the conduct of the plaintiff and that of the defendant such that it is quite reasonable to say that one of them has been responsible for the injury or harm to the exclusion of the other. In other words, the fact that the courts have the power to reduce the award of damages does not mean that they have to in every single case in which the plaintiff has somehow been at fault.

Accidents and injuries

It is important to note that what the defendant alleges is that the plaintiff has, by his fault or want of care, contributed in some measure to his injuries. A plaintiff in a civil action sues for damages in respect of the injury or damage he has suffered. He does not, properly speaking, sue in respect of the accident which has caused the damage; prosecution for carelessly caused accidents is the business of the police. Nowhere is the applicability of this observation more clear than in the cases in which plaintiffs have had their damages reduced through not having worn a seatbelt, even though the accidents in which they were injured were caused entirely as a result of the defendant's fault.

Just such a situation arose for decision in the case of *Froom* v. *Butcher* (1976). The plaintiff received neck and chest injuries in an accident caused by the negligence of the defendant. Liability for the accident was not disputed, but the defendant pleaded that the plaintiff, who was not wearing a seatbelt, should have his damages substantially reduced on that account. The Court of Appeal agreed to this proposition and reduced the plaintiff's damages by 25 per cent., it having been established that the injuries to the neck and chest would not have occurred if a seatbelt had been worn. The case is thus certainly not authority for the proposition that a failure to wear a belt is always contributory negligence, for some injuries would have happened in spite of a belt being worn. Indeed, this was Mr. Froom's argument towards an unreduced award of damages. He said that he had read the statistics and seriously considered the whole issue, and had come to the conclusion that he was better off not wearing a belt than wearing one.

Nevertheless Mr. Froom's damages were reduced. Indeed his neck and chest injuries would have been avoided altogether had a belt been worn. In a sense, it could seem odd that the plaintiff's failure to do something which would have avoided his injuries altogether led to a reduction of only 25 per cent.; but then, the defendant did cause the crash. It appears from other decisions that if the wearing of a belt would have reduced the severity of injury but would not have prevented it altogether, a reduction in damages of about 15 per cent. will be made. Certain exceptions to this principle have already been established: damages are not reduced in the case of pregnant women, or of excessively fat or unusually shaped people, or those who convince the court of seat belt phobia: *Condon* v. *Condon* (1978).

The function of contributory negligence

It is the function of the principle of contributory negligence to apportion blame, and consequently the financial responsibilities following it, in a just and fair manner. It is not its function to limit recovery of damages for past action by the defendant whose injurious actions have ceased to cause loss. In *McKew* v. *Holland and Hannen and Cubitts (Scotland) Ltd.* (1969) the pursuer (or plaintiff) had suffered an injury in an accident for which the firm was liable, and as a result he occasionally lost control of his left leg which gave way under him. Some days after this accident he went to look at a flat which was approached by a steep stair between two walls and without a handrail. On leaving the flat he started down the stair, holding his daughter by the hand and going ahead of his wife and brother-in-law who were with him. He suddenly lost control of his leg, threw his daughter back in order to save her, and tried to jump so as to land in an upright position instead of falling downstairs. In so doing he fractured his ankle badly.

The House of Lords decided that his act of jumping in the emergency in which he found himself did not itself break the chain of causation from the wrongful injury which had a few days earlier been caused by the defendant firm. So by itself, that injury would not have been too remote a consequence to attract compensation. However, what did break the chain of causation was the plaintiff's conduct in placing himself in an unnecessarily dangerous situation in the first place, knowing the condition of his leg and not taking more care, for instance by asking for assistance down the stairs. His fractured ankle was, therefore, too remote a consequence of the original injury. It is to be noted that although the plaintiff contributed through his own want of care to his ultimate condition, this was not a case of contributory negligence since this was a new and independent event, the negligence of the defendant firm being by that time already spent.

Chapter 9

RIGHTS, REMEDIES AND LIBERTIES

This chapter examines a variety of rights, remedies and liberties which are recognised by the law in respect of personal security and freedom from unwarranted interference, and also in respect of goods and property. One particular theme which runs through the greater part of this chapter is provided by the legal remedies which are available as a consequence of the commission of various forms of the tort of trespass. The tort of trespass, in its various forms of trespass to land, trespass to the person and trespass to goods, is the oldest established wrong known to the English legal system. As such it has also come to provide one of the very cornerstones of the liberty of the individual, as well as assisting in the protection of property rights whether over land or goods.

The rules and principles now to be discussed are, in general, equally applicable in the case of both health services staff and patients or others using health service premises. Thus, for instance, lawful means of defence against a violent patient will be discussed in the same broad examination of areas of law which also relate to a patient's remedies for unwarranted detention or restraint. Some, though not all, of the considerations affecting property are also visibly affected by principles of the law of trespass. Rights and wrongs relating to property in respect of both staff and patients will also be examined in this chapter.

I

Trespass to the person

While the victim of an assault, or a battery, or of false imprisonment, which are all forms of trespass to the person now to be discussed, is entitled to commence legal proceedings for the wrong, he may often in fact be much more concerned with what

he can do to retaliate. Indeed, from the viewpoint of someone
who is threatened with personal violence, the law of trespass is
not so much about whom you can sue as about whom you can hit.
In other words, it is useful to know what sort of legal retaliation
can be made to an attack or threatened attack. But to
understand that, we need to know what it is which constitutes a
trespass to the person. This section examines assault and
battery, and legitimate responses, giving particular attention to
the handling of violent patients who create difficult if relatively
infrequent problems. The law relating to personal restraint and
detention, including powers of arrest, are discussed in the following section.

The essentials of trespass

Trespass may be defined as a direct interference with the
person or goods of another without lawful justification; it is
actionable without proof that actual damage, in the sense of
injury or loss, has occurred. The essential ingredients of trespass
can conveniently be examined in turn. The first element is that
of the *directness* of the wrong.

The element of directness is the ingredient which serves to
distinguish trespass from negligence. Thus, if A throws a stone at
B's car when B is driving along the road, and the car is damaged,
this is a direct injury to B's property and he can sue A in
trespass, for damages. If, however, A leaves stones in the road to
await the arrival of B in his car, and B has to swerve to avoid the
obstacle and thus damages his car, B cannot sue in trespass
(whatever else he can sue in) for the damage to his property has
been caused indirectly, as a consequential effect. Nor would
trespass be applicable if B's car had actually hit the stones and
was damaged in that way; for the damage was, again, not
directly caused.

Without lawful justification

This simply means that no general or particular defence to an
action in tort for trespass is available, or that there is no
justification for the interference with another. Thus, in relation
to assault and battery, reasonable self-defence is an answer to a
plaintiff who has started a fight and the complains about the
natural response. That is to say, self-help or self-defence is a

defence of general application to this area of trespass. A particular justification can be found, for instance, in the Mental Health Act 1959 which in certain circumstances gives authority for the physical restraint of mentally disordered persons; or in the Criminal Law Act 1967 which sets out in detail powers of lawful arrest. Conversely, a person whose liberty is being lawfully restrained commits an assault, or battery, or both if he forcibly attempts to resist. Such would be the case with resisting lawful arrest, or forcibly resisting (or obstructing) medical officers or social workers in the course of restraining or detaining a mentally disordered person subject to relevant powers under the Mental Health Act 1959. Powers of arrest are discussed generally in the following section of this chapter; powers of restraint and detention in respect of mental patients are dealt with in Chapter 13.

To conclude this point, then: acting in the course of lawful arrest or restraint is not a trespass to the person. One who resists such arrest or restraint does commit a trespass, which can in turn be lawfully responded to with a reasonable amount of physical force which must be proportionate to the resistance shown.

Actionable without proof of special damage

Actionable simply means in respect of which a complaint may be made to a court of law, such court being prepared to entertain the complaint.

Without proof of special damage means that it is not necessary, in order for the court to be prepared to entertain the claim or complaint, that the plaintiff should have to prove actual injury or loss. In the example used above, in which A throws a stone at B's car and damages it, damage or loss has actually occurred. But the mere touching of something or someone can be a trespass. Thus, if A had pushed B's car a couple of feet in order to get his own car into a parking space, that would equally have been a trespass to B's property even if no actual physical or monetary loss ensued. Likewise it is just as much a battery to tap another on the shoulder as it is to hit another person or stab him.

Naturally, the damages (note the distinction: damage is what is wrongfully done; damages is what you get by way of redress) will differ considerably. If no actual physical damage or injury has been caused by the defendant the damages awarded against him may be purely nominal, say £1. However, this will not always be so, for in some cases, as we shall see, the law presumes general damage and awards damages in consequence which can be not only far from nominal, but sometimes very substantial. Such could be the case, say, in the tort of assault—a tort which we now examine in detail.

Assault

While battery is the intentional or negligent infliction of some degree of physical contact or force on another person, assault may be defined as an act of the defendant which causes to the plaintiff reasonable apprehension of the immediate infliction of a battery on him by the defendant. There is no such tort as a careless or negligent assault. The act mentioned in the definition is therefore to be taken as an intentional action. There need be no actual intention on the part of the defendant to use force or violence, or even the actual power to do so, provided that the plaintiff reasonably believes himself to be in imminent danger of violence.

There must be an act or some force of outwardly observable physical conduct. Thus words alone, unless accompanied by some act or threatening gesture, will not amount to an assault. Abuse may well amount to criminal libel insofar as it has a tendency to lead to a breach of the peace (a matter of public importance, and for that reason provided for by the criminal law), but it will not by itself amount to the tort of assault.

There are other torts which protect actual injuries to property, and the equitable remedy of injunction affords legal protection against the threat of damage to property. Other forms of threat may be covered by the criminal law, such as blackmail.

The present ability to inflict violence

Violence, it may be recalled, can be the merest touching of another. To shake one's fist in a man's face is an assault. To shake one's fist at someone a great distance away is (even assuming they can see you!) very unlikely to be an assault, but it is important to notice that the present ability to inflict violence is judged from the plaintiff's viewpoint. If a replica gun is pointed at you, you are unlikely to risk its being a real one by taking the threat lightly. Thus, pointing a replica firearm at someone is an assault even though it can, as it happens, do no harm.

The very important consequence of this last point is that a person threatened in a way which can (but unknown to the plaintiff) result in no actual harm, is legally at liberty to retaliate in reasonable proportion to the threat. In a recent unlawful occupation of a building in London the unlawful besiegers carried replica or imitation firearms. One was killed by a policeman, and the policeman who confronted the apparent gunmen was very properly commended—he was not going to get near enough to find out whether or not the firearms were real!

Battery

Battery is the application of force, maybe in the form of violence but not necessarily so, to another person.

A battery may be committed even when there is consent to physical contact. For instance in *Nash* v. *Sheen* (1953), it was held to be a battery to apply a tone-rinse to the plaintiff's hair without her consent. She had gone to her hairdresser's, the defendant, and asked for a permanent wave. There had thus been consent to some physical contact, but no consent in respect of the unwanted tone-rinse.

By the same token, a patient who has consented to have an injection for tetanus and is in fact given an injection for some completely different purpose, whether intentionally or negligently, will have an action in battery against the person giving the injection.

In contradistinction to assault, it is the actual application of force or physical contact which amounts to the tort of battery. Moreover, unlike assault, fear in the sense of alarm or apprehension is unnecessary. Is there unintentional battery? Such cases will usually fall within the category of risks normally consented to in everyday life, such as jostling in a tube train. There must, however, be either a negligent or an intentional act; a purely accidental touching or jostling without negligence is not a battery.

The violent patient

In the light of certain complaints in recent years about ill-treatment and manhandling of patients (especially mental patients) it would be unrealistic to pretend that the health service administrator's likely experience of violent people will be completely restricted to violence from patients. However this section is included because of the publication in March 1976 of Health Circular HC(76)11 for action by Regional and Area Health Authorities on the subject of the management of violent, or potentially violent, hospital patients.

The general drift of this important circular was summarised previously in Chapter 5. In this chapter extracts from the circular are given so as to show in practice the sort of situation with which staff may be faced. It is the administrator's function to circularise staff internally on the subject in such a way as to make procedures abundantly clear to all concerned. It should be noted that the problem is not confined by any means to psychiatric wards.

Serious acts of violence by patients in hospitals—attacks on other patients, staff or other persons, or damage to property—are relatively infrequent. Nevertheless, particularly in mental illness and mental handicap hospitals and units and in accident and emergency departments, they do present a problem on which staff require adequte guidance and help. This calls for both good professional practice and appropriate administrative arrangements.

Patients who may become violent

Some episodes of impulsive violent behaviour are unpredictable. However with patients whose diagnosis or behaviour patterns are already well known it may often be possible for staff to recognise those who present some degree of special risk and to note signs which may indicate the possibility of an outburst. Special consideration should be given to the arrangements for care of each such patient and to the kind of action—*e.g.* segregation, sedation, restraint—it may be most appropriate to take if violence is threatened or occurs.

Such patients require more supervision than others and this need must be taken into account in the staffing of the ward they are in. With enough staff it may be possible to manage a few potentially violent patients in a ward where most of the patients behave normally. The extent to which this can be done necessarily involves nursing judgment. In some hospitals grouping may be the best way of using special facilities and skilled staff although, if possible, special "disturbed wards" should be avoided. When used, groupings should be small, with a high staff ratio. Experience has shown that to group a large number of potentially violent patients in a single unit without sufficient facilities and staff is likely both to encourage violence and to make it more difficult to deal with. It is also important not to put patients who may be violent with patients who may be especially at risk of being bullied or assaulted.

Accident and Emergency departments

A somewhat different problem is presented by a new patient coming in a confused and potentially aggressive state to an accident or emergency department where he or she is not known. These departments have to deal with patients suffering from many different conditions, some of which by their nature may dispose a patient to violent behaviour, and the possibility that some may behave violently must be kept in mind when considering the department's organisation and arrangements. In the interests of the safety of staff, the safety and continued treatment of other patients and of preventing a violent patient from further injuring himself, physical restraint may on occasion be unavoidable. Professional staff, and other employees, working in such departments must be made aware of the type of problems which might arise, and be given appropriate guidance.

Patients suffering from the effects of alcohol or drugs

Violence may be associated with the use or misuse of drugs or alcohol (or both) or other toxic substances. Such patients may not always see themselves as ill and may feel threatened by, and react against, the alien environment in which they find themselves. In alcoholism treatment units acts of violence are uncommon; alcoholics are more likely to create a problem in a medical or surgical ward, or in the accident or emergency department, very occasionally by violence in the true sense, but more often through the restless agitated and disorientated behaviour characteristics of severe intoxication or withdrawal. Drug addicts may on occasion create violent disturbances as in-patients (though the drug dependence units have developed skill in reducing this to a minimum), or, more often, by arriving in a drugged state—aggressive, disorientated and confused—at accident and emergency departments.

The handling of patients in a state of temporary intoxication, whether caused by alcohol, drugs or poisons, in accident or emergency departments in such a way that violence can be prevented, or minimised, is a skill which those working in those departments should be enabled to acquire: the experience available in the drug dependence treatment units should, where practicable, be utilised in providing in-service training.

Patients suspected of possession of offensive weapons

If there are reasonable grounds for believing that a patient possesses an offensive weapon (such as a knife) he should be asked to hand this over for safe custody. If he refuses, or denies possession, it may be necessary to search the patient and his belongings and to remove the weapon in the interests of the safety of others; this applies whether or not he is subject to detention under the Mental Health Act.

II

Unlawful restraint or detention

This section will include an outline of the circumstances in which it may be lawful to detain or restrain someone against his or her will. The principles to be set out apply equally, in general terms, to staff, patients and visitors. Any of these groups might include a person who might lawfully be detained, say for suspected theft. Again, any group may include someone who was restrained or detained, but in respect of whom no lawful authority for such action existed and who could therefore commence civil proceedings for the wrong, or who could lawfully resist.

English law contains no such thing as a statute setting out all the circumstances in which the detention of someone against his will may be unlawful. In fact quite the reverse; for any such detention will be unlawful unless specifically permitted either by statute or as a result of a body of judicial decisions. Any detention or restraint, provided it is complete and not just an obstruction or hindrance which can be avoided, amounts to false imprisonment unless it is specifically permitted by the law.

False imprisonment

False imprisonment may be defined as arresting, imprisoning or otherwise completely restraining a person without lawful justification, and preventing that person from exercising his lawful right to leave the place where he is so restrained. It is a form of trespass to the person, like assault and battery, and is likewise subject to the same general legal principles applicable to those wrongs.

There is no requirement of actual imprisonment, though a person wrongfully imprisoned would certainly be within the ambit of the tort. The word false is simply an indication of wrongfulness: it does not mean untrue, for when a person is falsely imprisoned the detention is real enough! It means, simply, wrongful in law.

Lawful conditions on right to leave

It is no tort to prevent a person from leaving your premises because he will not fulfil a reasonable condition subject to which he entered them.

In *Robinson* v. *Balmain Ferry Co. Ltd.* (1910), the plaintiff paid a penny for entry to the defendants' wharf from which he proposed to cross the river on one of the defendants' ferry boats. A boat had just gone and since there was not another one for 20 minutes, the plaintiff wishes to leave the wharf and was directed to the turnstile which was its exit. There the plaintiff refused to pay another penny which was chargeable for exit, as was stated on a notice board, and so the defendants refused to let him leave the wharf until he did pay. The Judicial Committee of the Privy Council held that this was not false imprisonment. The following statement was made by the court: "There is no law requiring the defendants to make the exit from their premises gratuitous to people who come there on a definite contract which involves their leaving the wharf by another way. The question whether the notice which was affixed to these premises was brought home to the knowledge of the plaintiff is immaterial because the notice itself is immaterial." Furthermore, the court regarded the charge of one penny for exit a reasonable charge. Thus the decision is authority for the proposition that release only subject to reasonable condition is lawful (that is, the detention prior to such condition release is lawful).

Questions very similar to the one raised by this case are not confined to contractual conditions imposed as a reasonable condition of leaving. So, if a porter by mistake pushed a trolley into a theatre which was in fact in use, it could (subject to all the circumstances of the case) be reasonable for the surgeon in charge to permit his exit, with the trolley, only when a particularly delicate operation had been completed.

The presumption of damage

False imprisonment is actionable *per se*, that is, of itself. It does not require proof that the plaintiff has suffered actual injury or other loss or damage. If such actual injury or loss has in fact been caused by, say, the necessary expenditure on a taxi fare to make up the time lost by the wrongful detention, then special (that is, specifically claimed) damages will be awarded in addition to the general damages awarded for the interference with the plaintiff's liberty.

The tort of false imprisonment is thus a bulwark of the freedom of the citizen, whatever the circumstances of an unlawful detention. The plaintiff need not prove actual loss or injury; and, moreover, very heavy damages can be awarded. There is a case decided in 1914 in which a plaintiff who had been wrongfully detained on suspicion of shoplifting was awarded £75 for only about a quarter of an hour's detention. Increase that to take account of 60 years' inflation and you have a pretty hefty bill for damages!

The nature of the place or location of the wrongful detention or restraint is immaterial, provided that in all the circumstances the restraint is complete (and that it is not, as above, subject to a reasonable condition for release).

Completeness of restraint

The restriction of the plaintiff's liberty must be complete. If he is locked in a cell, or a room, or any other premises from which he cannot get out, false imprisonment is complete. It is not, therefore, false imprisonment merely to close a door on someone (as for instance, in temper) if the door is not locked. But it is no defence to say, if the door had actually been locked, that the plaintiff could have been resourceful and picked the lock, climbed out of a skylight or other such far-fetched or unreasonable means of escape.

Merely to have one's way blocked is not false imprisonment. So, if our porter and his trolley have their way barred by contractors who refuse to move until they have finished a job in a corridor, false imprisonment is not committed so long as the porter can, without an unreasonably great risk to his own safety, find an alternative route to his destination.

Plaintiff's knowledge of restraint?

Although a case decided in the last century laid down the rule that an ignorant plaintiff could not be awarded damages (that is, if he did not know his liberty was in fact totally restricted), a case decided in 1920 laid down a contrary rule and now seems to be the case to follow. Thus it appears to be the law that ignorance of one's total restraint (say, by being unaware that companions are in fact captors, or as a result of being asleep, drunk or unconscious) is no bar to the recovery of damages for false imprisonment: *Meering* v. *Grahame-White Aviation Co. Ltd.*

As long ago as 1834 it was held that it is possible to commit false imprisonment against a person too ill to move even in the absence of any restraint: *Grainger* v. *Hill* (1834). This case again, brings home the important point that the protection afforded by the tort of false imprisonment (or, at least, the compensation available after the event) is an important bulwark of civil liberty.

Detention of patients against their will

Having thus stated some essential points about the tort of false imprisonment, we now go on to give a list of situations in which involuntary restraint or detention can be lawfully justified provided proper procedures are observed for accomplishing it. Following that we go on to examine two major areas of the law which are concerned with the above-mentioned "proper procedure" for restraint if liability in tort is to be avoided. These areas are powers of arrest and detention of mental patients. Powers of arrest, in particular the very limited power of an ordinary citizen to make an arrest, may arise particularly, if infrequently, in relation to theft on health service premises or theft of health service property especially in large hospitals. The law of theft will be briefly explained in the context of powers of arrest generally, examined shortly.

Instances of lawful detention

As stated earlier, it is up to a person seeking to detain or restrain another against his will to point to a specific legal power to do this. Anyone who has committed an arrestable offence may, subject to the limitations on the right to make an arrest, be detained. So may a person reasonably suspected of having committed an offence, until police have time to arrive. Persons who are mentally disordered and subject to formal admission procedure under the Mental Health Act 1959 may be involuntarily detained, as may formal mental patients who abscond without leave. In the case of patients other than mental patients, persons insisting on discharging themselves against medical advice should be warned in the presence of witnesses and should be requested (but not forced) to sign a common form of declaration of election to accept the risk of discharge at that time which has been properly explained by staff.

Public health legislation has added categories of persons who may be involuntarily detained or otherwise dealt with against their will provided a justice's order is obtained. Such instances include principally the removal to a hospital of a person suffering from a notifiable infectious disease, pursuant to powers given by the Public Health Act 1936. The expression "notifiable disease" is defined in the Public Health Acts 1936 and 1961 and in the Health Services and Public Health Act 1968. It includes cholera, smallpox and typhus, acute meningitis, acute poliomyelitis, disentery, infective jaundice, whooping cough and malaria. Lassa fever and rabies have recently been added to the list of notifiable diseases. Notification, incidentally, must be made by medical practitioners to the local public health authority who in turn have the duty to inform the district (or area) health authority.

Furthermore, a person who is suffering from a grave chronic disease, or an old person who on account of age is infirm or physically incapacitated, or is unable to look after himself properly or have someone else do so, may be removed to a hospital or other suitable institution if the conditions of section 47 of the National Assistance Act 1948 are satisfied, and if a justice's order is obtained. The conditions required to satisfy section 47 are that the community physician certifies in writing to the local authority that he is satisfied after thorough inquiry and consideration that such removal is necessary in the interests of the person sought to be removed, or that it is necessary for preventing injury to the health of, or serious nuisance to, other people in the local authority's area.

Patients wishing to leave hospital

Health service staff may be faced with a difficult dilemma
when it is remembered, on the one hand, that wrongful detention
is actionable and may lead to heavy damages, and on the other,
that a duty of care is placed on them to see to the proper
treatment and surveillance of their patients. In this dilemma,
Circular HC(76)11 offers some useful guidance.

A nurse or other member of staff may occasionally be faced
with a situation where a mentally disordered patient who is not
already subject to detention seeks to leave hospital—whether
psychiatric or general—precipitately. This may occur in
circumstances where it seems likely that the patient may do
immediate injury either to himself or to some other person.
When these factors apply the nurse or other members of staff
may then take reasonable steps to prevent or minimise the harm
feared to the patient or to others. The particular action it is
appropriate to take will depend upon the particular situation.
Where it is practicable a junior member of staff should always
seek the assistance and support of a more senior nurse or doctor;
otherwise he must act on his own initiative with the help of
whomever else may be available. In some circumstances it will
not be appropriate to go beyond making a determined effort to
dissuade the patient from leaving. But if the nurse (or other
member of staff) considers that the danger to the patient or
others is both serious and immediate, he is entitled to take
proper and reasonable steps to restrain the patient for such time
as is necessary to consider whether an emergency application
should be made to authorise detention for observation under section 29(1) of the Mental Health Act 1959, or a report under section 30(2) by the doctor in charge of the patient's treatment.

If the patient has already left the hospital, the appropriate
action may be to ensure that a report is made to the police and to
the Social Services Department of the local authority or to take
prompt steps to secure the patient's compulsory readmission to
hospital by informing the mental welfare officer responsible
under the Mental Health Act and/or any available relatives of
the circumstances, in order that an application can be made
under section 29(1). It may not be appropriate for junior staff to
make such contact themselves. Health authorities should however ensure that appropriate instructions are issued in each
hospital indicating persons who may make such reports. Such
authorisation should be sufficiently wide to avoid any risk that
essential action might be delayed because of unavailability of
appropriate staff. It must be clearly brought to the attention of

all staff however that they have a responsibility when faced with such a situation to bring the facts directly to the attention of an appropriate officer.

In all cases where a situation of the kind referred to has arisen a doctor in charge of the patient's treatment should be informed at the earliest opportunity of the circumstances and the action taken. Care taken to comply with the advice given in this paragraph should greatly reduce the risk of subsequent legal proceedings, either by the patient personally for wrongful detention, or by members of the public for injury or damage due to the neglect of the hospital to take lawful steps to detain or otherwise control the patient who caused it.

Visitors, or patients, who refuse to leave

The converse case of a patient refusing to stay is that of one who refuses to leave. Refusal to leave health service premises, or refusal to leave until some future time or date, may apply in the case of patients though its more usual occurrence is in respect of visitors who refuse to leave. In either event the person refusing to leave becomes in law a trespasser and reasonable force or pressure can lawfully be brought to bear on him to leave. However, it will be readily appreciated that the solution to this difficulty lies more within the bounds of diplomacy and decency than in strictly legal rules. An appeal to the better judgment of a visitor refusing to leave, or to leave at the time appointed for the end of visiting hours, will in any case usually be much more effective than quoting legal chapter and verse.

It may happen that a visitor, in particular a near relative, has an apparently legitimate claim to remain on the premises, for instance if the relative wishes to ask a question about the patient's condition of a doctor or nurse who cannot immediately be found. Staff should in normal circumstances, their other duties reasonably permitting, deal with an anxious inquirer in a humane manner. Indeed, morally if not also legally speaking, the treatment of a trespasser who has such pressing reasons for not wishing to leave immediately could be regarded as a corollary of the duty, recognised by the House of Lords in *British Railways Board* v. *Herrington* (1972), to behave towards trespassers with "common decency and humanity," at least so far as their physical presence is concerned. A parent denied access, or continued access, to a child under 16 could in law withdraw that

child from the hospital, but is probable that a court would over-
look staff's refusal to allow access if such was medically vital to
the child's treatment.

It was seen in Chapter 2 that the Secretary of State's duty to
provide services, staff and equipment for the operation of the
National Health Service is not legally enforceable at the instance
of a private individual. In the *Hincks* case, discussed earlier, four
orthopaedic patients commenced civil proceedings against the
Secretary of State for Social Services as well as the regional and
area health authorities in whose area the hospital in question was
situated. They lost their action, and lost their appeal to the
Court of Appeal. In the course of his judgment, based on the
demands of longer term economic planning in the health
services, Lord Justice Bridge said:

> "I feel extremely sorry for the particular applicants in this
> case who had to wait a long time, not being emergency cases,
> for necessary surgery. They share that misfortune with
> thousands up and down the country. I only hope that they
> have not been encouraged to think that these proceedings
> offered any real prospects that this could enhance the
> standards of the National Health Service, because any such
> encouragement would be based upon manifest illusion."

So much is unfortunately clear. But what of a patient who was
an "emergency" case? Was Lord Justice Bridge thinking only of
patients who present themselves at an accident and emergency
department of a general hospital, or would he have given a wider
significance to "emergency"? In one recent widely publicised
instance a woman managed to find an empty bed in a hospital
ward, installed herself in it and refused to leave until treated.
She was in fact treated, but in law she went to occupy the bed as
a trespasser. She probably ceased to be a trespasser when treatment started, if a licence to remain on the premises would in law
be implied from the conduct of the medical and nursing staff to
her. Her case was not an emergency, but urgency of treatment
varies as a matter of degree and from person to person. While the
matter is not clear, it is just possible that a patient who chose
such a course of conduct, but whose condition could in some way
be said to be urgent, might attract duties of common decency
and humanity in the form of actual treatment. On the other
hand it is more than possible that the law would refuse to
countenance such a wide extension of what began as the duty of
an occupier in respect of the safe condition of occupied premises
to such an apparently far-fetched demand.

Powers of arrest

The extent of the power to arrest used to depend to a considerable extent on the very old distinction between felonies and misdemeanours, the power being greater for the former than the latter. However by the Criminal Law Act 1967 that distinction has been abolished, but a new distinction was created: between arrestable offences and non-arrestable offences. An arrestable offence is one for which the sentence is fixed by law or for which a person, on conviction, is liable to be imprisoned for five years. This includes theft. The Act sets out the extent of the power of arrest without a warrant.

Any person may arrest without warrant anyone who is, or whom he, with reasonable cause, suspects to be, in the act of committing an arrestable offence. Where an arrestable offence has been committed, any person may arrest without warrant anyone who is, or whom he, with reasonable cause, suspects to be, guilty of the offence.

Where a constable, with reasonable cause, suspects that an arrestable offence has been committed, he may arrest without warrant anyone whom he, with reasonable cause, suspects to be guilty of the offence. A constable may arrest without warrant any person who is, or whom he, with reasonable cause, suspects to be, about to commit an arrestable offence. For the purpose of arresting a person a constable may enter (if need be, by force) and search any place where that person is or where the constable, with reasonable cause, suspects him to be. A person may use such force as is reasonable in the circumstances in the prevention of crime, or in effecting or assisting in the lawful arrest of offenders or suspected offenders.

There are other statutory powers of arrest without warrant, in addition to the above. The above rules show that a private person can arrest in some circumstances involving theft and other "arrestable offences," but as this power can be exercised only in the circumstances laid down, it is risky to exercise it, as its exercise when those circumstances do not exist is unlawful and could result in an action for false imprisonment.

In *John Lewis & Co. Ltd.* v. *Tims* (1952) T was thought to have stolen from the shop. She was asked to come back in and was detained until the chief store detective and the managing director were able to be told the circumstances of the theft by the store detective who had arrested T (by requiring her to accompany them). Under the store's regulations only the general manager or managing director were authorised to institute proceedings. The latter decided to do so in this case, and the police were sent for. T was taken to the police station and charged. T's companion was found guilty, but the case against T was not proceeded with. She sued for false imprisonment. The House of Lords held that where a person arrested another without a warrant at common law he should take the arrestable person before a J.P. or a police officer as soon as reasonably possible. Here to take T to the managing director's office in order to prosecute did not constitute an unreasonable delay before handing T to the police. The store was not therefore liable for false imprisonment. Thus there would be no objection to a suspected person being brought before a matron or senior officer of the health authority if it was understood that a person suspected of having committed a crime (whether an employee or not) could not be prosecuted without the prior consent of the appropriate senior officer of the hospital or health authority.

Powers of police to arrest by warrant exist, of course, additionally to the powers just outlined. They are, however, beyond the scope of the present discussion, as are police powers of search and seizure by warrant. Search of persons and property by private individuals will now be explained.

Search of persons and property

Forced search of a suspected person can involve two possible legal wrongs: assault and battery, and false imprisonment. Even the discovery of stolen property on the person suspected does not technically free from liability those who conducted the unauthorised search, though there would then be little risk of an action by the wrongdoer. If such an illegal search is not followed by the discovery of stolen property, or if the person searched can give good account of his possession of stolen property, then there appear, on the face of things to be grounds for an action both for false imprisonment and for assault and battery, and very substantial damages may be awarded. The only effective defence to such an action is the prior consent of the person searched. A request to search could also lawfully be made a condition of entering premises, for instance in the event of a bomb scare or if offensive weapons are suspected. Such a practice is now unfortunately normal at many football matches, since the management find this the only effective way of reducing trouble in crowds. There is no question in this context of an enforced search, at least by a private individual. It is simply that a refusal to be searched may render the person refusing ineligible to enter.

Consent, at the time of search, must be real, genuine,

unforced, and with adequate opportunity of refusal. A suspect may, of course, demand to be searched, and while this may remove the possibility of action for assault the person who provoked the invitation may be faced with an action for slander. The right to inspect quarters, as for general cleanliness, does not include the right to search, even superficially as by feeling amongst folds of clothing. Consent to such search is required and in the absence of such consent the search will be actionable as trespass to goods. Such wrongful interference with the possession of goods is actionable in itself, even without proof of special damage, and in awarding aggravated damages a jury can thus express its opinion of the indignity suffered by the plaintiff.

In the event of an action's being brought for assault, wrongful imprisonment, trespass to goods, or other grounds, the plaintiff can sue the actual wrongdoer, those who assisted him and the health authority itself. "Superior orders" does not exonerate from such liability. The test of the hospital's or other authority's liability appears to be whether the officer concerned acted in the course of his employment. The same legal principles apply, with appropriate differentiation according to circumstances, to both staff and patients whose property is sought to be examined.

Hospitals and the Road Traffic Act 1967

This Act makes it an offence to drive with a proportion of alcohol in the blood exceeding the prescribed limit and enables the police in certain circumstances to require drivers to provide specimens of breath for breath tests and of blood or urine for laboratory tests. When, following a road accident, a driver is at a hospital as a patient the Act enables the police to require him to provide specimens for these tests while he is at the hospital, provided the doctor in immediate charge of the case does not object on the grounds that this would be prejudicial to the proper care or treatment of the patient. It is not intended that the police should seek to invoke these provisions of the Act in every case of a driver suspected of having been drinking who is at a hospital as a patient after an accident, for example a patient who is seriously injured or ill; on the other hand, a driver who has an accident after he has been drinking should not necessarily escape the provisions of the Act simply because he is at a hospital.

The procedure, so far as it may affect a driver who is at a hospital as a patient, whether an in-patient or an out-patient, following an accident, is given in greater detail in the following paragraphs. Apart from the need for the hospital doctor in immediate charge of the patient to be notified of the proposal to require provision of a specimen and his power to object, hospital staff will not be involved in the taking of the specimens or their evaluation for the purposes of the Act. Specimens of breath and urine will be taken by a police constable and specimens of blood by a police doctor and the laboratory tests will be carried out in forensic science laboratories. The necessary equipment for breath tests and for the taking of specimens of blood and urine will be provided by the police. There is no provision in the Act for the taking of urine specimens by catheter.

Circular HM(67)64 draws the attention of hospital authorities to the provisions of this Act enabling the police to require a driver, who following a road accident is at a hospital as a patient, to provide specimens of blood, breath or urine for the purposes of the Act. Procedure relating to police conduct are explained in some detail by the circular, but those procedures are not our principal concern here. What is of interest to medical, as well as nursing and administrative, staff are the following points:

> (i) Under the Act a patient at a hospital is not liable to arrest without warrant, nor can he be required to go elsewhere to give the specimens of breath, blood or urine.
>
> (ii) Specimens may not be taken from a patient without his consent, and a specimen may not be taken from an unconscious patient or by catheterisation.
>
> (iii) The constable must notify the doctor in immediate charge of the case of the intention to require a patient to provide a specimen and the doctor may object at any stage before a specimen has been provided if he considers that such action would be prejudicial to the proper care or treatment of the patient. He may also object to the patient being told of the requirement to provide a specimen, or warned of the penalty.
>
> (iv) Members of the hospital staff are not required to take part in the taking of specimens or in their evaluation, although the hospital is requested to arrange conditions of privacy under which patients may provide specimens.
>
> (v) Hospital equipment will not be used in the tests.

The Circular ends with the important reminder that the arrangements which it sets out shall be subject to the overriding consideration of the medical interest of the patients. This is a salutary reminder, since in the nature of events it is the medical and nursing staff in accident and emergency departments who are likely to be most frequently affected. In particular, the requirement incumbent on police to take specimens from patients is not, according to section 2 of the Act, to be made if the doctor in immediate charge of the case is not first notified of the proposal to make the requirement, or if he objects on the grounds that the provision of the specimen would be prejudicial to the proper care or treatment of the patient.

III

Patients' property: loss or damage

There is a variety of ways in which damage may be caused to patients' property, or in which that property may be lost, and there is also a variety of legal consequences flowing from damage or loss. In some circumstances, though they are restricted by legal provision, damage or loss may not lead to as wide or as serious consequences in some situations as in others, notably where an exemption notice exists which the law considers to be fair.

The ordinary law of negligence may be invoked in case of loss of, or damage to, patients' property. It will be recalled that negligence in law consists of the breach of a duty of care, causing the loss or damage which is complained of. But the undertaking of a duty on the part of the recipient of property, goods or valuables has a wider effect still, and can constitute what the law calls a *bailment*.

Bailment occurs when goods are delivered on a condition, express or implied, that they shall be restored by the bailee to the bailor, or according to his direction, as soon as the purpose for which they were bailed shall be fulfilled. The categories of bailment are very wide indeed and include not only bailments for reward to either bailor or bailee, as in the hire of garaging for a motor car, but also gratuitous loans or deposits, as where a bicycle is lent to a friend, or a man stores furniture for a neighbour without payment.

Furthermore we saw in Chapter 7 that an occupier owes a duty of care in respect of the safe condition of the occupied premises not only to the person of lawful visitors but also to their property. Damage to clothing or other immediate personal effects is within the ambit of the occupier's responsibility, and it is probable that damage to the property or goods even of a lawful visitor who remains personally uninjured is also the responsibility of the occupier or occupying authority; though it has been judicially decided that there is no legal duty, except by way of a contractual agreement, on an occupier to take care to prevent theft of the goods of lawful visitors. Such was the case in *Edwards* v. *West Herts. Group H.M.C.* (1957), relating to the property of a hospital doctor in premises of which the health authority was the legal occupier.

The bailment of property

It was held in *Martin* v. *L.C.C.* (1947) that a local authority hospital was a bailee for reward in respect of a paying patient's property handed over to the hospital authorities for safe keeping and, therefore, under a higher degree of responsibility for taking care of property deposited than that attached to a gratuitous bailment. This decision does not, however, preclude the possibility of limiting the property which will be accepted with the patient in other than emergency cases.

A "bailee for reward" has a duty to take the same care of the goods as a reasonable person would of goods of his own of a similar character, *i.e.* if the goods are of a character that would reasonably be expected to be kept in a safe, then the bailee is bound to provide a safe for them. A "gratuitous bailee" has a duty to take the same care of the goods as he does of his own goods of similar character; thus, if he has a safe for his own goods then he must keep his bailor's goods in a safe. On the other hand if he keeps his own goods in a locked cupboard then he can keep the bailor's goods in the same manner.

While a National Health Service hospital or other institution is certainly not an insurer of patients' property, once a bailment of property or goods is proved by the patient it is up to the bailee (the person or authority receiving the goods, in the case of a hospital the relevant health authority) to disprove negligence. But lest this apparently onerous burden seem too much for health service staff or authorities to shoulder, it must also be borne in mind that the opportunity has always existed for a person, or authority, to exempt itself from legal liability by agreement or, much more commonly, by a notice visibly displayed on the premises onto which the relevant property is brought by patients. It will be recalled that, as was explained in relation to premises liability in Chapter 7, the law no longer permits exemption notices relating to personal injury or death caused in the course of business, or the pursuit of a profession, by negligence. For the rest, exemption notice must be "fair" if they are to have any legal effect.

Exclusion notices

Fairness of exclusion or limitation of liability is something which cannot always be predicted with confidence in advance. One important factor which would certainly be prominent in all the circumstances of an individual case would be the opportunity, if any, for the patient to see to the safekeeping of his or her property as an alternative to care by the hospital, clinic or authority which was seeking to exempt itself from property loss or damage negligently caused. For instance, it would seem anything but fair if patients had (as they very frequently have to as in-patients) change into suitable clothing for bed occupation, but the hospital sought by notices on the premises to exclude negligence liability in respect of loss of, or damage to, clothes and everyday effects which the patient could not put anywhere else but in a locker or some such other suitable and recognised storage place. This consideration of fairness applies with particular force in the case of patients admitted as emergencies, and especially to unconscious patients. It is inconceivable that an exclusion (exemption) notice could now, in law, be said fairly to exonerate the hospital or other institution or authority from the duty to take reasonable care in such circumstances. Of course, the problem of fairness or otherwise might not arise at all in an emergency case, and could not possibly arise in the case of a patient admitted unconscious, since it is a fundamental rule that any such notice be proved to have been brought to the attention of the person whose claim is sought to be defeated or restricted by the terms of the notice.

Specific considerations

It must be remembered that bailment is founded on possession—there can be no bailment where a patient retains some control of the goods in question—and also it may be relevant to bear in mind that no one becomes a bailee against his will. Merely to send goods to a person, or leave them on his premises, does not make him a bailee; in such cases he has no duty at all with regard to the goods, save to refrain from wilfully damaging them.

Instructions have been issued to health authorities that arrangements should be made for the safe custody of money and other valuables brought by patients on admission and that they should be warned that if they do not take advantage of these arrangements Authorities cannot hold themselves liable for any loss. Health Authorities have also been instructed in the detailed accounting arrangements to be used in dealing with patients' moneys: HM(62)2 and HM(71)90.

In no circumstances has a health authority power on its own initiative to sell a patient's property. Such a sale would amount to the tort of conversion to which there would be no answer. It may be that the authority would consider taking the risk of disposing of articles of little, if any, value, but it might not be easy to show that the articles were of no importance to a claimant, and the onus of proof would be on the authority, though for the purposes of the Limitation Act 1939, time would run from the date of the conversion. If the goods were simply missing the cause of action would accrue from the time of demand for return. In the case of valuable articles, application can be made to the court for an order of sale.

The property of patients who die intestate and without next of kin belongs to the Crown—*bona vacantia*. The Treasury Solicitor (or the Duchy of Cornwall or the County Palatine of Lancaster as the case may be) deals with the matter. In the case of sums less than £20 a cheque should be sent direct to the Treasury Solicitor or as the case may be. Above that sum the matter is to be reported to him and he will send to the area health authority official forms for completion. Reasonable financial expenses may be deducted; for example, the payment of funeral expenses: HM(72)41.

Difficulty has sometimes arisen where health service property has been lent to patients on their discharge from hospital and patients have been reluctant to return it. The law is quite clear: the property must be returned on request. The Ministry has suggested the following practical action. Property lent should be marked "The property of . . . A.H.A." This eliminates doubt as to whether the property has been given or lent. Further, the patient should be asked to sign a document to the effect that he undertakes to return the property when it is no longer needed, and that he understands that failure to return it in good condition may render him liable to pay the cost of replacement or repair.

Finally, the often fine distinction between merely borrowing and actually taking property can cause problems in practice. The crime of theft consists of the dishonest appropriation (taking) of another's property with the intention of permanently depriving the other of it. A forgetful borrower is thus not a thief if there is no evidence of dishonest intent. Nor is the crime of theft committed even in the face of mischievous or malevolent intentions if there is no intention to permanently deprive the other person of their property. Special crimes exist under the Theft Act 1968 including taking and driving away a motor vehicle without the owner's consent, even if there is no intention to permanently deprive. This is the "joy-riding" offence introduced because of the difficulty, in most cases the impossibility, of proving that the joy-rider ever at any point intended to steal the vehicle.

Private institutions

The decision in *Edwards* v. *West Herts. Group H.M.C.* (1957) related to premises administered by a National Health Service authority. As such, the decision has a restricted application, if indeed any, to private institutions such as private hospitals or clinics. In the case of such institutions there is a legal contract between them and their private patients, and a contractual duty to take reasonable care of patient's clothing and belongings may be implied by law into the agreement even if such a duty is not actually expressed in the contract for care and treatment.

While, as in the case of exemption notices properly and visibly displayed on National Health Service premises, it is always legally open to a private institution to alter or exclude its liability in respect of negligent damage to, or loss of, patients' property by a clause in the contractual agreement, the overriding consideration of *fairness* once again applies; and, as in the case of alternative places to store clothing and normal immediate personal effects in National Health Service premises, so here, the fairness of the contractual term would be assessed in all the circumstances of each case. With the current growth in the provision of personal health services on a private basis it is probably important that conditions for the acceptance and admission of patients are seen to be at least as favourable as those available within the National Health Service. As in many areas, it should not be the legal minimum requirements which rule the day here, but rather a decent and humane system for the safekeeping of belongings which achieves a sensible balance between the interests of the patient in the security of his or her belongings, and the legitimate interest of the health care institution in avoiding being saddled with a responsibility in respect of patients' property which diverts valuable time and energy from the principal objectives of care and treatment.

As in the case of National Health Service institutions, a notice or contractual clause purporting to exclude or modify liability in respect of property damage or loss will not affect the personal liability of an individual member of the staff, however senior or junior, as a result of whose carelessness or other misconduct the complaint arises.

Chapter 10

PRIVACY, RECORDS AND CONFIDENTIALITY

I

Interests in privacy

Even though a plaintiff who makes a complaint against a defendant in a court of law may appear to be the object of the law's protection, such an impression can be misleading when the real operation of legal rules and principles is carefully investigated. A leading contender for the impression that it is a person himself who is protected (or at least compensated) by the law is the simple case in which the plaintiff pedestrian is knocked down and injured by the defendant motorist who negligently strays onto the pavement along which the plaintiff has been walking with all proper care for his own safety. The plaintiff who is injured may sue for *general* damages for such items as pain and suffering and loss of expectation of life, and for *special* damages (*i.e.* damages which are specifically pleaded or raised) such as damage to clothing, medical expenses and loss of prospective earnings, all of which can within certain limits be specifically quantified in actual cash terms. In such a case, then, the plaintiff has been injured and the plaintiff stands to be compensated.

But what are we to say of the situation if the same unfortunate plaintiff is not physically injured (in which case we could have said that "*he* was injured"), but suffers an unwarranted invasion of his private life by journalists, data-banks or other unwonted means? Unless he is actually defamed or his land (including his house) trespassed upon, or unless the plaintiff can show that the other interfering party has committed a legal nuisance against his property and himself, our unfortunate victim cannot recover damages at law. The simple legal reason for this is that there is no tort of "invasion of privacy" as such. True, the established torts of nuisance, defamation and trespass often in fact amount to invasion of privacy, but they can lead to an award of damages not for that reason alone but for the reason that they are definite and established legal wrongs. So someone whose way of life receives unsolicited investigation from another may very frequently be left without any remedy, despite any apparent moral or social claim which that person's situation may have to our attention. One even hears such expressions as "the right to privacy" and "the right to lead one's own life (within the law) as one pleases." Again, these expressions evince social or moral claims only, in a large number of cases. In a decision of the Court of Appeal (Criminal Division) in 1974 it was held that an agreement or joint operation designed to elicit information from building societies, banks and "finance houses" (moneylenders) amounts to a criminal conspiracy if "unlawful" means are used.

The word "unlawful"—which referred in the instant case to posing and telling lies in order to get hold of the desired information—is an obscure way which the judges have in this notoriously ill-defined area of the law to express their disapproval of the activity which is the subject-matter of the (in the event) criminal agreement, or "conspiracy." Whatever satisfaction the victim of the criminal conspiracy to interfere in this private life may have, that satisfaction will not lead to the award of any compensation in a civil action, even though a lot of damage and embarrassment may have resulted.

The law of defamation

This is not the place to embark on a detailed account of the vast area of the law which concerns defamation, in the more permanent (or usually written) form of libel or in the less permanent, and therefore more transient (and usually spoken) form of slander. But some of its principles must inevitably be stated in order to illuminate certain important and practical points of contact between this area of the law and the matters of professional confidence and privacy. It is, of course, by no means every case of breach of professional confidence that leads to an action for defamation. But some can, and do.

Defamation has over the many years, indeed centuries, of its development in the common law of tort received a variety of definitions. (In this context "common law" is used in contradistinction to statute law, which has impinged only rarely on the civil law relating to defamation.) A well-used and useful definition is as follows: Defamation is the publication of a statement which tends to lower a person in the estimation of right-thinking members of society generally, or which tends to make them shun or avoid that person. When defamation takes the form of written matter the law of libel may be invoked successfully against the person who has "published" it. This does not mean that the libel must have taken the form of a book, article, newspaper or magazine report—though those forms of "publication" clearly suffice. All it means is that A shall be proved to have issued defamatory matter about B to a third person C. Publication is thus from A to C. The same principle about the necessity of publication applies equally to slander, when the spoken word or other more transient (or "passing") form of communication will be uttered by A to C in respect of B, who again stands to become the plaintiff (against A) in an action for defamation.

The principal difference in effect between slander and libel is that in the latter case the plaintiff can be successful in his action for damages even if no damage, in the sense of lost business or suchlike, can actually be proved. In the case of slander, however, the general rule is that such actual damage as is quantifiable readily in financial or monetary terms, must be proved. To this general requirement in slander there are four exceptions, in which cases no actual or specific loss or damage need be proved by the successful plaintiff. These are: imputation of unchastity in a woman (*e.g.* saying that she is a whore—this sort of action is infrequent in our modern age); imputation of an infectious or contagious disease (this being limited in practice to venereal disease—information about which must be handled most carefully, as we shall see shortly in dealing with professional and medical confidence); imputation of unfitness or incompetence in the plaintiff's trade, profession or calling (which, it has been judicially decided, can also include an honorary or unpaid office); and imputation of a criminal offence punishable with imprisonment. In none of these four exceptional cases is it necessary that the successful plaintiff prove actual loss or damage, though if he does he will of course be awarded suitable damages as compensation.

Even at this early stage of our discussion we can already see that privacy and reputation are sometimes subject to socially or morally unwarranted interference (or "invasion") but in circumstances—in the case of many otherwise slanderous remarks which cannot be proved to have caused the plaintiff specific loss or injury—in which the existing law gives no redress.

Defences to defamation

There are a number of defences to an action for defamation. Certain of these defences are of particular relevance to our present dicussion. One is the defence of privilege, which can take the form either of absolute privilege or qualified privilege. The "privilege" in question amounts to the permission in law to make certain statements, even if they are published about the plaintiff and on the face of it defamatory of him, providing the bounds of the particular occasion in question are not exceeded. These permissible bounds vary and with them the matter of whether the privilege—which can, if pleaded successfully, amount to a complete defence—is absolute or qualified. The practical difference in effect between the two is that an absolutely privileged occasion is one on which the defendant could put up a successful and complete defence whatever his own personal motives or reasons, and even if he acted out of spite or malice towards the plaintiff. Such occasions include things said or done during the course of, and as a part of, judicial proceedings. If, for instance, a patient who brought an action in negligence against a member of a hospital's medical staff said something on its face defamatory about that member of staff, the occasion would be privileged and thus protected even if the plaintiff failed to prove his allegation of negligence. But a defamatory remark about the private life of the member of staff, quite unconnected with the matter in issue, would not receive the protection of such privilege.

The law relating to privilege as a defence also arises in cases where the giver of information has a duty to give it and the recipient has a related interest in receiving it, or when the two of them share a legitimate interest in the subject matter of the information. Such, typically, would be the case of an employer furnishing a testimonial in respect of an employee's application for a post with another employer. Statements which are apparently defamatory can be defended in this instance by an appeal to the principles of "qualified privilege." Here, unlike the case of absolute privilege, not everything is protected by the law but only that which is written or said in good faith and without personal spite or ill will. This is, in fact, the "qualification" which conditions the privilege of so saying or writing with impunity: namely, that the speech or writing is not "tainted" with malice. It may be a delicate and difficult question of evidence as to how to separate honest statements from those which may appear on their face to be the same sort of comment but which, on further investigation, are prompted by malevolent and therefore illegitimate motives. This is one of the rare occasions on which the law of tort looks to the motive as well as to the action produced by that motive on the part of the defendant.

The relevance of the principles relating to the maintenance of professional confidence is this. If a medical man were to broadcast erroneous information about the health (or, rather, ill-health) of a patient in such a way as to furnish people other than those legitimately entitled to it with information which might cause them to "shun or avoid" the subject of the statement (and that is for the courts to judge, on all the facts of the case if it comes to court), an action for defamation could conceivably lie if it could be said that the qualified privilege of the occasion had been breached, either out of motives of personal ill-will or, in this instance, from the implied restrictions of reasonable communications having been exceeded or breached.

It ought, of course, to be added that another defence to an action for defamation is the plea of justification, or truth. Unlike some other legal jurisdictions, English law contains no requirement that the plea of truth be supplemented by proof that the otherwise defamatory statement or other matter was published "in the public interest." All that need be proved is that it was true when uttered, that is, published to a third party.

Truth and discretion: an instance

Concerning venereal disease, the NHS (V.D.) Regulations 1948 laid an obligation on boards of governors and RHBs to take all necessary steps to secure that any information obtained by officers of the board with respect to persons examined or treated for venereal disease shall be treated as confidential. These regulations were replaced by regulations in 1968 and then in 1974. They retain the general obligation that such information should be treated as confidential, but remove any obstacle to the passing of information to doctors or any hospital or local authority staff in this country or persons abroad who may need it as part of their work in connection with treatment or contact tracing. HM(68)84 on Control of Venereal Disease says, in an accompanying memorandum:

"In order to comply with this obligation it is desirable that Boards should require medical and other staff of venereal disease clinics to keep strictly confidential any information they obtain about the identity of a patient, and not to disclose it except as permitted by the regulations. This should be done either by including a requirement to this effect in their contract of service or by subsequent written instruction.

"The Minister is advised that the regulations do not absolve any person from the existing obligation to give evidence in a court of law if required by law to do so, or prevent them from giving information about a patient when asked by that patient preferably in writing.

"The Minister is advised that the legal position of medical and other staff who are concerned with the process of contact tracing is that they are not liable for slander etc. in the absence of malice or improper motives, for anything done as part of their duty as imposed on them by the instructions of their employing authority in pursuance of that authority's functions."

The 1974 Regulations state:

"Every Regional Health Authority and every Area Health Authority shall take all necessary steps to secure that any information capable of identifying an individual obtained by officers of the Authority with respect to persons examined or treated for any sexually transmitted disease shall not be disclosed except—

(a) for the purpose of communicating that information to a medical practitioner, or to a person employed under the direction of a medical practitioner in connection with the treatment of persons suffering from such disease or the prevention of the spread thereof, and

(b) for the purpose of such treatment or prevention.

These regulations differ from the earlier ones (of 1948) in that they add to the earlier ones everything from the word "except."

The reason for such an expression as "the Minister is advised that . . ." is apparently that the further disclosure of information about venereal disease is lawfully permissible provided that the person who furnishes information has a duty to give it and that the recipient has a corresponding interest in receiving it. Information about such a matter as venereal disease must clearly be handled with the greatest care since (quite apart from claims of the patient to have such information kept quiet) the imputation of such an "infection or contagious disease" could, if unproven, amount to actionable defamation even if uttered by the spoken word and even if no actual damage in the sense of financially assessable loss can be proved by the plaintiff. But the change in practice brought about by the 1968 and 1974 regulations and advice clearly, and very wisely, takes into account the individual interest of other medical men in their attempts to contain such social diseases and, indeed, the concomitant public interests in the beneficial consequences of the success of such attempts.

Under the Abortion Regulations, certain information about the termination of a pregnancy has by law to be supplied to the chief medical officer. It is not, however, to be supplied to any other person except those specified in the regulations. Other examples of the obligation to keep confidential information obtained will be found in various statutes dealing in part with similar types of communications problems.

II

Medical records

The rules and regulations concerning the keeping and the confidentiality of medical records are considerable, and for the purposes of this book there is time only to point to some principal features of interest and concern, as well as to discuss an important recent decision of the House of Lords expressing a firm judicial policy of freedom of the patient to *receive* information as to his medical condition and its treatment. Nor is there time to discuss the vexed issue of the computerisation of medical records, which some fear as a threat to the preservation of their confidential nature, save to say that an efficient manual system of records can pose exactly the same *type* of threat, if misused, even if the degree of risk of breach of secrecy is in that case not as great.

Ownership of records

The question as to who exactly owns these or those medical records and notes is sometimes discussed as if it were conclusive as to the entirely separate issue of what can properly be disclosed from the content of the notes. But a distinction can and should be drawn between the physical property in the notes and the intellectual property in their contents. The concept of intellectual property is not a generalised concept in English law such as to afford an automatic remedy in case of breach of confidence as a result of wrongful disclosure; its application is reserved for broad yet specific areas of regulation such as copyright or patents. Nevertheless it should always be remembered that a right to disclose contents certainly does not automatically accompany physical possession of a document, even though it is not perhaps a legal but a moral obligation that would be breached by disclosure.

In private practice a patient's records and medical notes will normally belong to the practitioner, though it is perfectly open to the practitioner and his private patient to agree otherwise. In National Health Service practice the medical record card belongs to the Secretary of State, and this is also the case in hospitals so far as non-paying patients are concerned. In the case of private patients in hospital (whether NHS or private) the notes probably belong to the practitioner in charge of the patient's case.

Public Records Act 1958

This Act has an important effect on the preservation and destruction of health service records. Under the Act it is the duty of everyone responsible for public records of any description to arrange for the selection of those records which ought to be permanently preserved and for their safekeeping. Those public records selected for permanent preservation shall be transferred not later than 30 years after their creation to the Public Records Office or such other place as is approved by the Lord Chancellor (who has general responsibility for public records). However, those records can be retained if in the opinion of the person responsible for them they are required for administrative purposes. Public records not required for permanent preservation are to be destroyed. The definition of "public records" includes records kept by National Health Service authorities, but excludes records of private patients in NHS hospitals. Specific guidance on this matter may be found in Circular HM(61)73.

Patient's right to information

It would be as unreal as it would be unfortunate to suggest that a patient should have a right, either moral or legal, to receive exhaustive information about his complaint and its treatment from the medical staff in charge of his case. Large areas of human activity are properly left to be governed by the proper and reasonable exercise of judgment and discretion. Much attention is given to some of the many areas so governed in the following section of this chapter. But there are some cases in which a patient has a right to receive information. The receipt of information about the nature and treatment of the personal injuries received by a plaintiff who subsequently commences legal proceedings is one such instance.

In an important recent case decided by the House of Lords it was held that:

"Where a party to any proceedings in which a claim is made in respect of a person's personal injuries or death applies under the Administration of Justice Act 1970 for an order that a person who is not a party to the action produce 'to the applicant' documents in his possession, custody or power which are relevant to an issue arising out of that claim, then, having regard to the unequivocal words used in the Act, if the court considers that it is a proper case to exercise its discretion to make an order, the court making the order must order the documents to be produced to the applicant, and may not order the documents to be produced to some other person on the applicant's behalf on condition that the documents are not disclosed to the applicant himself.

"An order for discovery made under the 1970 Act, which gives the court power to order disclosure of documents before the commencement of proceedings, must likewise be made in favour of the applicant and not to someone else on the applicant's behalf on condition that disclosure is not made to the applicant himself."

It was so decided in *McIvor* v. *Southern Health and Social Services Board* (1978), a case which came to the House of Lords on appeal from Northern Ireland. In so deciding the House over-ruled two earlier decisions of 1973 and 1975, both rendered by the Court of Appeal and both involving hospitals, which indicated that disclosure could be restricted to someone other than the applicant. The two overruled cases were *Dunning* v. *Board of Governors of the United Liverpool Hospitals* (1973) and *Deistung* v. *South Western Metropolitan Regional Health Board* (1975). In the latter case the Court of Appeal (Civil Division) went as far as to hold as follows:

"Where hospital notes and records are disclosed to a medical expert selected by a person who is a prospective plaintiff in an action for personal injuries the plaintiff is not entitled to see them, nor are his legal advisers. The plaintiff is not bound by the report made by the medical expert on the basis of those documents. The report is to be regarded as one made by a potential witness for the plaintiff and if the plaintiff or his legal advisers feel that the report needs further explanation or reconsideration they may take it up with the expert. That may be followed by a conference between counsel and the expert at which counsel may ask further questions in order to determine whether the plaintiff has a case. In answering the questions the expert may refer to the hospital notes and records without showing them to counsel."

The hospital had argued in the *McIvor* case that the consequences of not confining the production of hospital records to the medical advisers of the applicant would be so dire (through misunderstandings and suchlike) that Parliament, in passing the Act of 1970 permitting disclosure, must have intended so to restrict the power. For instance, medical notes and records can be difficult for laymen to interpret; and they may contain the doctor's fears about the patient's prospects for the future which, if disclosed to the patient, might cause him distress or retard his recovery. The House of Lords not only decided that no such restriction was implicit in the Act, but also that such arguments in favour of any such restriction were unconvincing. There might be exceptional cases in which a court could exercise its discretion under the Act to restrict the circulation of information, *e.g.* to professional (including medical) advisers alone; but this was certainly not to be regarded as the general rule.

The merits of the new approach

In his leading judgment in the *McIvor* case Lord Diplock answered certain questions which had been raised in argument by counsel for the Board in relation to commonsense and humane limits to discovery of documents. He said:

"In their consideration of medical reports the legal advisers of the applicant can have the assistance of the medical adviser in interpreting them; and, if there is matter in them of which it would be better for the applicant himself not to know (which could only arise where he was the patient concerned), his legal adviser would no doubt take precautions to prevent the information becoming known to his client. This kind of situation can arise at the trial when the medical evidence about a party to an action is being given. It is dealt with by common sense and humanity. Furthermore, documents disclosed on discovery, unlike evidence given in court at the trial are confidential in the sense that they may not be used by those to whom they are disclosed for any other purpose than that of the action in which they are disclosed."

He had already made it clear in his judgment that every aspect of public and private interest in disclosure or non-disclosure, as the case might be, should be examined in relation to the particular circumstances of each case as it arose for determination on this issue. His judgment makes clear that here is an area in which, given the initial rule of the relevant statute, it was on a full consideration of principle and policy that the outcome of the (and indeed any) particular case turns. In so doing the courts are acting fully within the parameters of the discretion given to them by the relevant rule.

However, in a letter to *The Times* newspaper in May 1978 the following sentiment is expressed:

> "The medical profession's committee of inquiry into competence to practise strongly recommended that the study of the issue of confidentiality should include the concept of grading information. Perhaps their Lordships might sometimes more fully consider how degrees of disclosure could protect and benefit those who consult doctors without litigation in mind, for surely there was more than a touch of legal arrogance in their conclusion that legal advisers could safely be left to decide what knowledge of medical facts might be harmful to the individual concerned."

This, with respect, seems an unwarranted criticism of the stance adopted by the House of Lords in the *McIvor* case, for two reasons. First, even if their Lordships had indeed decided that the issue of permissible limits to disclosure were to be left entirely to the consideration of the House of Lords (or other court, in the event of an appeal not being made or at least not that far), it was because Parliament had left them the power to do so in all instances other than documents "relevant to an issue arising out of the claim in the action." There are many powers of discovery of documents given to the courts by statute and some of them are much wider than the specific power given by the relevant statutory provision in this case. Indeed, owing to the specific purpose which this statute envisaged, any irrelevant (*i.e.* irrelevant to an "issue arising *out of* a claim in the action"—) parts of a document which is subject to disclosure can be covered up when the document is produced. Secondly, it seems to have been quite contrary to the natural inference of Lord Diplock's judgment to interpret him as having countenanced a discretionary power for lawyers independent of medical consultation.

An issue in criminal evidence

In the context of evidence in criminal cases, the recent decision in *R.* v. *Crayden* (1978) is instructive. After burglaries at two houses in Eltham in April 1976 the appellant (this was a Court of Appeal decision) was arrested and taken to a police station where, according to the prosecution, he made an oral and later written confession of the burglaries. At his trial he alleged that the admissions had been obtained from him by the use of violence. He said that he had gone to a N.H.S. hospital and had been examined by a casualty officer and a radiographer. The prosecution at his trial had sought, under section 1 of the Criminal Evidence Act 1965, to put in evidence the records kept by the hospital, in order to deny the claim of Mr. Crayden that his admissions had been extracted by police violence. The judge admitted the records for evidence purposes, and they supported the prosecution's contention that the appellant had suffered no injury while at the police station.

The appellant appealed on the ground that the evidence should not have been admitted. Without section 1 of the 1965 Act the records would not have been admissible as they contained hearsay (normally excluded from evidence in a court of law).

Section 1 of the Criminal Evidence Act provides:

"(1) In any criminal proceedings where direct oral evidence of a fact would be admissible, any statement contained in a document and tending to establish that fact shall, on production of the document, be admissible as evidence of that fact if—(a) the document is, or forms part of, a record relating to any trade or business . . .; (b) the person who supplied the information recorded in the statement . . . cannot reasonably be expected . . . to have any recollection of the matters dealt with in the information he supplied . . . (4) In this section . . . 'business' includes any public transport, public utility or similar undertaking carried on by a local authority and the activities of the Post Office."

The question for the Court of Appeal was therefore whether a hospital was a "business" for the purposes of the Act. It was held by the Court of Appeal that it was not. Counsel for the prosecution had submitted that a hospital was still a "business" in the narrow sense of the term since its activities included appointing staff, maintaining premises and acquiring equipment and other property. But the Court of Appeal considered that such activities were ancillary to the main purpose of a hospital as set out in the National Health Service Act 1946, s. 1 (now NHS Act 1977—to much the same effect). Mr. Crayden's appeal was therefore allowed. An NHS hospital is therefore not a "business" within the meaning of the Criminal Evidence Act 1965. It is to be noted that the Court of Appeal stated that "hospitals outside the service did not arise for decision in this appeal."

III

Privacy and Professional Confidence

A discussion of issues in privacy and professional confidence affords the opportunity of doing two things. This section first examines the location of our area for investigation in the wider context of ethical and social standards and of legal regulation. The section then proceeds to look at a variety of separate, though not unrelated, situations in which theory is pointed up into practical form. Practitioners, and health care staff generally, are frequently faced with the demands and constraints inherent in enshrined values. Whether these values be expressed in a moral, a social or a legal form, it must always be hoped that they help and do not hinder. For their purpose in a modern age is surely to advance the arts and sciences of medical treatment, and not to provide obstruction where it is neither needed nor wished for. While questions involving the maintenance of professional secrecy and confidence tend to arise most frequently in relation to medical staff and especially to the doctors, whose judgment and evaluation in health care constantly involves the use of records and thus consideration of information gathered directly from the patient, the principles now to be discussed can be considered to apply also to administrative staff at all levels. The only differences in application of the principles of secrecy and confidentiality would arise from procedural and circumstantial modifications appropriate to the role of the particular administrator or manager in the provision of health care and services.

Confidentiality is considered as a value, in which deep and important interests may be held, or claimed. Indeed, the profession of medicine is itself a valued interest of any civilised community. Duty to patient and duty to the community, of which the patient is one member, may be coterminous; but equally, they may not. Varying interests and disparate values are apt to create tensions, tensions which are themselves conditioned by the very way in which basic interests and values are expressed. The tension, often experienced within the area under discussion, between pragmatism and principle creates a multitude of problems for both theorist and practitioner.

It is possible to assert that the disparity in values underlying the maintenance of professional confidence in medical treatment lies in two opposing stances: confidentiality as an ideal (more or less approaching to the absolute, according to taste and experience), and confidentiality as a practical expedient. Put baldly in this way, the statement of positions could quickly leave the impression that conclusions reached as a matter of practical expediency are rather disagreeable and lacking in respectability; and that the expression of an ideal is the only one acceptable standard. In other words, that any proper doctrine of confidentiality must aspire to an elevated standard rather than merely avoid a fall below the bare minimum of professional conduct.

This difference in attitude is rendered more complex when lawyers enter the arena of ethics. For while ethics can aspire, the law is usually concerned in any direct way only with the preservation of minimum standards of conduct. But even in the aspiration to a high standard of professional conduct, the attitude of practical expediency may not be so lacking in respectability as is sometimes made out. Indeed, the utilitarian ethic has a most respectable pedigree: that actions should be judged according to their consequences, and that those consequences should themselves be judged according to their capacity to lead to the "greatest happiness of the greatest number." Let us now examine the source of the obligation of confidence, then consider what sort of an obligation this is; and, finally and at greater length, examine the dictates and indeed the adequacy of that obligation as applied to practical problems.

The Hippocratic Oath, and the B.M.A. Handbook

The Hippocratic Oath can be traced to the fifth century B.C., and was intended to be affirmed by each doctor on entry to the medical profession. The Oath begins:

> "I swear by Apollo the physician, and Aesculapius and Health, and All-heal, and all the gods and godessess, that, according to my ability and judgment, I will keep this stipulation. . . ."

and continues later with the subject of our discussion:

> "Whatever, in connection with my professional practice, or not in connection with it, I see or hear, in the life of men, which ought not to be spoken of abroad, I will not divulge, as reckoning that all such should be kept secret."

The Oath ends with this sentiment:

> "While I continue to keep this Oath unviolated, may it be granted to me to enjoy life and practice of the Art, respected

by all men, in all times. But should I trespass and violate this Oath, may the reverse be my lot."

In the recently published *Handbook of Medical Ethics* of the British Medical Association (1980) the modern British equivalent of the Hippocratic Oath inasmuch as concerns confidentiality between donors and recipients of treatment is stated in a less startling form. While the British Medical Association's statement of ethical standards is certainly not the only code accepted, or at least published, in the medical profession itself, its availability to such large numbers as well as its recent revision makes it a suitable stepping-off point for use in the present discussion. The obligation of confidentiality admits of certain exceptions, and the stern judgments of disciplinary committees take the place of earlier hell fire and perdition. The statement (in paras. 1.5–1.7) is not in an absolute but in a contextual and qualified form:

(1.5) The nature of professional confidence varies according to the form of consultation or examination [patient, impartial examiner, researcher], but in each of the three forms of relationship the doctor is responsible to the patient or the person with whom he is in a professional relationship for the security and confidentiality of information given to him.

(1.6) The doctor must preserve secrecy on all he knows. There are five exceptions to this general principle: (1) The patient gives consent; (2) when it is undesirable on medical grounds to seek a patient's consent; (3) the doctor's overriding duty to society; (4) for the purposes of medical research, approved by the Chairman of the British Medical Association's Central Ethical Committee or his nominee; (5) the information is required by due legal process;

The practical incidence of the obligation of confidentiality and of the stated exceptions will occupy us in a moment when solutions to specific problems of confidentiality are canvassed. But we may usefully take time now to consider briefly the very nature of the obligation of confidentiality, and of the concept of obligation itself.

An obligation signifies a bond or tie (latin *ligare, obligare*). There is evidence that the obligation created originally by the taking of the Hippocratic Oath was a professional obligation, in keeping with a time when the practice of medicine was an esoteric art. It is still in part a professional obligation, but for different reasons. The most popular conception of confidentiality is that it results from, and creates, ethical bonds; hence it is a significant concern of medical ethics. Thirdly, the obligation certainly appears to partake of a social quality. As said, the practice of medicine is one of society's valued interests; and, in the exception which proves this rule, the "doctor's overriding duty to society" spells it out. Then there are the legal obligations into which social or ethical obligations are transformed by opera- tion of the legal process, either by statute or statutory instru- ment, or by the activities of judges.

Do these four categories, into any or all of which the obligation of confidentiality might on occasion fall, exhaust the possibilities? It is suggested that they do not, and that there is a further and somewhat anomalous category of obligations which consists of a general duty to act, reveal or withhold in whichever manner best serves the treatment of the particular patient whose dealings with the medical profession are in issue. There is no reason why this consideration should not be weighed in the balance, pondered in the utilitarian calculus, along with any other material consideration. Indeed, if the medical practioner's obligation of confidence is to remain in a recognisable form, the "doctor's overriding duty to society" (the third exception above) must surely be tempered by an equally comprehensive view of the overall interests of the patient. After all, it is the latter who has volunteered his disordered presence at the surgery or wherever.

To put all this in the context of specific problems, this section will examine six issues of concern and some difficulty, and pre- face all of them by a brief statement of what it is for the obliga- tion of secrecy and confidentiality to turn, via breach or wrongful disclosure, into a legal obligation.

Legal remedies for breach of confidence

Apart from the obvious case in which wrongful disclosure in breach of the obligation of confidentiality might lead to a disciplinary hearing or, in a very extreme case, striking off, a variety of forms of legal redress present themselves. A settled remedy for breach of confidence is the interlocutory injunction, by which one who threatens to break the obligation is enjoined to refrain from any such breach. Disobedience to an injunction amounts to a contempt of the court of law which issued it, and the penalty for that is a fine or even an unspecified term of imprisonment. A contempt is also, incidentally, committed by way of a practitioner's refusal to disclose to a court of law information about a patient which he point blank refuses to disclose. As to why more doctors do not go to prison rather than divulge the confidences of their patients, more in a moment. Damages can also be awarded instead of an injunction when what is needed is not so much prevention for the future but cure for the past. But thereby hangs a tale. For when are damages available in law for breach of confidence?

The breach of an implied, or even on occasion an express, term of the contract between a medical practitioner who is giving, and a patient who is receiving, private treatment outside the NHS will give grounds for damages for breach of contract. Furthermore, there is some ground for thinking that damages in tort could be available for a practitioner's relaying of information to a complainant in such a distasteful and mawkish way that the recipient suffered shock. But as for the rest of tort law, an area widening almost every day in response to alleged "breaches of duty" by defendants to plaintiffs, can breach of confidence be said with any degree of certainty to found an action for damages? Most of the books say it will, and some say so almost without argument. But decided cases are lacking. This is no surprise, for breach of confidence in the particular sphere under discussion usually causes distress rather than actual loss (for instance, of money). And since it would probably take the House of Lords, the highest appellate tribunal, to create or at least (if expressed by a lower court) confirm the existence of the tort of breach of confidence in a form wide enough to help us here, and since that takes time, and a great deal of money, then we might wait for a very long time indeed before seeing the realisation of what so many so confidently expect. In 1974 the Law Commission proposed to remedy this apparent deficiency in the law by the creation of a new tort of breach of confidence. But it has not arrived yet.

"Due legal process"

The confidentiality between doctor and patient is an obligation owed at least to the patient, if not on a broader basis also. If the doctor is under a duty, then the patient has a right, moral or social. This right is sometimes expressed as a privilege. But it should be emphasised that the privilege is that of the patient and not that of the doctor. For the purposes of this discussion the terminology of rights and duties is preferred. A privilege is indeed conferred upon the doctor when the patient abrogates his right to confidentiality and releases the doctor to that extent from his duty by conferring on him a privilege to reveal. The conferment of this privilege is achieved through the patient's consent to the relay of the information in question. In certain circumstances it is even possible for a patient, by his instruction, to alter the duty to preserve confidence into a duty to relay information; in such circumstances it is not open to the doctor to refuse to disclose the information, or so it would appear at least in some cases: *C. v. C.* (1946).

Our immediate concern under this heading—"Due legal process"—is to examine the tension injected into the doctor's legal duty to the patient when a court orders disclosure of what the doctor considers to be confidential information. Legally speaking, for the purpose of such an event in judicial proceedings, the court exercises what no court in this country seems to treat otherwise than as an established right. The doctor is put under a duty to disclose; and a privilege is given *vis-à-vis* the patient who, correlatively, has no right to resist the procedure.

Lawyers enjoy a privilege in judicial proceedings in relation to the withholding of evidence. Why do doctors and others engaged in health care activities not enjoy the same, or a similar, privilege to withhold? A rational reply, though not necessarily a completely convincing one, might be that any other answer in the case of lawyers might result in a trial within a trial, or a trial about a trial. That sort of reason is given in relation to a barrister's immunity from suit in negligence in relation to conduct directly connected with litigation: *Rondel* v. *Worsley* (1969). But the real reason for the lawyer's distinctive privilege—and this goes for solicitors, too—seems to be that the lawyers got in first. Lawyers, lawmakers and also those whose job it is to suggest reforms in the law, appear jealous of existing preserves and there is little or no readiness to extend privilege to doctors, or to priests.

So, if a doctor refuses point blank to answer a judge's request for specific information, he may be held in contempt of court. We asked the question earlier: Why do not more (if indeed, any) doctors go to prison rather than divulge their patients' secrets? That the facts of the matter are not unhappy ones is often taken, at least by the lawyers, as comfort and assurance that the system is working well and requires no change. A more realistic explanation might be that the brinkmanship in the relation between judge and doctor-witness is handled in such a way as to avoid a fall over the edge into the abyss of contempt.

It has been seen that the ethical duties owed in respect of a patient's confidences admit of certain exceptions in the way in which they are formulated, for instance in the BMA's *Handbook of Medical Ethics*. The "overriding public duty" deserves separate mention and will get it. Under this particular heading, "Due legal process," we are specifically concerned with aspects of the legal process. That includes the criminal law. Do the requirements of "due legal process" extend to a general duty to volunteer information, either to a court of law or to the police? The general answer in both cases is certainly not. The same should apply also to non-medical staff in health services.

Doctors are often asked to give evidence in court about the medical history of a patient. If the patient or his solicitor makes the request consent is implicit, but if a third party seeks evidence of his medical state, even if it be the husband or wife of a patient, in divorce or custody proceedings, he must first provide the doctor with the written consent of the patient. This rule applies to a preliminary medical report and to an attendance in court. Without the consent of the patient a report cannot be given, but a doctor can still be compelled to attend court by a witness summons. Having taken the oath, the doctor is still not free to give medical evidence about his patient unless he is so directed by the judge, coroner or magistrate. The doctor is free to say, after taking the oath, that he has not had his patient's permission to speak about him and that he would welcome the court's direction whether he is to answer questions which involve a breach of professional secrecy. There is an instructive instance cited in the Annual Report of the Medical Defence Union (1970).

A general practitioner had treated a man of 21 who was addicted to amphetamine and was prosecuted for stealing drugs. He was immature and irresponsible and the general practitioner considered that since there was no ground under the Mental Health Act for his compulsory admission to hospital the only way in which he could be helped would be for him to be committed to gaol. The Union advised him that before giving such evidence in the magistrates' court at the request of the police he should insist upon a witness summons being served upon him and should ask the magistrates whether he was directed to answer questions. The patient could not then object to his giving a frank opinion to the court.

So the doctor may not only be compelled by order of the court to make disclosure; he may actually prefer this procedure to be put in train so that he will be given a legitimate reason to provide the court with details which would otherwise be available only on the definite initiative of the court. Is there any wider duty on a doctor, deriving from the requirements of "due legal process," to

volunteer information which he thinks may lead to the prevention of a crime or the apprehension of a criminal? A comment in
the Report of the Medical Defence Union (1977) is instructive
but less than conclusive:

> "Doctors frequently have to decide whether to notify the police
> of confidential medical facts which suggest that a crime may
> have been committed. Even though not legally obliged to
> report a suspected crime, a doctor may feel bound in a given
> case to disclose what he knows about a patient as a means of
> preventing foreseeable harm to the public. The possibility that
> drugs may be sold to members of the public has sometimes
> influenced doctors to disclose information about patients
> whom they know to have drugs in their possession."

It may be that in such cases the doctor's "overriding duty to
society," exception (3) in the B.M.A. *Handbook*, dictates or at
least argues in the direction of disclosure. In any event, neither of
the two instances just mentioned gives any credence to the view
that disclosure should be made whenever the likelihood of crime,
to be committed or already committed, presents itself. Indeed, in
the former case, relating to mental disorder detention or alternatives to it, the requisite procedure for legitimate disclosure was
put in hand so that the patient himself could be helped, and thus
better treated— in the doctor's opinion.

Legal and moral obligation

In the sort of clash between judge and medical practitioner
which normally seems to be avoided, at least in the extreme form
of a contempt of court, the relationship between the obligations
of law and ethics is worthy of a short comment. Paragraphs 1.16
and 1.17 of the B.M.A.'s *Handbook* are interesting in this connection:

> 1.16 Medical information required by law or statute falls into
> two categories, that which is required by statutory instrument,
> and individual cases in which an order is made by a Court of
> Law.

> 1.17 In the United Kingdom no privilege attaches to com-
> munications between patient and doctor, and a doctor can
> therefore be directed by a court to disclose such information. A
> refusal to comply with such a direction could lead to the doctor
> being held to be in contempt of Court. When asked by a Court

to disclose information without the patient's consent, the doctor should refuse on the grounds of professional confidence and say why he feels that disclosure should not be enforced. The court would be expected to take the doctor's statement into consideration but if in spite of this he is ordered to answer the questions, the decision whether to comply or not must be for his own conscience. *A decision to refuse, while illegal, is not necessarily unethical.*

The final sentence (italicised for purposes of emphasis) is particularly noteworthy. There is a school of thought (though not a popular one these days) which holds that a breach of a legal stipulation is of itself immoral, unethical. To read the contrary view from the BMA is refreshingly reminiscent of Jeremy Bentham's utilitarian liberalism: "Obey punctually, censure freely." So the reverse proposition of that adopted in the BMA *Handbook* becomes: A decision to disclose, while legal, is not necessarily ethical. On this, the case of Dr. Hunter is instructive.

Disclosure and the Road Traffic Act

On the evening of January 3, 1973, Dr. Hunter, a registered medical practitioner, treated a man at his surgery. The patient asked him to visit his girl friend who mentioned that she had been in a car accident. The doctor advised both patients to inform the police but he did not seek their consent to disclose their identity if asked to do so. Three weeks later a police officer requested him to divulge the name and address of either or both patients or to give information that would lead to their identification. The facts were that a stolen car had been involved in an accident, the driver and passenger having run away immediately afterwards; it was alleged that the driver was guilty of dangerous driving. The doctor refused, both at the time and later in writing, to divulge this information on the ground that this would be a breach of professional confidence. He was prosecuted in the local magistrates' court under section 168(2)(*b*) of the Road Traffic Act 1972 which states "... any other person ... shall if required ... give any information which it is in his power to give and may lead to the identification of the driver." He was fined £5: *Hunter* v. *Mann* (1974).

On the advice of the Union he appealed against the conviction on the ground that he was not within the words "any other person" which were not to be construed as having an unrestricted meaning so as to cause a doctor to act in breach of the duty of confidence on which the patient was entitled to rely, and not within the words "in his power" because power must include a legal right and he had no legal right to disclose. The Divisional Court dismissed the appeal stating that a doctor acting within his professional capacity and carrying out his professional responsibility was within the words "any other person." As to "power" the court decided that there was no doubt that a practitioner in the circumstances in which the doctor found himself had the power. The doctor had only to disclose information which might lead to identification and which was not otherwise confidential. The appeal was dismissed with a certificate that a point of law of general public importance was involved in the decision. Leave to appeal to the House of Lords was refused. Although the member was found guilty of failing to give information to the police about his patients he maintained professional secrecy.

It will have been noticed that Dr. Hunter was faced, not with an order from a judge to disclose information, but with the stipulations of a statutory provision of the Road Traffic Act. Breach of the stipulation is punishable by fine, which was accordingly imposed on Dr. Hunter.

While leave to appeal was refused by the Divisional Court, such leave might have been sought independently from the House itself. But this approach was not made. Like as not, the same sort of result would have followed. One can, however, have more than a degree of sympathy with Dr. Hunter and with anyone faced with the same problem. Courts of law are not always at their strongest when they seek to rely on "the ordinary meaning" of words, especially when such words might constitute terms of art and not just terms of reference, still less ordinary verbiage. The doubtful point of the Divisional Court's judgment, delivered by Boreham J., reads:

"I am not going to attempt to define 'power.' It seems to me a word of fairly common understanding and reading it in its ordinary way I have no difficulty in coming to the conclusion that a doctor in the circumstances in which the appellant found himself had the power. It may be that but for the section in the Act he would not have exercised that power because of his duty to his patient, but that seems to me to beg the question, for that would have been in accordance with his duty not to make voluntary disclosure. Once it is decided that the appellant is a person to whom the statutory duty imposed by s. 168 applied, then I have no doubt that he had the power. I think it would be no injustice to counsel for the appellant to say that this was the least strenuously argued of his points and I find it a point without substance."

The particular point in issue—the meaning of one phrase (indeed, one word) in a statutory stipulation—may seem insignificant. But any apparent insignificance is overborne by the evidence we find here of a judicial unwillingness to admit legal consequences of a medical practitioner's ethical duty. The judge argued: the doctor had a "power" (in the "ordinary meaning"—presumably, "all he could, all within his memory or intellectual capacity"); then said "that" power would not, but for the statutory stipulations, have been exercised by the doctor because of his duty to his patient. But one may then ask: what power? The argument in defence of Dr. Hunter begged the question only if the judge refused outright to attach any ethical significance to "in his power." And that, apparently, is precisely what the judge did.

To recap: this was not a case of judicial order to divulge, merely of a statutory requirement, the breach of which attracted a fine. Dr. Hunter was accordingly fined £5. But during the court proceedings he was not called upon to disclose the information sought by the police. It cost him, but his ethics remained intact. The derisory fine can almost be seen, not as a criminal penalty, but as a tax on conscience.

The doctor's overriding duty to society

This expression is taken verbatim from the third "exception" to the duty to preserve secrecy in the B.M.A. *Handbook*. It is a convenient handle for this topic, and is not intended to prejudice or pre-empt any conclusions we might wish to reach.

While it is well that cases of disclosure of information can usually be kept away from judicial scrutiny, it would be interesting to predict judicial attitudes to the notion of an overriding public duty. Specifically, if legal action (for an injunction, or for damages, or both) were taken by a patient against a doctor for breach of confidence, and if the doctor defended himself by claiming to have acted in the overriding public or social interest, what would the judges do? The notions of "public good," "public policy" and other such variations are notoriously amorphous even within the operations of the law. Their interpretation in an ethical or social context promises to be even less predictable.

It will be noted that the duty to society is expressed to be "overriding"; it is not independent, but depends on a balance of interests. In achieving such a balance, the interests of the individual patient, including as but one element his interest in confidentiality, will be bound to weigh heavily, even if heavier interests tip the scales at the end of the day. Head-on collisions of interest, public and private, may be avoided by the use of a variety of permissible manoeuvres. For instance, the patient's consent to disclosure may properly be sought; and there may be circumstances in which it would be proper to go further and encourage the patient to come clean himself. Failing either such course succeeding, an approach might be made to the family doctor (if the doctor with the confidential information was some-one other), or vice versa, for instance, information given to the occupational health service at the patient's place of work. The latter course could be justifiable either by an appeal to the best interests of the patient, or to those of workmates who might be endangered by the patient's condition, or both. In most such cases, an encouragement to appreciate possible harm or danger to others seems preferable to condemnation, for instance by informing the police without having attempted other courses.

Instructive examples discussed in M.D.U. Annual Reports include these:

If a patient will not agree that his tendency to fits or fainting or his impaired muscle power or control be notified to the licensing authority, it is to this quarter rather than to the police that members are advised to give information. Where the risk lies in the nature of the patient's employment, the medical officer of the employing body may be appropriately contacted in the interests of the patient and of the public. Although a family doctor is naturally reluctant to inform the licensing authority, against the wishes of his patient, that a tendency to fits is being concealed, particularly when the livelihood of the individual depends on driving, the safety of the public is paramount.

Two general practitioners were advised by the Union that their patients, each employed as a police officer and driving a police car, should report their tendency to fits to their employers but that if they refused to agree to this the doctors should contact the senior police surgeons.

The family doctor of a British Rail engine driver who became subject to fits and wished to conceal the fact was advised to inform the principal medical officer for the region. Similar advice was given to the doctor of a colour-blind signalman. In each case the patient was given the opportunity to take this step himself or to authorize his doctor to disclose it in the public interest.

If all else fails, open disclosure might be made, and in a way which might directly attract the possibility of legal process. Such open disclosure could be considered a matter of last resort, but in some situations the last resort may occur very early. In any event, the doctor must be mindful of the general exhortation in the B.M.A. *Handbook*: "A doctor must be able to justify his decision to disclose information" (para. 1.7). Sometimes the doctor himself may be endangered, either singly or with others. The *British Medical Journal* of 1973 cites the example of a doctor who was about to catch a train and happened to walk past the engine, only to realise that the man who was about to drive him 450 miles was a patient suffering from syphilitic aneurysm of the aorta which was eroding his sternum and liable to perforate at any minute. The reaction of the doctor contained more than a degree of compromise:

> "I went on the train and later sent for him. He hadn't told us he was a train driver, but I persuaded the patient to go to see his G.P. and the railway doctor. The authorities were most reasonable about it, and gave him another job. But if he hadn't stopped it would have been my duty as a citizen to communicate not with authority—but with the doctor concerned."

Thus, as in the other cases, every attempt was made to keep the communication between doctors; the information remains within the medical circle.

Dual roles

If an overriding duty to the public presents possible conflicts of interest which loom on the horizon, so much nearer are the problems in cases where a doctor has a duty to an employer as well as a different duty to his patient. Medical practitioners engaged in occupational medicine and as employment medical advisers must take care to distinguish their roles. In relation to both situations the B.M.A. *Handbook* is very specific. For instance, in relation to the obligation of confidentiality in occupational medicine, paragraphs 3.11 and 3.12 read:

> "An occupational physician has to be particularly careful. He holds his appointment from the management, but his duties concern the health and welfare of the workers, individually and collectively. He deals constantly with other doctors' patients. But these considerations do not alter the doctor-patient relationship; the fact that the doctor is employed and paid by a company or other employer does not mean the

employer has the right to see the results of examinations or notes written by the doctor. Only with the consent of the person examined may the employer have access in specifically agreed circumstances to that person's medical records. It cannot be assumed that this consent has general applicability.

"If an employer explicitly or implicitly invites members of his staff to consult the occupational physician the latter must still regard such consultations as confidential."

Difficult problems of a similar type have a habit of occurring in relation to school, university and college medical services. An analogous problem arises in the case of the patient who is an employee of a hospital who is injured at work and who brings an action for damages against the hospital—the hospital which holds the patient's records.

Lawyers acting for hospitals have argued that the medical records are the property of the Secretary of State and that they are entitled to inspect the records. The Medical Defence Union has supported numbers of doctors who have objected to this attitude on the ground that it cuts across traditional rules in industrial medicine; an employee who consults the staff health doctor albeit in the firm's premises and the firm's time, is entitled to professional secrecy and can require his doctor to refuse to disclose his records or information contained in them without his permission.

The case of the family doctor

As a final case study, let us look at the situation in which Dr. Browne found himself in 1971. The case concerned a disciplinary hearing before the Disciplinary Committee of the General Medical Council. Dr. Browne was charged with improperly disclosing to the father of a girl then aged 16 that she had been prescribed an oral contraceptive by Birmingham Brook Advisory Centre. In a British Medical Journal editorial the dismissal of the charges against Dr. Browne by the General Medical Council Disciplinary Committee was hailed as a reaffirmation of "the principles of medical practice that the doctor has an obligation to act in the way he judges to be in the best interests of his patient." Given the fact that Dr. Browne thought it medically inadvisable for his patient to be given the particular oral contraceptive in question, it is argued that he was acting properly to inform the girl's father. In a later issue of the B.M.J. in 1973 a senior barrister argued that the earlier editorial's argument does not hold, that legally Dr. Browne had no right to violate his patient's confidence. He accuses the medical profession in effect of closing ranks over the defence of one of their colleagues and the sacrosanct principle of the independence of the doctor's clinical judgment. The case certainly falls far short of constituting anything like a precedent for future action: indeed the Disciplinary Committee was at pains to stress that the issue was decided very much on its own merits. In particular, the Committee (so far as can be juged from the report) was impressed by Dr. Browne's insistence that he, as the family doctor, was most familiar with the girl's medical history. Furthermore, in the event of any adverse reaction it would be likely, he thought, to be he who would be called in to offer treatment.

For the "senior barrister" boldly to state that the disclosure which Dr. Browne made as the result of a considered decision was "unethical" is, with respect, unhelpful. He points out that: "People over 16 are entitled to confidentiality *because* [italics for emphasis] the Family Law Reform Act 1969 has given them the right to treatment and hand in hand with this goes the right to secrecy. But with children under 16 the doctor is legally, and probably ethically, justified in telling parents if their child is getting into some sort of sexual difficulty."

Two questions may be asked about the decision of the General Medical Council's Disciplinary Committee in Dr. Browne's case. First, are all such judgments to be considered examples of mere ad hoc-ery? Second, upon what social or ethical basis are the Committee's favourable decision, and the barrister's unfavourable criticism, to be based. By his use of "because," the barrister is giving vent to the sentiment of many lawyers that there is a necessary consequential connection between the existence of a legal regulation and the maintenance of an ethical standard. Such an approach to the relation between law and ethics is apt to produce either simplistic statements of position or, at worst, proponents of opposing ethical stances shouting at each other across a vacuum. The alternative to such a situation is not, however, to insist that every situation is to be decided according to a sort of palm tree justice, each entirely on its own merits. Surely there is room for a utilitarian approach: that courses of action should be considered and judged according to their consequences; and that such consequences be judged according to their capacity in particular cases to contribute to the greatest happiness, or benefit, of the greatest number.

Finally, in the assessment of this calculus concerning the legitimate interests which are going to be best preserved, or least harmed, there is a consideration which receives further examination in the following chapter and which has from time to time appeared on the scene in the present discussion: that is, the patient's consent. Consent to disclosure, whether express or implied, attracts analogies from the field of "informed consent" to treatment. In particular, the purpose of disclosure may be examined in the wider context of effects of disclosure. A test of utility in this examination clearly has much to offer, and it would be good to see it getting the attention which it deserves.

Chapter 11

TREATMENT AND CONSENT IN MEDICAL PRACTICE

I

Consent: general principles

It will be convenient to summarise the general principles governing consent as a defence to a civil action before continuing with a more detailed discussion of the notion of consent as it specifically affects medical cases.

The assumption of a risk must be freely and willingly consented to; mere knowledge of a risk alone will not absolve a defendant from liability in tort if he has wronged the plaintiff. This principle is just and fair, especially in relation to accidents at work caused by the negligence of an employer. Since the decision of the House of Lords in *Smith* v. *Baker* (1891) the law has been that an employer cannot set up the defence of consent to a known risk if that risk was not freely and voluntarily assented to.

In recent years it has become apparent that the defence of *volenti non fit injuria* will not protect against the defendant's neligence. It has already been seen that this defence is never available in cases of an employer's breach of a statutory duty (or, indeed, anybody else's breach of such a duty). It may be asked: What does this defence protect against? The answer seems to be that while consent to the general negligent conduct of the defendant will not absolve the latter from liability, consent to specific acts of negligence can do so. Authority for this proposition can be found in another, more recent, decision of the House of Lords in *I.C.I. Ltd.* v. *Shatwell* (1965), in which the employers (I.C.I.) would have been vicariously liable for the negligent conduct of an employee who blew up his brother (a fellow employee) as a direct result of a failure of both employees to observe safety procedures specifically provided by statute for explosives.

The defence of consent or *volenti non fit injuria* is not applicable unless the plaintiff has already made out a case that a tort has been committed. The example may be given of a window cleaner injured when falling from a ladder. True, a person in such an occupation voluntarily and knowingly consents to the risks involved. He does not (or the law does not allow him to) consent generally to another's negligence, and if the injury is caused by the negligence of the owner of the premises then the defence of consent is inapplicable in law. If there is no negligence or other liability in tort on the part of any other, the window cleaner being injured either by carelessness or plain misfortune, the defence of consent is in such a case inapplicable in fact.

Volenti non fit injuria as a defence should be distinguished from the partial defence of contributory negligence. The defence of contributory negligence operates to reduce the damages awarded to a plaintiff in proportion to his own fault in causing the injury. In the relatively restricted number of cases in which it applies, the defence of consent, if successful, is a complete defence. Thus, if a patient consents to undergo certain surgery, and further and substantially different surgery is carried out to which the patient could not reasonably be presumed to have consented, the further surgical operations will amount to battery. To the procedure consented to there is a defence; to others in which there is, in fact or in law, no consent, there is no defence. There is no halfway house as there is in the case of contributory negligence.

Absence of consent

Our initial concern, under the heading of "consent to treatment," is with the ingredients of the tort of *battery*. A word about terminology will be helpful. In criminal law the term *assault* is invariably used to denote an attack or other similar conduct on the part of an accused person, in which the victim suffers at least some physical harm by having come into contact with the accused, or with an object—perhaps a weapon—held by the accused. In the civil law (meaning here the non-criminal law) of the torts of assault and battery, a distinction is to be made. An assault is, strictly speaking, the threat (by actions or by words and actions combined) of the immediate application of physical force (which in this context may amount to no more than mere physical contact) to the person who complains of the assault. The actual application of that force or other contact is called battery.

Any unlawful physical instrusion on the body of a person constitutes a trespass. But there are occasions on which "interference" with the person of another will not amount to trespass to the person. One example is that of the physical contact which may be necessary when a person is lawfully arrested. The hallmarks of a lawful arrest are complex and this is not the occasion for a detailed examination of that particular area of the law. The essentials of lawful arrest were examined in Chapter 9. Suffice it to say that if a policeman, or in different circumstances a private citizen (in the case of a so-called "citizen's arrest") did not fulfil the necessary conditions for a lawful arrest, the involuntary detention of the person so detained would amount to the tort of trespass, in the form known as false imprisonment, and this tort would be likely to lead to heavy damages having to be paid to the victim.

To kiss a girl against her will is a trespass; likewise to subject a person to medical or surgical treatment without his consent is a trespass. But if the girl consents, or if the patient consents, the treatment is not a tort and is not wrongful. What, then, is the meaning of consent? What forms may it take? How is it properly to be obtained? And, most importantly, who is to be the judge of whether full and free consent—indeed informed consent—has been given: is it the giver of the "consent" or the recipient? These are some of the questions which give rise to some complexity in the area of consent to medical or surgical treatment.

Consent: express or implied

Consent may be, as the law puts it, express or implied. In either form, its existence will be a bar, a defence, to an allegation of trespass to the person (usually a battery, though the sight of an unsolicited hypodermic coming at you could amount to an assault). Consent is expressed if a person agrees in so many words that he agrees to the proposed treatment. Consent is implied where a person's conduct is such that we can naturally conclude from his behaviour and the surrounding circumstances of the particular situation that he consents to the act being done, the treatment being given. An example of implied consent would be a situation in which a person came, in a state of consciousness, to an accident and emergency department with a bleeding wound requiring medical attention. And where a person presents himself for medical examination his consent to what is necessary to carry out the proper examination in question will be implied. Good sense must be used here. If there is any doubt at all whether consent may be implied to everything that is proposed to be done to the patient, his or her express permission should be obtained. An example might be the pelvic examination of a patient of the opposite sex.

Where express consent is sought, oral consent is in law as effective as written consent. But there are obvious advantages of written consent, the principal advantage being that of the ready availability of proof in the event of the actions of the examiner or other giver of treatment being called in question later. Hence the model consent forms, as designed by the Medical Defence Union and the Medical Protection Society, which are used in hospitals and other appropriate health care institutions as a matter of daily routine.

Further procedures

There will be found in the model forms a clause to the effect that the patient accepts that no undertaking has been given that the operation will be performed by any particular person. This is to meet the situation disclosed by a case in 1950 in which a patient got nominal damages against the surgeon whom he had consulted in the first place, alleging an oral contract to operate personally and that by allowing the house surgeon to operate the surgeon had procured a trespass to the patient's person.

Another aspect of consent is this. Suppose a person is undergoing an operation for which he has given his consent. During the operation a condition is discovered that is unconnected with the condition in respect of which he consented to be operated on. If this condition is treated, will it be a battery, or will the consent given to the treatment of one condition be deemed to extend to treatment in respect of the newly discovered condition? (It is assumed of course that the patient is unconscious).

In *Murray* v. *McMurchy* (a Canadian case) the patient was undergoing a Caesarian operation. Tumours were discovered in the walls of the uterus. The surgeon tied off the patient's fallopian tubes thereby rendering her sterile. The reason he gave for doing so was the risk involved in further child-bearing. He was liable in battery. The court said that the only evidence was the tumours might have constituted a hazard in the event of further pregnancy. This was not enough justification for taking such a drastic step without the patient's consent.

In *Mohr* v. *Williams* (an American case) M consulted W an ear surgeon because of trouble in her right ear. The recommended operation was agreed on. Whilst M was under anaesthetic W examined the left ear, found it in a worse state than the other and operated on it. The court found for M: the evidence did not show any emergency which required immediate action. An operation done without the consent of the patient, said the court, was lawful only if necessary to preserve the life or the health of the patient.

In a case in England in 1969 a woman sued a doctor and the Birmingham RHB in respect of a sterilisation carried out on her whilst having a Caesarian. The defendants did not dispute liability, and the plaintiff was awarded £750 damages. The judge said he found it very difficult to decide on the amount of damages. The plaintiff had three children, and was a Roman Catholic.

In this connection the model consent form put out by the MDU and the MPS has this phrase:

"I also consent to such further or alternative operative measures or treatment as may be found necessary during the course of the operation. . . ."

We cannot be certain what the effect of this wording is, but the view expressed here is that this would not justify the doctor in doing the kind of thing done in the cases referred to above, but only those things necessarily related to what was consented to.

Informed consent

The picture given so far is a simple one. But we must now return to the question: by whose standards is the consent judged to be full and free consent? Clearly, no one in his right senses would allege that a patient "consented" to treatment if such "consent" had been obtained under threat or other form of compulsion. The area of the law under discussion is designed to protect against, or at least to compensate, unwarranted instrusions into the physical personal interests of patients. These interests would be ill-served if their scope could be dictated by the authority of others. So in the case of a sane, conscious adult, the only person who can give full and free consent is the patient himself. The law does not recognise even the nearest and closest relative as having authority to act on the patient's behalf (except in the perhaps unusual case of the patient who states specifically that a certain other person is to make the decision on his or her behalf).

The patient must be given a full and comprehensible explanation of the treatment which is proposed. The language of the explanation should be as simple and as nontechnical as is possible in all the circumstances. For only if a patient can truly be said to know just what he or she is consenting to can such consent be valid in law. Even if a patient signed a form of consent containing a statement by the patient that the effect and nature of the operation has been explained, this would not necessarily prevent that patient from later arguing that a full and comprehensible explanation had not been given. This is the point, mentioned earlier, about who is to judge the adequacy of communication between medical staff and patient. Is it the member of the medical, or nursing, staff; or is it the patient? Any problem of communications, or of an alleged breakdown in communications, is likely to cause problems. What can the law do usefully in this situation, without appearing to be partial to either of the sides in a dispute? We encounter here the vexed issue of "informed consent."

The principal point of difference between the specific area of "informed consent" and consent generally is that, while the response to treatment given in the absence of consent would be a trespass action (battery), it is the law of negligence which the courts use in order to respond to treatment following incomplete explanation of risks.

In respect of a sane and conscious adult, the only person who can give a valid consent is the patient himself. The law does not recognise even the nearest and closest relative as endowed with authority to act for the patient.

The patient must be given a full and comprehensible explanation, in language as simple and nontechnical as possible. Only if he knows what he is being asked to consent to can the patient's consent be valid. Even if the patient signs a consent form which contains a statement by the patient that the effect of the operation has been explained to him this would not prevent him from later arguing that he had not in fact been given a full explanation.

Where express consent is sought, oral consent is as effective as written consent, but the latter is obviously preferable. The uncertainties of oral communication are notorious. With writing there is no doubt that some consent has been given, and what its exact terms are. The Medical Defence Union has advised its members:

> "It should be the invariable practice to obtain the patient's written consent to any operation which requires a general anaesthetic or to any procedure which may involve a special risk."

The Union and the Medical Protection Society have published model consent forms.

The importance of consent, we have seen, is that it is a defence to an action against a doctor or nurse for assault or battery. For this to be a good defence, however, there are a number of points to be observed. Or to put it another way, even though apparent consent has been got, the patient might be able to show that his consent was in some way not a true consent, that the act done to him was done without his consent, and, therefore, amounted to an assault.

The MDU and MPS consent forms provide for the medical practitioner to sign on it, below the patient's signature, his confirmation that he has explained the nature and effect of the treatment to the patient. There seems to be no legal necessity for this. It is, however, a useful reminder that the nature and effect of the treatment should be explained to the patient by a medical practitioner. If he leaves it to a nurse to do so he might find later that the patient was challenging the accuracy of the account given him by the nurse on the doctor's behalf. There is less likelihood of such a challenge succeeding where the explanation is given by the doctor. It seems clear that a doctor should not confirm that he has explained the treatment to a patient if he has not, but, say, left it to a nurse.

The Medical Defence Union Annual Report for 1969 refers to an important aspect of consent. A senior surgeon had written:

"Some of our house surgeons could not explain the nature and effect of treatment to our patients. One of them at present is a Greek and his English is simply not good enough."

The MDU commented:

"This surgeon was informed that his observations were disturbing, that it could be argued that a doctor whose command of the English tongue is so poor that he cannot explain the nature and effect of an operation is also incapable of taking a proper medical history."

The MDU advised the surgeon that if any house surgeon has such limited command of English, the situation was both serious and dangerous and should be reported to the hospital authorities without delay. In the same year, 1969, the Ministry introduced stricter rules to ensure that doctors with overseas qualifications have an adequate understanding of English. Further action was called for in 1973 and was later taken.

It is very much to be hoped that the Government's 1980 decision to abandon language tests for doctors who are nationals of EEC member states as a condition of registration in this country does not produce any problems such as the one just outlined. There are about 400 such doctors practising in this country.

While a breakdown in communications may be the result of

carelessness on the part of medical or nursing staff, or even accidental with no-one being to blame, there are some situations in which information about certain details of proposed medical or surgical treatment may be deliberately withheld if such withholding is considered to be in the best interests of the particular patient. Indeed, some details of procedures or effects may be particularly worrying or frightening to many patients. How far are those giving the treatment permitted in law to withhold detail of procedures, or effects, or both and still be able to maintain that the patient "consented" to the treatment in question? English law on the point is rather sketchy insofar as there have been very few judicial decisions concerned with this specific issue of consent.

A case in 1954 concerned alternative treatments for goitre. These were either drugs, or an operation. The defendant doctor decided that an operation would be the better course. Before the operation the doctor prevaricated about the risk to her voice, although he in fact knew that there was a slight risk. He did this for the patient's own good, since he considered it to be important that the patient should not worry. The doctor's approach was justified in the light of all the circumstances of the case. The plaintiff, a singer, claimed damages for alleged negligence by her doctor, a surgeon and the hospital, in relation to advice and treatment and the performance of a partial thyroidectomy. After the operation it was discovered that the plaintiff's left vocal chord was paralysed. The plaintiff alleged that the doctor was *negligent* in advising her that the operation involved no risk to her voice and that the surgeon was negligent in damaging the laryngeal nerve during the operation. The judge, Lord Justice Denning, said that the surgeon should not be considered negligent merely because one of the risks inherent in an operation actually materialised, but only if he had fallen short of the standard of reasonable medical care. With regard to the doctor, whose position in law is more important for the purposes of the present discussion, the court had to consider whether the doctor had said there would be no risk to her voice or whether he merely prevaricated. In the event, it was decided that his conduct amounted only to prevarication and that such prevarication did not amount to the tort of negligence.

The case of *Smith* v. *Auckland Hospital Board* (1965) must be considered. This was a New Zealand case, but it is of relevance as the English law on the point was considered. S entered hospital for examination and, if necessary, surgical treatment for suspected aortic aneurism. In the course of the examination he was subject to aortography in which a catheter is inserted in the

femoral artery and guided towards the aorta into which a fluid is
then injected for the purpose of X-ray. In the course of this procedure a mishap occurred: the catheter dislodged some material
from the interior of the artery wall. Clotting resulted, and despite
all proper efforts, S's right leg degenerated into a gangrenous
condition and had to be amputated below the knee.

In this action S alleged that the defendants were negligent in a
number of respects. The jury found for the Board in all matters
relating to the way the aortography had been carried out. S also
alleged that the Board was negligent in failing to warn him of the
risks inherent in the procedure. The jury found the Board
negligent in that respect, but the judge held that that conclusion
was one which the jury was not, in law, entitled to arrive at. The
Court of Appeal reversed his decision on that point, thereby
restoring the jury's decision that the Board was negligent
(through its employees). In doing so the court emphasised
strongly that it was dealing with a situation in which the patient
had actually asked about the risks involved.

> "On no account must it be thought that we are laying down a
> general rule as to what a doctor should tell his patient before
> performing an operation or carrying out an exploratory proce-
> dure. Still less are we saying what information should be
> volunteered by the doctor if he is merely explaining the nature
> and purpose of what is proposed and no question is asked of
> him as to the risk involved. But here S had asked 'Is there any
> risk attached to this procedure?' "

What the doctor (one of the members of the surgical team) in
fact said was:

> "Old chap, within a couple of days you will be back home. You
> will be under a slight anaesthetic and will know nothing about
> it."

This answer was meant to be reassuring, but it was, said the
court, capable of the construction that there was no risk, and it
was not disputed that there was some risk (especially as the
plaintiff was a man of 64 with an arterio-sclerotic condition). It
was not, therefore, a true and complete answer. It is not in fact
always necessary to give such an answer, and the question here
was: was it a negligent answer?

Now in any allegations of negligence against a professional
man, the opinions of his colleagues are always relevant in deciding whether the defendant has failed to exercise reasonable care.
In this case doctors giving evidence for the Board unanimously
said that if asked that question by S they would have answered

reassuringly but that there was also some risk. The defendants were therefore in breach of their duty to answer the question carefully. But in order to succeed S had to show also that if he had been told of the risk he would not have consented to undergo the examination. The court was satisfied from the evidence that S would not have consented, and his action therefore succeeded.

It should be noted that this case relates to the duty of a doctor which arises when he is asked a question, the answer to which will assist the patient to decide whether or not to consent to the treatment. It is not a case about the doctor's duty when asked by the patient about his condition, such as "Am I going to get better?" Nor is it a case of medical negligence as such, the principles of which were examined in Chapter 6 since the procedures in this case were not carried out negligently.

In *Chadwick* v. *Parsons* (1971) the plaintiff was totally deaf. The defendant, an E.N.T. surgeon, heard of a device which if implanted into the mastoid cavity of the skull and connected to the ear with gold wires would restore hearing. The defendant was enthusiastic as to the success of this operation, and being anxious, the court said, to do his best to help humanity, suggested it to the plaintiff, who agreed. At this time no such operation had been carried out, so that it was not in fact possible to say how successful it might be. The defendant did not warn the plaintiff of the serious risks which the operation carried with it, that is, that if it failed there would be disastrous effects. It failed, the defendant did not contest liability and an award of almost £20,000 damages was upheld by the Court of Appeal.

Neglience or battery?

Before the end of January 1980 there was no English case on the point whether the absence of full and informed consent makes any ensuing treatment a trespass to the person, a battery. But now a judicial decision on the matter exists for our guidance.

In the case of *Chatterton* v. *Gerson* the facts were as follows. The plaintiff, a healthy middle-aged woman, underwent a small hernia operation in her right groin. She later suffered pain in the operation site, and it was discovered that a nerve had been trapped in the course of the repair. A further operation failed to free the trapped nerve, and repeated injections of local anaesthetic failed to give more than temporary relief. The plaintiff's pain was such that she could not bear the touch of clothing on the scar site, had to have a cradle over it in bed, and could bear to wear nothing but a loose cotton dress over the affected area.

She was sent for treatment to a pain clinic at a large county hospital. Her doctor was a specialist in the treatment of chronic intractable pain. He administered an intrathecal phenol solution injection to block the sensory nerve which transmitted the pain signals from the scar site to the brain. This is a procedure designed only for the relief of chronic intractable pain, where the only available alternative is the ever increasing doses of narcotic drugs. As such it is a treatment of last resort, and some doctors will use it hardly ever or not at all.

The consultant did not pretend to recollect exactly what he had said to the plaintiff in particular in the conversations prior to her injections, but it was his regular practice to explain the general nature of the process and to explain that the effects would involve numbness in the area from which the pain signals had been transmitted. This numbness, he normally explained, would cover an area larger than the pain source itself, and it might involve temporary loss of muscle power. The plaintiff did not, in her evidence in the present case, recollect this detail. There was, however, said the court, no particular reason to believe that the doctor departed from his normal practice of explanation in the present case. The injection failed to have more than a temporary effect, and a second injection was given.

The success of the procedure could not, it may be deduced, be guaranteed, and indeed no such guarantee could have been given in respect of the second injection. Following the second injection the plaintiff continued to experience acute agony in the scar area, and in addition lost the feeling in her right leg. Did the doctor's choice not explain in detail that the procedure was not a guaranteed success amount to such misinformation as to render the plaintiff's alleged consent ineffectual, with the result that his treatment of her was in law a battery?

In the event it was decided that, in what he said, any good doctor had to take into account the personality of the patient, the likelihood of the medical or surgical procedure going wrong, and what in the way of warning was for a particular patient's welfare. In this case the doctor had fulfilled his duty to explain. The whole picture in this case was of an unfortunate lady desperate for pain relief. Had the claim been based in negligence (like the case which was mentioned earlier), the plaintiff would have had to prove not only a "breach of duty to inform," but also that had that duty not been broken she would have decided against having the operation. Here was a case of an operative procedure the success of which could not in all cases be

guaranteed. But it was not a trespass to the person, in the form of
battery, by the doctor not to have spelled this out; and it is
probably that an action in negligence would also have failed
since the poor lady would probably have gone ahead with the
operation anyway, given her unfortunate condition. She would
not then be able to complain of the *damage* which, as we saw in
Chapter 6, is one of the essentials of success in an action for
negligence.

Consent: special cases

Accident and emergency cases present few problems. The
patient's consent is required, if he is in a fit condition to give it;
otherwise the spouse's or nearest relative's consent should preferably be obtained. Failing this, a medical officer or doctor can
only act for the best, exercising due and reasonable care.

The question of treatment of minors is rather more
problematical. The Family Law Reform Act 1969 specifically
provides for this eventuality in section 8:

S.8(1) The consent of a minor who has attained the age of
sixteen years to any surgical, medical or dental treatment
which, in the absence of consent, would constitute a trespass
to his person, shall be as effective as it would be if he were of
full age; and where a minor has by virtue of this section given
an effective consent to any treatment it shall not be necessary
to obtain any consent for it from his parent or guardian.

(2) In this section "surgical, medical or dental treatment"
includes any procedures undertaken for the purposes of
diagnosis, and this section applies to any procedure (including, in particular, the administration of an anaesthetic) which
is ancillary to any treatment as it applies to that treatment.

(3) Nothing in this section shall be construed as making
ineffective any consent which would have been effective if this
section had not been enacted.

The implications of this seem to be that if a minor (of 16 or 17)
gives his consent to treatment, and the parent purports to override that consent, the parent's views can be safely ignored as far
as the law is concerned. Further, if the minor refuses his consent,
and the parent purports to give his, the minor's refusal must be
given effect. Third, the effect of section 8(3) seems to be this: at
common law it might have been possible for a person under 16 to
give a valid consent to treatment, and the fact that 8(1) validates
the consent of a person of 16 is not to be take to impliedly

invalidate the consent of a person under 16. (Such a consent would, of course, only be valid where it could be shown that the child very clearly understood what was involved in the treatment.)

In the case of mentally disordered persons, consent of the patient and (or) of the patient's "nearest relative" (see Chapter 13) should normally be obtained. Even where a person, though mentally disordered, appears to be capable of giving valid consent, it is a prudent course to obtain also the consent of the nearest relative. In an emergency the Responsible Medical Officer (see Chapter 14) may act without consent.

The problem of members of such sects as Jehovah's Witnesses refusing blood transfusion arises not infrequently. The first thing to be said is that there is no general legal duty to submit *oneself* to medical treatment: one can normally withhold consent to treatment on any ground one chooses, including the ground that it involves an unacceptable procedure such as transfusion. Where the operation necessarily involves a transfusion then it clearly cannot be undertaken in such circumstances. However, in cases where a transfusion may or may not be necessary the patient who refuses to agree to it can be asked to sign a consent form by which he acknowledges his understanding of the advice given him, confirms his refusal to undergo transfusion, and exonerates from any possible liability for not giving the transfusion the hospital authority and all relevant members of the nursing and medical staff. What if such a consent form is signed and during the operation the theatre staff nevertheless, acting from a desire to save life, do give a transfusion? It is difficult to resist the conclusion that they have committed an assault on the patient. One may wonder how much, or how little, damages a court would award such a patient if he were to sue for an act which, let us assume, saved his life.

Particular moral and legal difficulties seem to arise where a parent refuses to allow a child (under 16) to have a blood transfusion. Some years ago some hospital authorities brought children before a juvenile court as being in need of care, protection or control in such circumstances, with a view to a fit person order being made and to such person then giving the necessary permission to the transfusion (or operation, where an operation is refused). The Government expressed the view that it was not right to use this procedure for that purpose, and authorities were advised to rely on the clinical judgment of the consultants concerned after full discussion with the parents. A suitable consent form is available.

In the criminal case of *R.* v. *Blaue* (1975) the Court of Appeal held that the attacker of an 18-year-old Jehovah's Witness, who died in hospital from knife wounds after refusing a blood transfusion which might have saved her life, had indeed caused the girl's death despite her refusal of the treatment offered to her. It has long been the policy of the law that those who use violence on other people have to take their victims as they find them, and an assailant cannot say that his victim's religious beliefs which inhibit him from accepting certain kinds of treatment are unreasonable.

Where an operation is to be carried out on a married person, the consent of the spouse does not have to be got. What, however, where the operation will affect the reproductive capacity of the patient? Should the spouse's consent be got? It appears to be the practice to seek it. However in reply to a question in Parliament in February 1973, a Minister said:

> "I am advised there is no legal requirement that the consent of the spouse must be obtained for the sterilisation of the partner."

In a case in May 1978, a judge of the Family Division ruled that a husband had no legal right to prevent his wife having an abortion when the operation was undesired by him.

Teaching on patients

Another issue which bears on the topic of consent, though which attracts somewhat different consideration from those which we have been examining so far in this section, is the matter of teaching on patients. In many hospitals, including especially those designated for teaching purposes, the cooperation of patients in the practical experience of trainee medical and surgical staff is an essential part of their training. Even when there is no physical contact between medical student and patient (and thus assault and battery are not relevant to the issue) a certain interest of the patient is nevertheless to be considered.

English law gives no remedy to invasion of, or interference with, privacy as such. There are torts such as trespass, including the elements of trespass to the person which we have already examined, and there is defamation which compensates interference with, or injury to, reputation. But there is no such tort as invasion of privacy, despite the facts that other parts of the law of tort in fact compensate such invasions or interferences. So when a patient is, without warning, confronted by a group of medical students accompanying the doctor or consultant, there is no remedy in damages even though the circumstances of the examination might be very embarrassing to the patient (that is, not unless the patient, in an unlikely and extreme case, suffers nervous shock involving adverse physical symptoms).

In 1973 the DHSS issued a health circular for action by area health authorities and boards of governors on the subject of teaching on patients. The model paragraphs for information to be given to patients about teaching procedures were criticised on the ground that they contained no explicit reference to a patient's right to decline to take part in teaching procedures without prejudice to treatment, even though this right was in fact recognised by one of these model paragraphs. A revised version of information to be given to patients was therefore prepared and is attached to HC(77)18 issued to area health authorities and boards of governors in May 1977.

There follows the full wording of the revised model paragraphs for information to patients, and following that is the text of the explanatory circular HC(77)18. It will be noticed that the explanatory notes make it clear that the information to patients is to be applicable to any teaching situation, not only to doctors and medical students.

"In-Patient
We are sure you will realise that it would be impossible to train future members of the health professions without the help and cooperation of patients. This is a hospital where such staff are trained. A few students will normally be attached to the medical team which will be treating you; one of them may be allocated to take a personal interest in your case. They will usually accompany the other members of the team on their rounds. One or two may assist in other ways in looking after you. During your stay in hospital you may also be asked whether you would be willing to take part in a teaching session attended by a number of medical students.

Patients therefore play a very important part in the teaching work of the hospital. We hope you will agree to cooperate in this work if we need your help. If, however, you do not wish to take part in any teaching work, it is open to you to refuse without your treatment being affected in any way. In this case you should, as soon as possible, inform the Ward Sister, or the doctor.

Out-Patient
We are sure you will realise that it would be impossible to train future members of the health professions without the

help and cooperation of patients. This is a hospital where such staff are trained. Instruction takes place in the out-patients department as well as in the wards. This means that a small number of students may be present during consultations with patients, which form a most valuable part of their training.

Patients therefore play a very important part in the teaching work of the hospital. We hope you will cooperate in this work if we need your help. If, however, you do not wish to take part in any of this teaching work it is open to you to refuse without your treatment being affected in any way. In this case you let your general practitioner know so that he can make other arrangements with the hospital.

The distribution of explanatory literature should, however, be regarded as no more than an insurance that a patient has been made aware that the hospital he is to attend is engaged in teaching; it should not be looked upon as an acceptable substitute for personal explanation by the teacher.

On the first occasion that a student is present during the examination or treatment of a patient, or himself attends the patient, his status and the reason for his attendance should be explained to the patient whose cooperation should be sought. When practicable, this explanation should be given by the teacher but may be given by the student or a member of the nursing staff. Whenever a teacher proposes to discuss a patient's condition with a student in the presence of the patient, or to demonstrate the condition to a group of students or doctors, he should ensure that the patient understands the situation and consents. He should also ensure that patient's consent and cooperation where the demonstration is to be given wholly or partly by means of closed-circuit television or is to be recorded on videotape or still photographs for later showing to students.

This guidance applies not only to doctors and medical students but to all teachers and students, subject to such modifications as may be appropriate in the case of students other than medical students.

A special situation arises at dental teaching hospitals and units where a high proportion of work carried out by students under supervision is work that would normally be done by general dental practitioners. A patient who is referred by a general dental practitioner for specialist dental treatment should be treated under this circular in the same way as a patient referred by a general medical practitioner for specialised medical treatment. But an out-patient who seeks dental treatment at hospital that would normally be provided by a general dental practitioner may have to be told that he must seek such treatment from a general dental practitioner if he declines to participate in teaching at the dental hospital or unit."

II

Organ transplants and consent

The complex issues involved in consent to treatment are not limited to the bounds of one's own body, for the currently much-debated question of organ transplants is also widely dependent on the presence or absence of consent. Consent can be an issue of fundamental importance in the case of both live and cadaveric organs which are sought to be transplanted. In the case of donors of organs who are living, the requirements of the law relating to consent which were examined in the foregoing sections must be very carefully observed. This is almost to state the obvious, for it goes without saying that an extremely full explanation should be given, in all normal circumstances, to both the would-be donor and the would-be recipient of a live organ. Such transplantation can be of great value especially within family groups where tissues can frequently have a good chance of being matched in such a way as to reduce the chances of rejection of the transplanted organ or tissue by the body of the recipient.

Questions of consent affect not only the legitimate claims of live donors and recipients to appreciate the probable outcome of transplant surgery. They affect also the legitimate desires of potential donors who wish to aid others after their death by consenting prospectively, during life, to the removal of organs after death. Here the Human Tissue Act 1961 enters the arena, together with the many difficulties of interpretation and practice with which provisions of the Act are associated. These difficulties have caused a variety of practical problems over the years since 1961, including especially the question of who is in lawful possession of a body, such as to give consent to the removal of cadaveric organs, and the question as to the precise function of the coroner whose formal permission must be sought before removal. The outcome has been a rather untidy array of specific pieces of advice or guidance which have been produced each in response to one practical problem, even crisis, or another. Finally, a very legitimate question of consent involves the claims of a would-be donor in respect of privacy and non-disclosure of identity following death, breach of which can make life a misery for unfortunate relatives.

The Human Tissue Act 1961

This Act provides for the use of the bodies of deceased persons for therapeutic purposes and purposes of medical examination and research.

Section 1(1) provides that if a person requests, either in writing (made at any time) or orally in the presence of two witnesses during his last illness, that his body or any specified part of it be used for therapeutic purposes or for purposes of medical education or research then the person in lawful possession of his body may—unless he believes that the request was subsequently withdrawn—authorise the removal for the stated purpose(s).

The request may be made orally or in writing, and it is to be noted that a written statement does not require to be witnessed, being different in this respect from a will, as well as from the oral statement. It should also be noted that whoever is in lawful possession of the body *may*, not must, authorise the removal.

Who is *in lawful possession?* There is no authoritative ruling on this, but, where the person dies in hospital, it seems to be the deceased's next of kin, and not the hospital (subject to 1975 Circular noted below). If this is so, then even if the deceased has made a written request within this subsection the hospital cannot use his body for this purpose without first getting the authority of the next of kin who may then authorise the removal unless he believes the request was subsequently withdrawn.

Section 1(3) provides that the removal of the body on the above authority shall be lawful if it is effected by a fully registered medical practitioner who has satisfied himself that the person is dead, and that there is no reason to believe an inquest or post mortem will be required.

The authority under sections 1(1) and 1(2) cannot be given by a person having possession of the body for interment or cremation only.

Section 1(7) provides that in the case of a body lying in a hospital or similar establishment the authority can be given by a person designated by the hospital board or committee. However, where a person dies in hospital the person lawfully in possession is normally the deceased's personal representative.

Any body so used must be decently and properly interred or

cremated, and a certificate of interment or cremation sent to the appropriate Inspector of Anatomy within six weeks. (Human Tissue Act 1961, s.3, and Anatomy Act 1832, s.13). The Anatomy Act 1832 remains on the statute books, and a reason for this is apparently that the Act allows for the removal of the whole body whereas the Human Tissue Act applies to any part of the body. Secondly the latter Act permits retention of part of the body whereas the 1832 Act requires that the whole body must be buried or cremated.

What if no such request as is mentioned in section 1(1) is made? Section 1(2) says that the person in lawful possession may permit the body to be used if he has no reason to believe that the deceased had not expressed an objection, or that the surviving spouse or any surviving relative objects to the body being so dealt with. A DHSS circular of 1975 deals with this topic. It says, amongst other things:

"(i) Some uncertainty has been expressed on the interpretation of 'the person lawfully in possession of the body.' The Secretary of State hopes that the following guidance will be helpful. If a person dies in hospital, the person lawfully in possession of the body, at least until the executors or relatives ask for the body to be handed to them, is the Area Health Authority responsible for the hospital. In the case of a private institution, the person lawfully in possession would be the managers.

If a person dies elsewhere than in hospital the question of who is lawfully in possession should not normally give rise to difficulty. Thus, it may be the husband in the case of a deceased wife, the parent in the case of a deceased child, the executor, if any, or even the householder on whose premises the body lies. If a person is brought into hospital dead the health authority will be lawfully in possession of the body as in the paragraph above, although in such cases the Coroner will normally be involved.

(ii) Whether or not a request has been made (that is, whether removal is under section 1(1) or 1(2) of the Act), authority for the removal of organs or tissue must be given in each case by the person lawfully in possession of the body, and the receiving of such authorisation should be recorded and timed in the patient's notes by the person receiving it. The authority may be given on behalf of the area health authority by any person or persons designated for the purposes. Area health authorities should authorise certain specified persons to exercise this responsibility for them.

Persons so designated will be responsible for ensuring that the necessary enquiries have been made and should be of sufficient seniority to exercise that important function. It would be appropriate to designate senior administrators; doctors or nurses and authorities should bear in mind that it will often be necessary to contact the officer urgently at night and at weekends. Before a person is designated, authorities should be satisfied that he or she is fully conversant with the requirements of the Act. The designation may be by name or by post and may cover more than one person or post.

A person lawfully in possession of the body of a patient who has not requested that his body or parts of it be used (that is, where s. 1(2) applies) may only authorise removal of parts if, having made such reasonable enquiry as may be practicable, he has no reason to believe that the donor would have objected or that the surviving spouse or any surviving relative objects to the body or the specified part being so dealt with. Specific consent is not necessary, merely a lack of objection. What enquiry is reasonable and practicable must depend on the facts of each particular case. However, in most instances it will be sufficient to discuss the matter with any one relative who had been in close contact with the deceased, asking him his own views, the views of the deceased and also if he has any reason to believe that any other relative would be likely to object. In certain circumstances it might be necessary for such discussion to take place on the telephone. Potential organ donors will often have spent some hours or even days in hospital and in such cases hospitals will have sufficient opportunity to take steps to contact relatives. Where after such reasonable enquiry as may be practicable, there is no evidence that the donor has any relatives, authority may be given under s. 1(2) in the absence of any other evidence which suggests to the contrary. Where it is known that a potential donor has relatives but it has not been possible to contact any of them, a person giving authority for organ removal must be especially careful to ensure that the requirements of the Act with regard to the making of enquiries have been met. It is not enough to say in a case where organs must be removed very soon after death that no enquiry is practicable. Any objections made by patients or relatives should be noted immediately in the patient's notes. The word 'relatives' is not defined in the Act, but there are some circumstances in which it ought to be interpreted in the widest sense, e.g. to include those who although claiming only a distant relationship are nevertheless closely concerned with the deceased.

In cases where the health authority is the person lawfully in possession of the body, and an authorisation under s. 1 has been given, the relatives or executors may subsequently ask that the body be handed over to them; but this action does not revoke the authorisation which continues to be legally effective. If the deceased during his lifetime had recorded an appropriate request, then it would be reasonable for the authorisation under s. 1(1) to be acted upon. But if the authorisation depended on s. 1(2) then despite the legal position set out above, the surgeon should be asked not to proceed if it comes to be known that a surviving relative does object to the use of the body or some part of it. Where no authorisation had been given to the surgeon before a request for the body is received from the relatives, the health authority should ask them to give their agreement to the removal of organs.

Where there is reason to believe that the Coroner may require an inquest or post-mortem examination to be held, authority to remove parts of the body may not be given nor may a part be removed without the Coroner's consent. In law a Coroner has no jurisdiction until death has taken place but in cases where organs, e.g. kidneys, must be removed very soon after death, Coroners may wish to be informed of the proposed course of action before death is reported. It is essential that complete confidence exists between the hospital and the Coroner, and authorities should do all they can to see that this obtains in all cases. Where a Coroner has given consent, it remains the responsibility of the person designated by the health authority, not the Coroner, to ensure that the provisions of the Act with regard to the making of enquiries, as specified in s. 1 of the Act, are complied with.''

Law and practice in transplantation

A code of practice, designed to allay public fears about the circumstances in which organs may be removed from dead patients for the purpose of transplantation was issued by the Department of Health in December 1979. The code has two principal purposes: to set out the precise procedure which should be followed by doctors in deciding whether a person is clinically dead; and to set out the manner in which doctors should properly approach relatives for permission to remove organs.

A code of criteria for the diagnosis of brain death was drawn up by the Royal Colleges in 1976, and their code for transplants issued in 1978 was able to build on the 1976 criteria in the specific application to transplants. The transplant code of 1978 is intended to reassure the public over fears which had been expressed in some quarters that ventilators or life-support machines might be turned off when a doctor knows that a potential recipient is waiting for a vital organ. In fact, one of the greatest problems facing transplant surgeons having the care of a potential recipient is the shortage of suitable organs and tissue available, due in some part to the very natural and usually very proper unwillingness on the part of doctors treating a critically ill patient actually to declare that patient dead. Nonetheless, the code on transplants indicates a proper response to possible fears, if only to confirm assurance.

The procedure to be adopted specifies that two doctors must certify the brain death of a possible donor and each doctor must complete a checklist independently. The code reads:

"When death is determined on the basis of brain death, or where it is proposed to remove organs within an hour after respiration and circulation have ceased, death should be diagnosed by the following combination of doctors:

(a) A consultant who is in charge of the case, or in the absence of a consultant, his deputy, who should have been registered for five years or more and who should have had adequate previous experience in the care of such cases, and

(b) one other doctor.

Neither of these doctors should be a member of the transplant team and the result of the examination and the diagnosis should be recorded in the case notes relating to the deceased patient."

A patient must, states the code, be presumed to be alive until it is clearly established that he is dead. The time of death should be recorded as the time when death was conclusively established and not when artificial ventilation was withdrawn or the heart beat ceased. It states emphatically that any tests or treatment carried out on a patient before death must be for the benefit of the patient and not solely to preserve organs. But after the patient is dead according to the criteria specified in the code (above) there is no *legal* objection to administering any drugs necessary to maintain the condition of organs. The code is right to make the point in this way for two reasons. First, it states that when death is established there is no legal reason to wait to inject organ-maintaining drugs, not that any particular practitioner ought to have no objection or reservations of a non-legal variety.

Second, an injection, or other application, of organ-maintaining drugs into a living patient with the sole or even the primary purpose of maintaining organs for the benefit of a potential recipient would constitute a battery in the absence of the potential donor's consent. And in the circumstances in which critically ill potential donors find themselves, such consent is most unlikely to be decently obtainable. Nor would any such consent by next-of-kin or other relative suffice; while a relative can consent on behalf of an unconscious or emergency patient, or on behalf of a minor under 16, to treatment of that patient, the injection of organ-maintaining drugs could hardly be said to constitute "treatment" of *that* patient: see also HC(77)28.

The role of the Coroner

In February 1980 a furore developed following the decision of the Leicester and South Leicestershire coroner that written permission should be obtained from him in order that organs could be properly removed from a deceased person. While he had in the past given oral consent (*some* form of consent from the coroner being one of the conditions in the Human Tissue Act for a legitimate organ removal) for quite a number of organ transplants (or, to be precise, organ removals) he claimed properly to insist on written permission in the case of the removal of the heart of a sixteen-year-old girl killed in a road accident. The whole issue was clouded with misfortune owing to the fact that reporters from a daily newspaper had already behaved in a thoroughly disgusting manner in pestering the relatives of the deceased girl. It could not have been a more fraught atmosphere in which the Coroner came to make his decision, especially when it was suspected that the girl's relatives had not in fact given specific permission for the removal of the heart, though permission had been given in respect of certain other organs.

Guidance sent to all coroners from the Home Office recognises that the coroner's discretion to give or refuse consent appears to be absolute, but expresses the hope that Coroners will not place obstacles in the way of doctors, or indeed take moral or ethical decisions upon themselves. It is difficult to see, however, how any adequate exercise of discretion could possibly be exercised without the possible canvassing of ethical considerations in the general context. A number of health regions are now drawing up policy documents relating to transplantation policy and procedure.

Donor cards, and confidentiality

Debates have been carried on for some years as to whether a "contracting in" or a "contracting out" scheme for the expression of willingness prospectively to donate organs after one's death is the preferable course. The current practice, facilitated by the availability of blank organ donor cards which become effective when signed, amounts to a "contracting in" scheme in the sense that someone must specifically express a willingness, though this might also be the nearest relative if no such signature of the potential donor had been given. Transplant surgeons themselves differ as between the two alternatives, but there is a very substantial body of medical opinion opposed to a "contracting out" scheme.

An innovation in 1980 was the introduction of so-called "all part" organ donor cards. These cards are designed to be signed by the potential donor, who has the option to delete one or more of the specified organs. The scheme is thus still an opting-in scheme, and it may be said that it possesses the distinct advantages that the reader of such a card found in the possession of a deceased person can be quite specific about the consent to remove certain organs or tissue, and the way of the alarmed coroner, who has his job to do, may thus be eased.

Finally, as a result of the distasteful treatment by the press and news media of mawkish details of deceased donors, some cards now carry the inscription "I desire confidentiality in respect of my identity and that of my relatives," or some other such sentiment. It was seen in Chapter 10 that English law provides no remedy for invasion of privacy as such; an injunction is usually too little and too late. Such a wish expressed on an organ donor card might conceivably act as an indication of the desirable conduct of press, radio and television, assuming of course that they were made aware of the desire for secrecy in the first place. Unfortunately, the grotesque treatment during 1979 and 1980 by the press and media of many intimate details which are utterly irrelevant to the information of any decent human being, let alone the future benefit of transplant surgery, has left thousands of otherwise willing and public-spirited donors with grave doubts as to whether they should, by a signification of desire to donate organs after death, risk subjecting their already grief-striken relatives with the tastlessness of some elements within the press and news media.

Chapter 12

PRESERVATION AND TERMINATION OF LIFE

This chapter is concerned in a variety of ways with aspects of the preservation and termination of life, the latter including natural death. The preservation and the termination of life both present legal and ethical problems for the practitioner and the lawyer alike. And though some problems are now largely solved to the satisfaction of medical practitioners, including the issue of determination of brain stem death, upon which general agreement was reached only quite recently, certain other problems continue to press for the attention of lawyers, medical practitioners and lay people; not least, the issue of the medical and ethical justifications underpinning the abortion law continues to cause controversy and disagreement. Only in early 1981 was an authoritative judicial determination made as to the question, which had for a long time worried nurses and their professional bodies, whether nurses could lawfully participate in the process of abortion by medical induction.

I

The crime of murder

In the context of the provision of health services one hardly expects to have to comment on the law governing murder in the sense of a deliberate malevolent killing. Nevertheless the ingredients of this crime must be briefly considered since in English law a benevolent killing can be as much murder as a killing which is malevolent. The crime of murder is therefore normally committed equally by a doctor or nurse who, with the best of intentions, puts an end to the life of a patient in great pain, in circumstances in which normal life could otherwise have continued. The extremely difficult ethical and practical issues involved in varieties of what is frequently called "euthanasia" will be canvassed briefly after an examination of the criminal law relating to murder and also to manslaughter.

Murder is unlawful homicide with "malice aforethought," while manslaughter is unlawful homicide without "malice aforethought." Malice aforethought is an ancient concept of the criminal law, and it should be noted that it has never meant that murder necessarily involves premeditation in the sense of malevolent planning, or indeed prior planning with any form of motive. Its modern significance, as the necessary mental element without which murder cannot be committed (whichever other crime is), is that the accused must intend to kill, or to cause the victim really serious bodily harm, or that he must intend to do an act which he reasonably foresaw, or must reasonably have foreseen in all the circumstances, would cause really serious bodily harm.

For murder to be committed, death must occur within a year and a day of the unlawful act. The reason for this arbitrary rule lies in the difficulty seen by the law in tracing the links between cause and effect where there is a long interval between the act and the death. This may have been a sound enough basis for the "year and a day" rule in former times, but the retention of the rule in the present much more advanced state of medical science can be justified only on the ground that one who has injured another should not remain indefinitely at risk of prosecution for murder. Nevertheless, the rule remains applicable in both murder and manslaughter (discussed below).

Death after medical treatment

Some consternation in the medical profession was caused by the decision of the Court of Criminal Appeal (as it was then called) in the case of *R.* v. *Jordan* (1956). In that case, the accused stabbed the victim who was admitted to hospital. It did not, apparently, occur to the prosecution, the defence, the judge or the jury that there could be any doubt but that the stab caused the death.

In the Court of Criminal Appeal, the fresh evidence of two doctors was allowed to the effect that in their opinion death had not been caused by the stab wound, which was mainly healed at the time of death, but by the introduction (with a view to preventing infection) of terramycin after the deceased man had shown he was intolerant to it and by the intravenous introduction of large quantities of liquid. This treatment, according to the evidence, was "palpably wrong." The court held that if the jury had heard this evidence they would have felt precluded from saying that they were satisfied that the death was caused by the stab wound and they quashed the conviction.

The court did not say in express terms that there was evidence of negligence, gross or otherwise, though it may reasonably be inferred that "palpably wrong" treatment is negligent.

The case gave rise to some concern in the medical profession and it was predicted that the result of it would be that if, in future, the victim of a homicidal assault died as a result of the medical treatment instituted to save his life, it would not be considered homicide by the assailant if the treatment could be shown to be "not normal."

The Court of Appeal in the case of the Jehovah's Witness who refused medical treatment in the form of a blood transfusion (*R. v. Blaue* discussed in Chapter 11) distinguished (that is, in effect, refused to follow) the earlier decision in *R. v. Jordan* on the ground that it was "a very particular case depending upon its exact facts" although the court in the later case was inclined to think that *Jordan* was in fact correctly decided, given the particular circumstances which obtained there.

In conclusion it may be added that in order that a new and intervening cause of death be judged to have arisen, medical treatment should have been grossly (simply meaning "very") negligent; while the reasonableness, in the opinion of certain others, of a victim's refusal to undergo medical treatment or treatment of an appropriate kind does not affect the criminality of the accused's act.

The crime of manslaughter

Manslaughter may be committed in a variety of ways from the law's point of view, but only one such mode of commission is of direct concern to us here, in a discussion of treatment and the patient. A negligent act causing the death of another can lead to a charge of manslaughter. However, how negligent must one be to be guilty of manslaughter?

The crime of manslaughter may be committed by an act of gross negligence resulting in death. In *R. v. Bateman* (1925) a doctor was convicted of manslaughter. He had attended the deceased upon her giving birth to a dead child. The evidence of negligence concerned ignorance of medical technique and failure to cause the deceased to be removed to hospital as soon as he should. His appeal against conviction was successful on the ground that the judge had not correctly directed the jury as to the degree of negligence which has to be proved for a finding of guilty of manslaughter. It will be appreciated that negligence may lead to civil liability, that is, to the defendant having to pay damages to compensate the person he injured. Here, however, we are concerned with criminal liability for negligence, that is, with punishment for the negligent act. The Court said in *R*. v. *Bateman*,

> "in order to establish criminal liability the facts must be such that, in the opinion of the jury, the negligence of the accused went beyond a mere matter of compensation between subjects and showed such disregard for the life and safety of others as to amount to a crime against the State and conduct deserving punishment."

Can it be manslaughter to omit to do an act, such omission leading to death? Take the case of a parent refusing to get medical aid for a child. First, it must be said that under the Children and Young Persons Act 1933 it is an offence for any person who is at least 16 and who has the care of any child to wilfully neglect the child in a manner likely to cause him unnecessary suffering or injury to health. If the child dies as a result of such neglect is it manslaughter?

Manslaughter and failure of care

In *R*. v. *Senior* (1899) a parent belonged to a sect whose beliefs did not permit him to seek aid. He failed to get help for his child who died. He was convicted of manslaughter. However, in *R*. v. *Lowe* (1973) parents of low intelligence so neglected a baby that it died. The father was charged under the 1933 Act and with manslaughter. His conviction on the first charge was affirmed. To be guilty of that the sole question was whether the failure to get a doctor was deliberate (wilful) and caused the child suffering. However, the conviction for manslaughter was quashed. Mere neglect, even though deliberate, which resulted in death, did not (as the trial judge had told the jury) necessarily constitute manslaughter where, as here, the accused failed to foresee the consequences of his neglect.

The Court of Appeal said:

> "If I strike a child in a manner likely to harm it it is right that if the child dies I may be charged with manslaughter. If I omit to do anything with the result that it suffers injury to health

which results in death, we think that a charge of manslaughter should not be an inevitable consequence, even if the omission is deliberate."

However the Court gave leave to appeal on this point to the House of Lords. Phillimore L.J. said:

"This court thinks there is something inherently unattractive in a theory of constrictive manslaughter. It seems strange that an omission which is wilful solely in the sense that it is not inadvertent, the consequences of which are not in fact foreseen by the person who is neglectful should, if death results, automatically give rise to an indeterminate sentence instead of the maximum of two years which would otherwise be the limit imposed."

Whilst it is, therefore, necessary to prove more than mere neglect which happens to result in death, a decision in 1977 shows that the prosecution, in order to secure a conviction for manslaughter does not have to go as far as to prove the accused's foresight of the likelihood or the possibility of death or serious injury. All that need be proved is gross negligence in the sense of a *reckless disregard* of danger to the health and welfare of an infirm person under the care of the accused: *R. v. Stone* (1977).

This decision is also of interest to those involved in the health services for the following reason. A relative of a family which lived in very poor circumstances—an old man who was almost blind and deaf, his mistress and the man's 34-year-old mentally subnormal son—came to live with them. She had, or developed, anorexia nervosa which stopped her eating properly and, in her last days, at all. She became helplessly infirm, and from that time onwards the law regarded the relatives with whom she lived as having assumed the duty of caring for her. The decision—that they (man and mistress) were guilty of manslaughter—seems less harsh when it is remembered (as the Court of Appeal pointed out) that this was a duty which they could have discharged not only by looking after her properly themselves, but also by summoning help, which the neighbours (knowing the filthy conditions of the woman) had urged.

Euthanasia

It might have been possible to entitle this section "Withdrawal of life-support measures," but for the fact that the word "euthanasia" frequently carries connotations much wider than that above, and is understood by some to refer also to "mercy killing." In fact, mercy killing is as much unlawful homicide as any other deliberate killing. Motive may affect sentence, but it does not affect the criminal nature of the act. Under certain circumstances a killing which might otherwise have been outright murder might be reduced to manslaughter if the accused could prove to a jury the onset of such a mental state as to amount to diminished responsibility. But it would still be an unlawful homicide, albeit manslaughter.

The word "euthanasia" comes from the Greek *eu*, meaning "good" with the association of "easy," and *thanatos* meaning death. The use of the very word is enough to engender a storm of protest in some quarters, for there are those who believe that a taking of a life in any circumstances is profoundly wrong. Such sections of opinion are apt to identify euthanasia with merely killing to the exclusion of other possible defences such as the termination of artificial life-support measures. But even a declaration issued by the Vatican, from the Sacred Congregation for the Doctrine of the Faith, in June 1980 concedes:

> "When inevitable death is imminent in spite of the means used, it is permitted in conscience to take the decision to refuse forms of treatment that would only secure a precarious and burdensome prolongation of life, so long as the normal care due to the sick person in similar cases is not interrupted."

Doctors and nurses are reminded that they should "neglect no means of making all their skill available to the sick and dying; but they should also remember how much more necessary it is to provide them with the comfort of boundless kindness and heartfelt charity."

Medical science is even now so advanced that a body can be kept functioning in respect of circulation and respiration even when the person whose body it was is clinically dead, that is, when brain stem death has been diagnosed according to procedures which since 1978 have received general agreement among the practitioners. So switching off a ventilator or other machine having artificial life support functions is certainly not necessarily unlawful. It *may* be unlawful, depending on the condition of the patient and the stage of clinical diagnosis.

Various attempts have been made for a number of years to alter the law relating to the "mercy killing" aspect of euthanasia, but without eventual legislative success. A maximum two year jail sentence was proposed in 1976 but the law remained unchanged. A more elegant reform of the law of homicide, if any reform were indeed to be desired, would be the abandonment of the present mandatory life sentence for murder. This would retain the same element of criminality and would thus avoid trivialising the taking of a human life, without making the offender subject to a fixed sentence (the sentence for murder being fixed by law, albeit varying in many cases in accordance with judicial discretion and that of the Home Secretary of the day).

Conclusion

To conclude: euthanasia in the sense of what is sometimes referred to as "passive" euthanasia, that is by abandoning or otherwise failing to take measures which could enable life to continue, is not murder but at worst manslaughter in the form of a grossly negligent omission to take those steps which would reasonably have prolonged life. But the withdrawal of artificial life support measures following a firm and clear diagnosis of brain stem death does not constitute an unlawful killing since life has already passed from the body. On the other hand, "active euthanasia" may well amount to murder and at present carries the sentence of life imprisonment. The only ways in which the imposition of such a sentence could be avoided would be either a choice not to prosecute in the first place, or a pardon following conviction. The first course is practically far easier though it is ethically not without objections.

II

The Law of Abortion

It is murder to kill, in certain circumstances, another human who is in being. There can, therefore, be no murder of a child until the extrusion of its body from that of the mother is complete, though it is not necessary that the umbilical cord should be severed.

The Infant Life Preservation Act 1929 created the offence of child destruction. The Act makes it an offence for any person who, with intent to destroy the life of a child capable of being born alive, by any wilful act causes a child to die before it has an existence independent of its mother. However, this is subject to a

proviso that the prosecution must prove that the act was not
done in good faith for the purpose only of preserving the life of
the mother. Pregnancy for 28 weeks is prima facie proof that the
child was capable of being born alive.

Under the Offences Against the Person Act 1858, s. 58:

(a) a pregnant woman, who, with intent to procure her own
miscarriage, unlawfully administers to herself any poison or
noxious thing or unlawfully uses any instrument or other means,
and

(b) any person who, with intent to procure the miscarriage of
any woman, unlawfully administers to her or causes to be taken
by her any poison or noxious thing or *unlawfully* uses any instrument or other means, is guilty of *abortion*.

In *R.* v. *Bourne* (1939), B, an eminent gynaecologist performed
an operation which caused the abortion of a 14-year-old girl who
was pregnant as the result of a rape. He performed the operation
without fee, with the consent of the girl's parents, and after consulting another doctor. He was charged with an offence under
section 58 of the 1858 Act. He stated that he had formed the
opinion that the continuance of the pregnancy would cause the
girl serious injury and lead to her being a physical wreck for the
rest of her life.

It will be noted that section 58 does not contain the proviso
noted above to the offence of child destruction. However, section
58 does contain the word "unlawfully." The judge directed the
jury that the effect of the word was to read into section 58 the
proviso referred to, so that in a prosecution under section 58 it is
up to the Crown to satisfy the jury that the defendant did not
procure the miscarriage in good faith for the purpose only of preserving the mother's life; preserving life, he said, should be
reasonably construed, so that if the doctor was of the opinion on
reasonable grounds and with adequate knowledge, that the
probably consequence of the continuance of the pregnancy would
be to make the woman a physical or mental wreck, the jury could
take the view that he operated for the purpose of preserving the
mother's life. He was held to be not guilty.

The Abortion Act 1967

Under section 1 a person is not guilty of the offence of abortion
when a pregnancy is terminated by a registered medical
practitioner if two registered medical practitioners are of the
opinion, formed in good faith that:

(a) the continuance of the pregnancy would involve risk to the

life of the pregnant woman, or of injury to the physical or mental
health of the pregnant woman or any existing children of her
family, greater than if the pregnancy were terminated; or

(b) there is a substantial risk that if the child were born it
would suffer from such physical or mental abnormalities as to be
seriously handicapped.

In determining whether the continuance of a pregnancy would
involve such risk of injury to health as is mentioned in (a) above,
account may be taken of the pregnant woman's actual or
reasonably foreseeable environment.

Any treatment for the termination of pregnancy must be
carried out in a hospital vested in the Minister or in a place
approved by him for this purpose. However, this (and the
requirement as to the opinion of the two registered medical
practitioners) does not apply to termination of pregnancy by a
registered medical practitioner where he is of the bona fide opinion that the termination is immediately necessary to save the life
or to prevent grave permanent injury to the physical or mental
health of the pregnant woman.

By section 2 the Minister must make regulations providing for
the opinion mentioned in section 1 to be given in the form and at
the time to be prescribed, and for a practitioner who terminates a
pregnancy to give specified information thereof.

By section 4 no person is under a duty to participate in any
treatment authorised by this Act to which he has a conscientious
objection but this is not to affect any duty imposed by law to
participate in treatment which is necessary to save the life or to
prevent grave permanent injury to the physical or mental health
of a pregnant woman.

Nothing in the Abortion Act 1967 affects the provisions of the
1929 Act.

The Abortion Regulations 1968

The opinion to which section 1 of the Act refers must be in the
form prescribed in the regulations. It requires the full names,
qualifications and addresses of the two practitioners who give
their opinion, the full name and usual place of residence of the
woman, and must indicate the ground on which pregnancy
should be terminated. The certificate must be given before the
commencement of the treatment for the termination of pregnancy, and must be signed and dated by the two practitioners.

However, in the case of an emergency abortion ("immediately
necessary, etc.") the certificate may be given by one practitioner,

and may be given before treatment or if that is reasonably impractical not later than 24 hours after termination.

Any certificate must be preserved by the practitioner who terminated the pregnancy to which it relates for a period of three years from the date of termination and may then be destroyed.

Any practitioner who terminates a pregnancy must, within seven days, give to the Chief Medical Officer of the Ministry notice thereof, in the form specified. This requires name and address of practitioner and patient, the ground for terminating pregnancy, and the place and date of termination. Particulars of the practitioners who joined in giving the certificate (in non-emergency cases) must be given. Other information relating to the termination must be given—the woman's marital status, previous pregnancies, number of children, type of termination of pregnancy, whether sterilization was performed, etc.

The information given to the Chief Medical Officer is not to be disclosed to anyone else except:

(a) for the purpose of carrying out their duties:
    (i) to an officer of the Ministry authorised by the C.M.O.; or
    (ii) to the Registrar General or a member of his staff authorised by him; or

(b) for the purposes of carrying out his duties in relation to offences against the Act or the law relating to abortion, to the Director of Public Prosecutions or a member of his staff authorised by him; or

(c) for the purposes of investigating whether an offence has been committed against the Act or the law relating to abortion, to a police officer not below the rank of Superintendent or a person authorised by him; or

(d) for the purposes of bona fide scientific research; or,

(e) for the purposes of criminal proceedings which have begun; or

(f) to the practitioner who terminated the pregnancy; or

(g) to a practitioner with the written consent of the woman whose pregnancy was terminated.

Nurses' participation in abortion

The case of *Royal College of Nursing* v. *Department of Health and Social Security* (1980) concerned the anxiety which had for some years been expressed by and on behalf of nurses called to assist in medically induced abortions. Since 1972, with increasing frequency, operations had been carried out in hospitals and clinics by nurses and midwives, acting under the general supervision of doctors, by the prostoglandin method of inducing labour. The College advised its members that what they were doing was unlawful, and in this case sought a High Court declaration to that effect. In refusing the declaration, Mr. Justice Woolf established the principle as follows:

Where a nurse participates in the process of abortion by medical induction, the treatment is nevertheless conducted by a registered medical practitioner as long as the process is initiated by a registered medical practitioner who remains responsible throughout for its conduct and control in the sense that any actions needed to bring it to a conclusion are done by appropriately skilled staff acting on his specific instructions, and he or another registered medical practitioner is available to be called if required.

The reasons underlying the first decision

Section 1(1) of the Abortion Act 1967, provides: "Subject to the provisions of this section, a person shall not be guilty of an offence under the law relating to abortion when a pregnancy is terminated by a registered medical practitioner."

The judge said that the reason the college had commenced the present proceedings was that its opinion differed from that of the Department on what activities were lawful for nurses to perform in relation to the termination of pregnancy by medical induction. The defence to the criminal offence of abortion provided by section 1(1) of the Abortion Act only applied when pregnancy was determined by a registered medical practitioner. At the time when the Act was passed the normal method of termination adopted by medical practitioners involved surgical intervention, and no difficulty had arisen as to whether or not the termination was by a registered medical practitioner as required by the Act.

However, in recent times there had been increasing reliance on medical methods of induction, one method being the extra-amniotic process. That process was initiated by the registered medical practitioner inserting a catheter through which the prostoglandin solution was to be administered to the patient, and the subsequent steps in the process were either in whole or in part carried out by nurses who would sometimes be responsible for connecting the prostin pump to the catheter so that the abortifacients could be fed into the patient and who would monitor progress of the process which lasted on average about 18 hours and could last for up to 30 hours.

In the medical induction process the registered medical practitioner and the nurse performed the same roles as they did in relation to a normal birth where labour had to be induced by medical means. It could not therefore be suggested that the nurse was not fully qualified from a professional point of view to perform the role which she was called upon to perform in relation to abortions.

Nor did an issue arise as to any conscientious objection which a nurse might have to being involved in the process. The right of conscientious objection was fully recognized in section 4 of the Act which provided that (apart from cases of necessity) no person should be under any duty, whether by contract or by any statutory or other legal requirements, to participate in any treatment authorized by the Act to which he had a conscientious objection.

The Department had circulated a letter with two annexes advising that providing a registered medical practitioner personally decided on and initiated the process of medical induction, and remained responsible for it throughout, it was not necessary for him personally to perform each and every action which was needed for the treatment to achieve its intended objective.

The judge concluded that although a nurse might play a large part in the process, the treatment was still carried out by a registered medical practitioner. No doubt the time was not far ahead when a pregnancy could be terminated merely by the patient taking a pill. If in such circumstances the doctor, having examined the patient, decided that it was a case where, in accordance with section 1, the pregnancy should be terminated, and he complied with the other conditions of section 2, then the fact that the pill might be handed to the patient by the nurse rather than the doctor so that the patient could take the pill, would not mean that the treatment was not that of the doctor. If such a patient were asked who was treating her she would say that it was the doctor, and that the nurse was assisting the doctor in the treatment.

The procedure laid down by the Department made it clear that the registered medical practitioner must decide upon the termination and the process must be initiated by him. He must also remain responsible throughout for its overall conduct and control in the sense that any actions needed to bring it to a conclusion were done by appropriately skilled staff acting on his specific instructions, but not necessarily in his presence, and that he or another registered medical practitioner must be available to be called if required. There was no reason for interpreting the provision of section 1 so narrowly that if anyone other than the registered medical practitioner participated in the treatment, the defence to a charge of unlawful abortion was not available.

The Court of Appeal's disagreement

The view of the Court of Appeal can be neatly summed up in the words of Lord Justice Brightman:

> "It would be a misuse of language to describe such a termination of pregnancy as 'carried out by' a registered medical practitioner, however detailed the instructions he gave to the nurse. The true analysis is that the doctor has provided the nurses with the means to terminate the pregnancy, not that he has terminated it."

This view was amplified by Lord Denning, Master of the Rolls, who, after saying that here was an area in which emotions run very high, added:

> "'Treatment' . . . means the actual act of terminating the pregnancy. When the medical induction method is used it means the continuous act of administering the prostoglandin, from the moment the administering is started until the moment the unborn child is expelled from the mother's body. *That continuous act* has to be done by the doctor personally. It is not sufficient that it is done by a nurse when he is not present."

The House of Lords' decision

In December 1980 it was announced that the Appeal Court's decision had been overturned by the Law Lords, who gave their detailed reasons for the decision in February 1981. The Law Lords' decision was reached by the narrowest majority, of three opinions to two. Nevertheless, that is enough to make a definitive statement of the legal position of nurse participation in extra-amniotic abortion unless and until Parliament steps in. And Parliament is unlikely to step in, given the emotionally-charged disputes which have been created by a number of recent attempts by private members to get the abortion laws changed.

While the reasons given by all five Law Lords differed to a greater or lesser degree from each other, the majority opinion can be seen representatively in the judgment of Lord Diplock, whose conclusion read as follows:

> "What limitation on this exoneration is imposed by the qualif- ying phrase: "when a pregnancy is terminated by a registered medical practitioner"? In my opinion in the context of the Act, what it requires is that a registered medical practitioner, whom I will refer to as a doctor, should accept responsibility for all stages of the treatment for the termination of the preg- nancy. The particular method to be used should be decided by the doctor in charge of the treatment for termination of the pregnancy; he should carry out any physical acts, forming part of the treatment, that in accordance with accepted medical practice are done only by qualified medical practitioners, and should give specific instructions as to the carrying out of such parts of the treatment as in accordance with accepted medical practice are carried out by nurses or other members of the hospital staff without medical qualifications. To each of them, the doctor, or his substitute, should be available to be con- sulted or called on for assistance from beginning to end of the treatment. In other words, the doctor need not do everything with his own hands; the requirements of the subsection are satisfied when the treatment for termination of a pregnancy is one prescribed by a registered medical practitioner carried out in accordance with his directions and of which a registered medical practitioner remains in charge throughout."

By contrast Lord Wilberforce, in a strong dissenting judgment, said:

> "I am of opinion that the development of prostaglandin induc- tion methods invites and indeed merits, the attention of Parliament. It has justly given rise to perplexity in the nursing profession. I doubt whether this will be allayed when it is seen that a majority of the judges who have considered the problem share their views. On this appeal I agree with the judgments in the Court of Appeal that an extension of the Act of 1967 so as to include all persons, including nurses, involved in the administration of prostaglandin is not something which ought to, or can, be effected by judicial decision."

So there the matter rests, unless and until Parliament sees fit to legislate specifically to accommodate procedures which were not, and could not have been, envisaged at the time it passed the 1967 Act.

Conscientious objection to participation in treatment

There are many nurses and midwives who object to having to participate in the process of abortion, at least in some if not in all cases. The objection, a very legitimate one, is envisaged by section 4 of the 1967 Act itself. That section reads as follows:

4.—(1) "Subject to subsection (2) of this section, no person shall be under any duty, whether by contract or by any statutory or other legal requirement, to participate in any treatment authorised by this Act to which he has a conscientious objection:

Provided that in any legal proceedings the burden of proof of conscientious objection shall rest on the person claiming to rely on it.

(2) Nothing in subsection (1) of this section shall affect any duty to participate in treatment which is necessary to save the life or to prevent grave permanent injury to the physical or mental health of a pregnant woman.

It is to be noticed that the exemption from a duty to participate in the process of abortion is itself excluded where the health or life of the pregnant woman is in grave danger. What is more, even in cases where there is no such grave danger, the nurse must adduce evidence of conscientious objection.

As to what amounts to "grave" danger, and what amounts to cogent evidence of conscientious objection, these questions which are essentially ones of fact should be determined according to common sense and common humanity. It testifies to the credit of the nursing profession as a whole that conscientious objectors frequently finish up by assisting in abortions or in treatment connected therewith in order to avoid unnecessary or undesirable further trauma to the patient, with only their own consciences to wrestle with afterwards.

Chapter 13

ADMISSION OF MENTAL PATIENTS

I

Social attitudes to mental disorder

We are now long past the stage of mankind's development when madness or lesser forms of mental disorder were apt to be categorised as "brutish." In consequence the treatment which could be expected to be meted out to the mentally disordered has itself undergone major changes, though it is only in the last two decades that really major advances in attitude and practice, suited to the sophistications and indeed the stresses of modern complex society, have been made. We refer, of course, to the Royal Commission which worked between 1954 and 1957 and whose recommendations formed the major *corpus* of the Mental Health Act 1959. A particularly remarkable difference in attitude between ancient times and ours is found in the view taken of "possession," for instance by evil spirits, now usually classified under one of the organic or functional heads of psychosis. Old skeletons have been found whose skulls contain small bore holes through which the possessing spirits have been enabled to escape. Such "patients" will frequently have been taken to greener pastures simply by the absence of proper sterilisation! Nowadays the treatment of psychotics can, at least in the first instance, be carried out via their own senses and not through a hole in the skull.

It is not necessary, however, to revert to an ancient terminology to classify forms of mental disorder under a variety of labels including "idiot," "imbeciles" and "lunatics." It can be fairly stated that the Mental Health Act 1959 not only facilitated major advances in the structure for the treatment of mental disorder but also advanced a more enlightened and tolerant attitude to the variation of such mental differences from the norm as seen through the eyes of the "ordinary man." It is often the function of the legislature to improve on existing attitudes and practices as distinct from merely reflecting actual views and

280

developments current at the time its legislation is in course of preparation. The whole history of the law relating to the treatment of mental disorder is one of the search for the most appropriate balance which can be struck between the values of, on the one hand, individual (if one wishes, civil) liberty and, on the other, the protection of other members of society from the actions of those who might cause harm to innocent people.

Restraint and freedom

In striking the balance between liberty and restraint for protection's sake, the 1959 Act lays its emphasis on the informal nature of mental treatment. Both this policy and the Act's terminology for the classification of mental disorder serve to remove the social stigma which has, regrettably, long been associated with mental abnormality. Within the overall framework of the Act there are, perforce, some provisions which specifically empower various authorities to restrain certain disordered persons when such restraint is in their own interest, or that of others, or both. A patient's nearest relative may, with the support of medical opinion, set in motion a number of procedures which lead to the admission of the patient for observation or for treatment. The more pressing needs of emergency admission are also catered for. Furthermore the "criminally insane" may be committed to specially secure hospitals, and courts are given the power to specify that treatment in an institution catering for the mentally disordered shall be an alternative to simple, non-treated, incarceration.

This is perhaps not the place to examine the complications which may very well arise if the staff at such a treatment institution are for some reason unwilling to accept such a patient for treatment. A recent instance which has hit the headlines demonstrates the *impasse* which ensues, and shows up in a clear way the operation of the judicial maxim that "the court will not act in vain." The usual instance of the operation of this maxim occurs in cases where an injunction is applied for but is not awarded because the court considers that the order requested is in some way unenforceable. The alternative to treatment is simple incarceration and without commenting on the merits or demerits of a staff refusal of a patient one may at least reflect on the proven statistics relating to the treatment in prisons, which indicate that the very experience of incarceration may constitute one of the steps in the causal process leading to recidivism or a life of crime.

Historical background

As long ago as the reign of Edward II an Act relating to the property of the mentally afflicted distinguished between "lunatics" and "natural fools" but later, this distinction was lost sight of and the series of Lunacy Acts passed during the nineteenth century covered "idiots" and "persons of unsound mind" together. It was not until 1913 that a separate Mental Deficiency Act was passed providing for mental deficiency institutions separate from mental hospitals and for a different system of administration of services for the care of the mentally defective. The lower grade defectives (idiots and imbeciles) could be dealt with either under the Lunacy Acts or under the Mental Deficiency Acts and such patients were sometimes admitted to mental hospitals, as distinct from mental deficiency institutions.

Under the Lunacy Acts provision was made for detention in the lunatic asylums of idiots and imbeciles as well as those who are defined as lunatics. There was an Idiots Act in 1886 and the later Mental Deficiency Acts defined these classes of people. However, the consolidating Lunacy Act of 1890, which was the principal Act for Lunacy and Mental Treatment, applied to all lunatics and included idiots. Under the Mental Deficiency Act of 1913 idiots were defined as

"persons in whose case there exists mental defectiveness of such a degree that they are unable to guard themselves against common physical dangers."

Imbeciles were defined as

"persons in whose case there exists mental defectiveness which, though not amounting to idiocy, is yet so pronounced that they are incapable of managing themselves or their affairs or, in the case of children, of being taught to do so."

The other classes of mentally defective patients, that is feeble-minded and moral defectives, could only be admitted to mental deficiency institutions.

Mental "illness" is, broadly speaking, a disorder of the mind which has previously functioned normally, whereas mental "defectiveness" was defined as a state of arrested or incomplete mental development of such a kind or degree that the individual was incapable of adapting himself to the normal environment of his fellows in such a way as to maintain existence independent of supervision, control, or external support. A person suffering from mental illness can often be restored to normal health, whereas though training can improve the social behaviour of a "mentally defective" person the basic effect is more likely to be permanent. In other words a defective person is not an insane person; he is a person who has never been normal and can never be "cured" although much can be done to help him by training.

The Mental Health Act 1959 contains within its scope both mental illness and mental deficiency. The term "mentally disordered" is used to cover persons suffering from "mental illness, arrested or incomplete development of mind, psychopathic disorder, and any other disorder or disability of mind." (Mental Health Act 1959, s. 4). "Severe subnormality" and "subnormality" are terms introduced by the new Act and replace, in some measure, the classifications used in the Mental Deficiency Acts.

From early times until the present century, legislation for the mentally afflicted was primarily concerned with the protection of the person and his property and the safety of the public, and assumed the need for custody rather than treatment. During the nineteenth century responsibility for providing "asylums" for "pauper lunatics" was given to the Poor Law authorities. The local justices were responsible for licensing and visiting private establishments for the insane outside the metropolitan area, specially appointed commissioners being responsible for the same function in the metropolitan area. In 1845 a permanent Board of Commissioners in Lunacy was established to exercise general supervision over all arrangements for the custody of lunatics; from this developed the Board of Control which was dissolved by section 2 of the Mental Health Act 1959.

The Lunacy Act 1890 consolidated the law in relation to lunatics, and the Mental Treatment Act 1930 introduced treatment of voluntary and temporary patients. Formality was still required and even under the National Health Service Act 1946, when mental health services came under the general framework of hospital services, the procedures for admission, discharge and all other forms of care remained unchanged.

The report of the Royal Commission on the Law relating to Mental Illness and Mental Deficiency (1954–1957: the Percy Commission) is an informative document on this subject, and formed the basis of the Mental Health Act 1959. The fact that the law existing in 1954, when the Commission began work, was very complicated was one of the reasons for the inquiry. Additionally, there had been considerable advances in medical knowledge, the social services had improved, and public opinion towards mental disorder had changed. The terms of reference for the Royal Commission were:

"to inquire, as regards England and Wales, into the existing law and administrative machinery governing the certification, detention, care (other than hospital care or treatment under the National Health Service Acts, 1946–52), absence on trial or licence, discharge and supervision of persons who are or are alleged to be suffering from mental illness or mental defect, other than Broadmoor patients; to consider as regards England and Wales, the extent to which it is now, or should be made, statutorily possible for such persons to be treated, as voluntary patients, without certification; and to make recommendations."

Procedures for admission to Mental Hospitals were more complicated than for other types of hospital and were a deterrent to patients and relatives. In some cases of mental disorder compulsory powers are required but the idea that treatment involved detention had been the underlying principle in former legislation. Prior to the 1959 Act compulsory powers for "certification" required an order from a Justice of the Peace as well as medical evidence and procedures were comparable to persons being taken into custody. The Royal Commission's leading recommendations included:

(a) Recognition of three main groups of patients for legal and administrative purposes: that is, mentally ill; psychopathic; and patients of several subnormal personality.

(b) All forms of hospital and community care should be available without use of compulsory powers and procedures. Compulsory powers should only be used to override the patient's own unwillingness or the unwillingness of relatives for the welfare of the patient or others. There would be special safeguards, and except in an emergency there would be no judicial order except in special circumstances.

(c) Establishment of Mental Health Review Tribunals to provide independent investigation into patients' detention.

(d) A large expansion of local authority community care services.

(e) The abolition of the Board of Control. (This body had been responsible until 1948 for supervising local authorities in discharge of their duties under Lunacy and Mental Deficiency

Acts. Since the 1946 Act, its functions had been mainly the receipt of documents, authority to discharge, visits and inspections.)

The mental deficiency services were launched as separate services, distinct from those for the mentally ill, in the Mental Deficiency Act 1913. This Act provided for the supervision by local authorities of defectives living in the community and where necessary, for defectives to be put under control with powers of detention either by individuals (guardianship) or in institutions managed by local authorities or private bodies. The Act provided for close central control of these new services by the Board of Control, particularly in regard to the detention of patients in institutions or under guardianship—power of discharge (with one exception) and power to continue Orders were given solely to the Board or its Commissioners—and in regard to the reception of defectives into the care of other persons even when there was no power of detention.

Most of the mental deficiency institutions were transferred into the NHS as hospitals vested in the Minister of Health. A few institutions ("certified institutions") remained under private control, the majority being run by religious bodies, and there were also Approved Homes approved by the Minister of Health where private persons received defectives without powers of detention. Other private individuals could receive small numbers of defectives into their care if they obtained the consent of the Board of Control. The Mental Deficiency Act 1927 amended the 1913 Act in several important respects, notably in the definition of mental defectiveness and in an extension of the circumstances in which a defective might be sent to an institution or given into guardianship.

Since the last Mental Deficiency Act was passed, local health authorities were constituted under the NHS Act 1946 with wide powers for the care and after-care of mental defectives (among others). The National Assistance Act 1948 has given to the same local authorities powers to provide residential accommodation for those in need because of "infirmity", and a wide range of services for the handicapped.

The Mental Health Act 1959, by repealing the Mental Deficiency Acts, has removed many criticisms directed against the procedure for admission to mental deficiency institutions and to guardianship and for detention and discharge. The Act brings mental illness and mental deficiency, as previously understood (so far as procedures are concerned), under the same regulations and gives access by patients and relatives to Mental Health Review Tribunals.

The Mental Health Act 1959

> "An Act to repeal the Lunacy and Mental Treatment Acts 1890 to 1930 and the Mental Deficiency Acts 1913 to 1938 and to make fresh provision with respect to the treatment and care of mentally disordered persons and with respect to their property and affairs; and for the purposes connected with the matters aforesaid."

The Act of 1959 was a major piece of legislation which resulted in particular from the three-year long labours of a Royal Commission. The three main principles upon which the Act, following in the main the recommendations of the Royal Commission on the Law Relating to Mental Illness and Mental Deficiency, was based are these: (1) that as much treatment as possible, both in hospital and outside, should be given on a voluntary basis; (2) that the emphasis in mental cases should be shifted as far as possible from institutional care to care within the community; and (3) that "proper" provision should be made for the residual category of cases in which compulsion is necessary, in the interest either of the patient or of society.

Voluntary admissions

In section 5 of the Act it is made clear that there are informal arrangements for admission of patients "without any application, order or direction rendering him liable to be detained under this Act." Formerly, a voluntary patient had to be willing to have treatment and make out an application for admission and discharge. To be admitted it is not necessary to be able to express willingness. Informal admission to mental deficiency hospitals was introduced in 1958 (Circular HM (58)5) and to designated psychiatric establishments in October 1959 under Commencement Order No. 1 of the Mental Health Act. Because section 5 deals with informal arrangements for admission, it is wrong to say that patients admitted informally were admitted "under section 5" of that Act. Under former legislation, informal treatment of mental illness was not allowed because section 315 of the Lunacy Act forbade treatment otherwise than under the provisions of that Act. The Minister of Health, over a year before the introduction of the 1959 Mental Health Act, took a stance leading to the repeal of section 315 of the Lunacy Act, and so mental hospitals were admitting informally without section 5 of the Act being operative at all. An additional point to be noted at this stage is that the Lunacy Act applied to mental hospitals, but under the Mental Health Act 1959 compulsory admission is to a "hospital" are defined in section 147 as "any hospital vested in the Minister under the National Health Services Act 1946."

Balancing interests

In treating the question of freedom or restraint in matters of mental disorder, two complementary aspects of our subject should be kept in mind. The first concerns the extent, if any, to which restrictions may justifiably be placed on individual liberty as a result of the mental condition of a person who is considered to deviate thus wise from some "norm." The other aspect concerns the degree of freedom which may be expected to be exercised, and which in law can be exercised, by those in charge of the restrictive or other treatment of such "deviants." To put the matter crudely: how free may mental deviants expect to be, and how free, in turn, can those people be who are in some way concerned with the preservation of conformity to the "norm"? The vast literature, legal and sociological, on the first question tends to detract attention from the second—as to how free a hand may be exercised in treatment or enforcement of conformity—unfortunately so, because of the complementary nature of the two questions.

One of the principal and avowed aims of a legal system is the preservation of order. In preserving order, or at least in seeking to do so, the law is concerned with the creation and enforcement of norms. In some instances the norms to be enforced are the creation of the law itself, via major legal organs such as the courts and Parliament. In others, while legal organs certainly have their say, and indeed the final say when it comes to the lawfulness or otherwise of certain standards or conduct, it is the function of the law to form an adequate reflection of standards and norms engendered in the first instance by other disciplines. The law, at least the law of England—and in all probability most other legal systems, too—bears witness to the reflection of both these sources of norms. With the relatively recent major advances in psychiatric knowledge the law has had to come to terms with norms engendered in a discipline outside itself and to do its best to accommodate concepts and norms which are in many cases alien to the law as such but which are certainly not unacceptable to it and which can, in a number of ways, be taken over by the law and translated from a non-legal to a legal status.

The Mental Health Act 1959 was based on the Report of the

Royal Commission on the Law Relating to Mental Illness and Mental Deficiency (the Percy Report). One of the basic premises of the report was that people suffering from mental disorder should, as far as possible, be treated in the same way as those suffering from physical illnesses and that compulsion and custody should be used as little as possible. A range of safeguards was proposed for those patients who had to be the subject of compulsory powers and the Commission suggested that decisions on compulsory admission to hospital or guardianship should be a medical instead of a judicial matter. These proposals were embodied in the 1959 Act. The Act also contained a number of general provisions for the mentally ill and handicapped, but over the course of the interim years many of these have been removed from the Act and incorporated in other legislation. For example, Parts II and III have largely been replaced by other Acts, such as the Health Services and Public Health Act 1968 (the relevant provisions of which have been replaced in the National Health Service Act 1977), the Education (Handicapped Children) Act 1970 and the Nursing Homes Act 1975.

Outdated terminology and concepts

The Report of the Royal Commission on Law relating to Mental Illness and Mental Deficiency (1954–1957) dealt in great detail with the various groups of patients and the terminology in use. The Report reviewed the definitions in Mental Deficiency Acts and felt that such terms as "idiot" and "imbecile" were generally regarded as offensive and, in common speech, terms of ridicule or abuse. It also considered that the term "moral defective" was misunderstood as it was felt that the words "moral" and "immoral" generally referred to sexual morality only. The term "person of unsound mind" used in the Lunacy Acts was also criticised as it gave many people the false impression that it implied a state of permanent mental instability. The Commission considered that new terminology was needed to mark a step forward from ancient prejudices and fears, and be an outward sign of a real advance in public sympathy. Although the Mental Health Act of 1959 has four groups in the definition of mental disorder (mental illness, severe subnormality, subnormality and psychopathic disorder) the Royal Commission in fact recommended only three groups.

Their first group was patients suffering from mental illness, including those who became mentally infirm in old age; the second group comprised those patients suffering from personality disorder which did not make them severely subnormal but for whom the term psychopathic personality was used; and their third group was all those patients formerly described as idiots and imbeciles and some who were classified as feeble minded, under a general heading of severely subnormal. The definition of mental disorder under section 4 of the 1959 Act is to be studied carefully. It will be noted that the definition of mental disorder does not include promiscuity or other immoral conduct. At one time, such conduct was considered evidence of disorder: how times have changed! It is recognised that personality defects are not automatically mental disorders, and because people's behaviour does not automatically conform to the established pattern, the Act does not intend that they shall be dealt with as mentally disordered persons, unless requiring medical treatment.

II

Mental disorder

The whole of the Mental Health Act 1959 uses and is based upon a concept of mental disorder, the definition of which is set out in section 4. In particular, powers in respect of involuntary detention are differentiated with specific reference to the categories of disorder set out in section 4. The definition reads:

(1) In this Act "mental disorder" means mental illness, arrested or incomplete development of mind, psychopathic disorder, and any other disorder or disability of mind; and "mentally disordered" shall be construed accordingly.

(2) In this Act "severe subnormality" means a state of arrested or incomplete development of mind which includes subnormality of intelligence and is of such a nature or degree that the patient is incapable of living an independent life or of guarding himself against serious exploitation, or will be so incapable when of an age to do so.

(3) In this Act "subnormality" means a state of arrested or incomplete development of mind (not amounting to severe subnormality) which includes subnormality of intelligence and is of a nature or degree which requires or is susceptible to medical treatment or other special care or training of the patient.

(4) In this Act "psychopathic disorder" means a persistent disorder of disability of mind (whether or not including subnor-

mality of intelligence) which results in abnormally aggressive or
seriously irresponsible conduct on the part of the patient, and
requires or is susceptible to medical treatment.

(5) Nothing in this section shall be construed as implying that
a person may be dealt with under this Act as suffering from
mental disorder described in this section, by reason only of
promiscuity or other immoral conduct.

Powers of detention

Powers of involuntary detention in a suitable institution,
either a mental hospital or a mental unit in a general hospital,
are given by the 1959 Act to the persons specified and by the
procedures outlined principally in sections 25, 26 and 29,
together with other explanatory sections. Powers of involuntary
detention in cases where the mentally disordered person has
fallen foul of the criminal law are governed, in the first instance,
principally by sections 60 and 65. Furthermore, powers are given
by section 136 to policemen to take a mentally disordered person
found in a public place to a "place of safety." The present section
of this chapter examines involuntary detention in civil (non-
criminal) cases, and the following section gives an overview of
the criminal law relating to mentally disordered offenders.

Admission in civil cases "under section" constitutes an infringement of liberty and therefore requires strict observance of
procedures if it is to be a legal infringement.

An application for admission pursuant of s. 25 of the Act may
be made in respect of a patient on the grounds—

(a) that he is suffering from mental disorder to a nature or
degree which warrants the detention of the patient in a hospital
under observation (with or without other medical treatment) for
at least a limited period; and

(b) that he ought to be so detained in the interests of his own
health or safety or with a view to the protection of other persons.

The application under section 25 must ordinarily be found on
the written recommendations in prescribed form of two medical
practitioners including in each case a statement that in the opinion of the practitioner the conditions set out in (a) and (b) above
are complied with. The application may be made by the
patient's "nearest relative" (defined at length in section 49), a
person authorised by a county court or by an officer of a local
social services authority appointed to act as a "mental welfare
officer" for the purposes of the Act (a social worker, usually a
specialist in psychiatric work).

In any case of urgent necessity, an application for admission for observation supported by only one medical recommendation—called an "emergency application"—may be made pursuant to section 29 in respect of a patient either by a mental welfare officer or by *any* relative of the patient, and every such application must include a statement (to be verified in the medical recommendation) that it is of urgent necessity that the patient be admitted and detained for observation and that compliance with the ordinary required formalities would involve undesirable delay. It suffices if such an emergency admission is in the first instance founded on a single medical recommendation given, if practicable, by a practitioner who has had previous acquaintance with the patient. The circularity involved in both these procedures on admission for observation is that detention is permitted only in pursuance of the terms of sections 25 and 29, respectively; but those sections allow of such detention only if there exists "mental disorder of a nature or degree which warrants detention." One might be forgiven for asserting that Parliament did not seem to have made up its mind as to who or what it was that should ultimately authorise detention—the statutory provision itself, or the opinion, referred to in the section, of whichever person is designated to decide upon what is "warranted." The authorised periods of detention are up to 28 days, in the case of section 25, and up to 72 hours in the case of section 29, but it can be extended to 28 days if a second medical recommendation is obtained within the 72 hours.

The nature of, and period of authorised detention specified in section 26 is rather different. Section 26 provides for admission for treatment of patients for one year, and an application under this section may be made in respect of a patient on the grounds:

(a) that he is suffering from mental disorder, being—

    (i) in the case of a patient of any age, mental illness or severe subnormality;

    (ii) in the case of a patient under the age of 21 years, psychopathic disorder or subnormality;

and that the said disorder is of a nature or degree which warrants the detention of the patient in a hospital for medical treatment under this section; and

(b) that it is necessary in the interests of the patient's health or safety or for the protection of others that the patient should be so detained, provided that the application is founded on the written recommendation in the prescribed form of two medical practitioners each stating that, in the opinion of the practitioner, the conditions set out in (a) and (b) above are complied with; and each such recommendation must include such particulars of the grounds for the opinion that the above conditions are fulfilled and also a statement of the reasons for that opinion; and it must also specify whether other methods of dealing with the patient are available, and, if so, why they are not appropriate. Once a patient has been admitted under section 26, he may in the first instance be detained up to one year, although he may be discharged from compulsion at any time by the appropriate authorities including his nearest relative. After one year, authority for detention may be renewed for a further year and thereafter for periods of two years at a time. Further detention may be recommended by the Responsible Medical Officer to the managers if he considers that detention remains necessary in the interests of the patient's own health or safety, or for the protection of others.

The problem of psychopathy

The medical superintendent of Broadmoor recently commented that if four psychiatrists sitting round a table were asked to give a definition of "psychopathy" the questioner would receive five different answers! It is not necessary to enter into the finer points of such lateral humour to appreciate the difficulty which lies in the way of a once-for-all definition of psychopathy. The problem has long faced the medical profession, but lawyers have the particular difficulty of drawing a simple line which will hopefully serve to mark off such disorder from other disorders and from "normality." The definition which is to be found in section 4 of the Mental Health Act 1959 is entirely in behavioural terms:

"In this Act 'psychopathic disorder' means a persistent disorder or disability of mind (whether or not including subnormality of intelligence) which results in abnormally aggressive or seriously irresponsible conduct on the part of the patient, and requires or is susceptible to medical treatment."

The reference in section 4 to treatment is purely consequential and has no real effect on the preceding definition, couched as it is in behavioural terms. In the interests of such patients and in the interests of others with whom such patients are likely to come into contact, it is thought desirable in the legislation which now operates in this area that psychopaths should therefore be susceptible to some form of restraint. The Royal Commission which presented its final report in 1957 specifically examined the problem of psychopathy and its attendant dangers to the sufferer and to others, and recommended that psychopaths should not (in cases other than those involving the commission of a crime) be admitted for treatment after the age of 21; but that if admitted by that age, treatment under some form of restraint could be allowed lawfully to continue up to the age of 25. The problems of adolescence and those of adulthood were compared by the Commission, and it was resolved that a line should be drawn, in the interests of individual freedom, beyond which treatment under restraint should not be permitted (except, as stated, in the case of criminal action by a person who happened to be psychopathic, in which case other restraining provisions of the 1959 Act as mentioned above would operate).

Psychopathy and prevalent attitudes

There are those who consider that a narrowing of opportunities for the lawful restraint of such disordered persons is something to be wished for; there are others, indeed many others, who consider that the age limits in section 26 of the 1959 Act should be removed altogether to facilitate the restrained treatment of "abnormally aggressive" or "seriously irresponsible" patients of *any* age. The latter argue that since the concept of psychopathy is defined in essentially behavioural terms, the risk to other members of society (as well as to the patient himself) is just as great whatever age he happens to be. The division of opinion outlined above is not, however, so clear cut as we chose initially to state it; for it is quite consistent to hold that the definition of "psychopathy" itself be done away with in legislation affecting future trends in the treatment and restraint of the mentally disordered, and at the same time to demand that other members of society receive adequate protection from the dangerous or harmful actions of persons who are, on any medical view, likely to produce such adverse manifestations in behaviour.

The case and the statute

In the case of *Re V.E.* (mental health patient) in 1972, the Divisional Court of the Queen's Bench Division, on appeal by way of special case stated for it by the chairman of a mental

health review tribunal in South West London, had to consider
the outcome of a situation which transpired not to have been
covered by any of the complex provisions of the Mental Health
Act 1959.

A woman aged 40 was admitted in June 1971 for treatment for
mental disorder pursuant to section 26 of the 1959 Act, her
particular mental disorder being labelled "mental illness." As a
result of tubercular meningitis she had suffered irreversible
organic brain damage and this had subsequently led to seriously
irresponsible conduct amounting to a hazard to her own health
and safety and to at least the safety, if not also the health, of
others. She had become an uncontrolled alcoholic and drug taker
and had on occasions been so incapable in the street as to be a
hazard to traffic. In November 1971 the woman applied to the
mental health review tribunal for discharge. At the hearing of her
application the tribunal, being dissatisfied with the original
diagnosis on her admission, directed that the classification
shown in the authority for her detention be amended by sub-
stituting "psychopathic disorder" for "mental illness" pursuant
to section 123(3) of the Act. "Psychopathic disorder" is defined
by section 4(4) of the Act as "a persistent disorder or disability of
mind (whether or not including subnormality of intelligence)
which results in abnormally aggressive or seriously irresponsible
conduct on the part of the patient, and requires or is susceptible
to medical treatment." Not all such patients constitute a danger
to themselves or to others, but it is in the nature of things that
many happen to do so, as did V.E.

The question of law thus arose, whether by reason of this substitution (effectively a reclassification) by the tribunal of
"psychopathic disorder" for "mental illness" in an application
made under section 26 of the Act, the patient might nevertheless
be thereafter detained; or whether, in the words of Lord Widgery
C.J. "notwithstanding that the tribunal refused to order the
patient's discharge on medical grounds she was nevertheless
entitled to be discharged on the ground that as a person over 21
suffering from psychopathic disorder she was never liable to be
detained . . . at all." "The Act," he continued,

> "is conspicuously silent whether the tribunal should itself
> order the discharge of the patient whose release is undesirable
> in his own or the public interest and who still suffers from *some*
> mental disorder, merely because the nature of that disorder
> would not justify a new application for admission made at the
> present time. In substance the argument for the hospital board
> is that if a patient is once detained by virtue of a valid applica-

tion, his detention can be continued so long as he continues to suffer from *some* mental disorder and his release is undesirable in his own or the public interest."

His Lordship indicated that he would not have been surprised if the 1959 Act did indeed have this effect, implying that the balance between liberty and protection would not thus be imperilled. However, he and his two brethren reached the decision on the strict construction of the Act that such was not its intention and the Court ordered, not without regret, that the woman was entitled to be discharged.

The loophole which the 1972 decision exposed has now been filled by the Mental Health (Amendment) Act of 1975. This Act provides for the continued detention of psychopathic patients, if such is the label which now attaches to them following a reclassification, at an age above 25 years, from "mental illness" or "severe subnormality" down, as it were, to the mental disorder which attracts considerably less lawful opportunity for detentive treatment. The purpose of the 1975 Act is to provide for the examination of all such reclassified patients to see whether they would be likely to act in a dangerous manner (to themselves or to others) if discharged. If so, the responsible medical officer may make a report recommending continued detention. Both the patient and the patient's nearest relative will be informed of the contents of such a report, and the patient will, of course, have the right to apply to a mental health review tribunal in the event of dissatisfaction. The onus of making the report is placed squarely on the medical officer; if he does not make a report stating that the patient will be likely to act in a manner dangerous to himself or others if released, the authority for detention will *ipso facto* automatically lapse and the patient will be discharged. If the patient is detained for such a continued period, there will also be the two-yearly report by the doctor, and if not considered dangerous the patient will be released.

Guardianship

Guardianship under the 1959 Act replaces to some extent the provisions for guardianship under the repealed Mental Deficiency Acts.

Guardianship is intended to provide power of control over the patient's residence and everyday life, should it be necessary in the case of a small minority of patients, for their own welfare or protection of others. It may also be used as a form of control over mentally disordered persons who do not need to be in hospital.

Section 33 of the Act details the grounds for making an application for guardianship, which are the same as those for treatment under section 26. Applications are made to the local authority with two medical recommendations, and the guardian (which may be the local authority) will be named in the application.

When an application is accepted by the authority, the guardian may exercise such powers in relation to the patient as if he were the father of the patient and the patient was under 14 years of age (section 34). Specific powers conferred on guardians, generally, include control of correspondence and leave and local authorities specifically have duties in relation to acceptance of applications (section 34), absence without leave (section 40), transfer of guardianship in case of death of a guardian (section 42), renewal of authority (section 43), discharge (section 47) and also transfers, visits and supervision. The guardian must appoint a medical attendant and make arrangements for occupation, training, welfare, etc., of the patient in accordance with the provisions of Mental Health (Hospital and Guardianship) Regulations 1960.

Guardianship, under the 1959 Act, replaced (with some differences) the provisions of guardianship under the Mental Deficiency Acts. It can also be used as a form of control over mentally ill patients who do not need to be in hospital and, to this extent, it replaced provision of the Lunacy and Mental Treatment Acts. It was anticipated that, in almost all cases, it would be possible for patients to receive care in the community *without* being subject to the control of guardianship. It was felt, however, that the powers of control over a patient's place of residence and his everyday life may be necessary in a minority of cases for the welfare of patients or protection of others. The provisions of the Act relating to guardianship have not been widely used in most areas of the country and the extent to which guardianship has been applied no doubt has varied according to the attitude of the officers concerned and the circumstances of the local authority.

Many cases of mentally subnormal patients have been resolved without recourse to guardianship by personal efforts of social workers and others involved. In some cases it may have been considered that in order to protect the finances of a patient, guardianship would be appropriate, but more often the Court of Protection services are used for this purpose. If the local authority officers considered it would be necessary to go into a home to visit a mentally disordered person, and it was likely that admission would be refused, then the use of guardianship could override this objection.

III

Mental disorder and criminal law

One of the marks of a civilised society is the degree to which it is prepared to exculpate offenders against the criminal law who are, in some major respect, different from the ordinary category of wrongdoers. A clear and necessary exception is that of the minor who is lacking in the so-called "mischievous discretion" necessary for the commission of a crime. Over the course of development of the English criminal law it has become increasingly clear that even adult offenders may also include categories which deserve exceptional treatment. In the case of mentally disordered persons, English law has shown a growing tendency to make special rules for such people both in respect of the principles of criminal liability and in respect of the method of treatment. The purpose of this section is, after some historical comments, to give a brief survey of the attitude of the legislature and the judiciary to mentally disordered persons who come into contact with the criminal law.

In Greek and Roman literature there occur references to the principle that people not in possession of mental faculties should not be treated as if they were perfectly normal. However, English law as it stood before the Norman Conquest displayed no such indulgence, and the laws of these times reflected the principle of absolute liability for wrongdoing, regardless of inadvertence, infancy and insanity. Such a policy no doubt resulted from the cumulative effect of two factors: the relatively rough-and-ready system of trial with its unsophisticated modes of proof, and the lack of understanding of the nature and causes of mental disorder. In the thirteenth century exceptions began to appear, and the celebrated commentator on the early common law, Henry Bracton, wrote that "an insane one is one who does not know what he is doing, is lacking in mind and reason, and is not far removed from the brutes." In these early times the plea of insanity was not frequent, but its use increased with the growth of relatively minor offences which nevertheless attracted the death penalty. As late as the seventeenth century it was necessary in order that the accused should be excused from normal criminal liability, to prove that he suffered from mental abnormality to an extreme degree. The analogy with "brutes" occurs in a case tried in 1724 in which the judge ruled that "in order to be excused from criminal liability the accused must not know what he is doing, no more than an infant, a brute or a wild beast."

The M'Naghten Rules

The next major development in this area, namely the formation of the M'Naghten (variously spelt) Rules, occurred in 1843. In that year, Daniel M'Naghten was tried for the murder of Henry Drummond, private secretary to Sir Robert Peel, the Prime Minister. It was found that the accused suffered from delusions and he was found not guilty on the grounds of insanity. The M'Naghten Rules are the result of the recommendations of a large number of judges to the House of Lords in consequence of the widespread discussion which followed the acquittal. The Rules are not laid down in a case *decided* by the House of Lords, but they have been recognised again and again as representing the law, in this jurisdiction and in others.

The burden of proof of insanity lies on the person who alleges it, namely the accused, though the weight of this burden is not as great as that on the prosecution who must prove criminal liability beyond reasonable doubt. To be exempt from normal criminal liability the accused must show: that he was suffering from a disease of the mind, and from a "defect of reason" due to such disease, with the result that he did not appreciate the nature and quality of his act. That is to say, on account of his mental condition he did not know what he was doing. The accused will also come within the Rules when, even if he knew what he was doing, nevertheless he did not know it was wrong. "Wrong" in this context has been held to mean "legally wrong," so that a belief (resulting from a defect of reason due to disease of the mind) that the criminal act was justifiable in the opinion of most ordinary people would not suffice to excuse from liability. Finally, under the M'Naghten Rules, where a man commits a criminal act under an insane delusion, he is responsible to the same degree as he would have been on the facts as he imagined them to be. Thus it will be no excuse to show that the accused suffered from the delusion that someone had defamed his good name and that he killed that person in consequence of the delusion.

It can be seen that the wording of these Rules, which still represent the English criminal law relating to insanity in spite of their antiquity, bears a strong resemblance to the phraseology used by courts in earlier times when knowledge and understanding of mental disorder was minimal. The Rules have time and again attracted criticism for their crudeness and for their drawing of distinctions which are thoroughly inadequate in the light of modern psychiatric medicine. There is clearly much truth in such criticisms, but despite the recommendations of the Royal Commission on Capital Punishment which reported to Parliament in 1953, the Rules themselves remain unchanged. It is, however, fair to say that while medicine is concerned with the treatment of individual cases according to their own particular nature, the criminal law as such must confine its attention to the drawing of a line between those forms of mental disorder which will exempt from criminal liability, and those which will not.

Consequences of a plea of insanity

When the accused is found to have been insane at the time of the act for which he is charged, he is ordered to be detained under the provisions of the Criminal Procedure (Insanity) Act 1964, according to which he is detained at the Queen's pleasure in a hospital to be specified by the Home Secretary. Nowadays, after the effective abolition of the death penalty for murder and all lesser crimes, the plea of insanity is rarely raised. To take 1970 as an example, there were only two cases in which the M'Naghten Rules were successfully pleaded by adults. In the none-too-distant and relatively barbaric days of the English criminal law when a whole host of capital offences existed the plea of insanity had a far greater part to play. Unless there is a question of possible execution, the accused will usually prefer a sentence of imprisonment of fairly definite duration to an unspecified period of detention consequent on a verdict of insanity.

Diminished responsibility

The introduction into the law of the plea of diminished responsibility to a charge of murder very greatly reduced the practical effects of such shortcomings in the area of the criminal law in which the question of insanity is most likely to arise. Section 2 of the Homicide Act 1957 provides that where a person kills, or is a party to the killing of another, he shall not be convicted of murder if he was suffering from such abnormality of mind (whether arising from a condition of arrested or retarded development of mind or any inherent causes or induced by disease or injury) as substantially impaired his responsibility for his acts and omissions in doing or being a party to the killing. A person who, but for this provision, would be liable to be convicted of murder is liable to be convicted of manslaughter. Thus, while insanity is as a matter of fact pleaded by the accused only in cases of murder, the plea of diminished responsibility is so restricted as matter of law. It should be noted that diminished responsibility is a plea in mitigation and does not amount to an exculpation from criminal liability. Its effect is that, since murder is the only crime for which the sentence is fixed (life imprisonment), a verdict of manslaughter can be followed by a variety of forms of treatment of the offender. Any sentence may be imposed, ranging from life imprisonment to an unconditional discharge. What is of much more significance for our present purposes is that a hospital or guardianship order may be made under section 60 of the Mental Health Act 1959. Additionally a restriction order may be placed on such an order with the result that the accused cannot be discharged for a fixed or indefinite period without consent of the Secretary of State. Hospital orders are made as a result of medical evidence that the accused is suffering from one of the four types of mental disorder defined in section 4 of the Mental Health Act 1959, namely mental illness, subnormality, severe subnormality and psychopathic disorder.

Such orders may be made also, of course, in the case of other crimes where the offender is found to be in need of treatment for his disorder. Section 60(2) of the 1959 Act provides, furthermore:

"Where a person is charged before a magistrates' court with any act or omission as an offence and the court would have power, on convicting him of that offence, to make [a hospital or guardianship order] in his case as being a person suffering from mental illness or severe subnormality, then, if the court is satisfied that the accused did the act or made the omission charged, the court may, if it thinks fit, make such an order without convicting him."

An alternative mode of treatment for the mentally disordered offender is provided for by the Powers of Criminal Courts Act 1973, as amended. In cases other than those in which the sentence is fixed by law (*i.e.* other than murder cases), the court may make a probation order, on condition that the accused undergoes a period of mental treatment not exceeding one year, either taken in or out of hospital. As is the case with hospital and guardianship orders, these orders are made on the basis of medical reports. In the case of a person already serving a sentence of imprisonment, if the Secretary of State is satisfied by reports from at least two medical practitioners that the person is suffering from one of the four forms of mental disorder specified in section 4 of the 1959 Act, and that such disorder is of a nature or degree which warrants the detention of the patient in a hospital for medical treatment, an order may be made for transference to such an institution.

The development of English law relating to the treatment of the mentally disordered offender has achieved a degree of sophistication only in comparatively recent times. The principle of treatment, upon which hospital and guardianship orders are based, is clearly differentiated from that of punishment. Major developments in modern psychiatric medicine provide a realistic background against which courts of law are empowered to exercise their discretion. Yet the law still embodies the M'Naghten Rules which, although relevant only to a numerically insignificant number of cases, can be linked with an age when little if any distinction was made between madmen and wild beasts.

The legitimacy of section 65

In the summer of 1980 the European Commission on Human Rights delivered an opinion critical of the procedure by which restriction orders under section 65 are administered under English law. Article 5, para. 4 of the European Convention on Human Rights (which the United Kingdom has signed) says that "Everyone who is deprived of his liberty by arrest or detention shall be entitled to take legal proceedings by which the lawfulness of his detention shall be speedily decided by a court and his release ordered if the detention is not lawful." Restricted patients can appeal to a mental health review tribunal which is independent and hears evidence from both sides; but the final decision is that of the Home Secretary, to whom the tribunal makes its recommendation, and it is the discretionary nature of that final decision which poses the problem of its legitimacy.

Chapter 14

THE MENTAL PATIENT

I

Administration of psychiatric hospitals

The administration of psychiatric hospitals is mainly the same as for other hospitals, and the law relating to mental disorder must be understood by those working in other than psychiatric hospitals. As the number of psychiatric units in general hospitals increases and amalgamation of general and psychiatric hospitals continues, the differences between psychiatric and other hospitals will decrease. With the introduction of the National Health Service in 1948 many psychiatric hospitals became groups by themselves, and their size, location, history and legal requirements tended to make the differences more apparent. One of the main differences, however, was that mental hospitals were required to have a superintendent who would be a medical practitioner unless the Minister directed otherwise. The N.H.S. (Superintendent of Mental Hospitals) Regulations 1960 removed the statutory obligation to have a superintendent, although hospital authorities are allowed to have one if they wish.

The modern tendency is now towards the "running down" of large mental hospitals and in the direction of greater integration of the treatment of mental disorder in (i) general hospitals and (ii) the community, by means of available social services.

Functions of managers

The managers of a hospital were defined in section 59 of the Mental Health Act 1959 as the Hospital Management Committee or Board of Governors, and, in relation to a special hospital, the Minister of Health. The special hospitals are dealt with in Part VII of the Act, and are those institutions which appear to the Minister to be necessary for persons subject to detention who, in the opinion of the Minister, require treatment under conditions of special security on account of their dangerous, violent or criminal propensities. In relation to a mental nursing home registered under the Nursing Homes Act 1975, the person or persons registered in respect of the home are the managers.

Section 14 of the N.H.S. Reorganisation Act 1973 abolished (*inter alia*) Hospital Management Committees, and the definition of the "managers" in section 59 became the Area Health Authority or special authority responsible for the administration of the hospital. Section 47 of the 1959 Act (referring to discharge of patients) was also amended to provide for the new definition of the authorities. "Regional Hospital Board" becomes "Regional Health Authority."

Managers have various functions, some of which may be delegated to officers, but some which they must carry out by themselves. The power to *detain* patients admitted under the Act rests *entirely* with the managers, and the managers, along with others, have power to *discharge* these patients. The powers to detain patients admitted under the Act are in sections 31(2) and 63(1). The power of the managers to discharge under section 47 can be exercised by three members and these functions *cannot* be delegated to officers. Generally, all hospital management committee members are authorised to discharge patients, and normally any three acting together deal with requests for discharge. It is in fact rare for managers themselves to discharge, and this function is normally carried out by the Responsible Medical Officer (for whom see later). Managers are also required to consider reports renewing the authority for detention of patients under section 43.

Regulation 24 of the Mental Health (Hospital and Guardianship) Regulations 1960 permit the delegation to individual officers or to a class of officers of particular functions. These relate to the rectification of documents under section 32 of the Act and to the retaking of patients under section 40. The view of the Minister of Health was that both medical and senior administrative officers should be so authorised.

Regulation 20 provides that any document which is to be sent or furnished to the managers may either be sent by post or delivered personally to the managers or to any person authorised by them to receive documents on their behalf. Some of the documents may need to be received at night or at other times when staff who would normally receive them during the day are not on duty. The patient's relative may wish to hand a notice of intention to discharge the patient to a nurse or psychiatric social

worker when visiting the hospital. The managers are required to
ensure that suitable officers or classes of officers are authorised to
receive documents bearing these circumstances in mind.

Local Authority Services

Local authority services are now provided for by Schedule 8 of
the National Health Service Act 1977:

"A local social services authority may, with the Secretary of
State's approval, and to such extent as he may direct, shall
make arrangements for the purpose of the prevention of illness
and for the care of persons suffering from illness and for the
after-care of persons who have been so suffering and in
particular . . . for:

- (a) the provision, equipment and maintenance of
  residential accommodation for the care of persons
  with a view to preventing them from becoming ill,
  the care of persons suffering from illness and the
  after-care of persons who have been so suffering;
- (b) the provision, for persons whose care is undertaken
  with a view to preventing them from becoming ill,
  persons suffering from illness and persons who have
  been suffering, of centres or other facilities for training them or keeping them suitably occupied and the
  equipment and maintenance of such centres;
- (c) the provision, for the benefit of such persons as are
  mentioned in the last foregoing paragraph, of
  ancillary or supplementary services; and
- (d) as regards persons suffering from mental disorder
  within the meaning of the Mental Health Act 1959,
  the appointment of officers to act as mental welfare
  officers under the Act and, in the case of such
  persons so suffering as are received into
  guardianship under Part IV of that Act (whether the
  guardianship of the local health authority or of other
  persons) the exercise of the functions of the
  authority in respect of them."

Further parts of section 12 of the 1968 Act include extension of
local authority functions under the National Health Service Act
1946. Local authorities have to make provision for care and training of children in lieu of education where it appears necessary.

The process of change

One of the basic principles of the 1959 Act was to ensure that there was a comprehensive community care service to meet the needs of all types of mentally disordered persons not needing hospital treatment.

The progress which has been made varies in different parts of the country, and whilst a number of hostels have been provided, it could hardly be expected that local authorities would be able to rehouse all the patients who did not need the full facilities of hospitals. The hospitals had mainly been provided by the local authorities, and hostels for elderly people as well as handicapped adults and children are high in their priorities. The "mental welfare officers" appointed by local authorities replaced to some extent the "duly authorised officers" but their duties and responsibilities have increased. Whilst they had previously been able to obtain a judicial order to admit a person to hospital, the 1959 Act only provides for an application to a specified hospital. The hospital is not obliged to admit any patient but regional health authorities do have to ensure that there are sufficient beds to enable general practitioners and local authorities to obtain admission of patients in emergency. Local arrangements in most parts of the country have covered this need without difficulty.

Sections 11 to 13 of the Mental Health Act 1959, refer to provisions for care and training of children in lieu of education, and the responsibilities of local authorities in this context cover children of compulsory school age. Until 1971 the responsibility for mentally subnormal children in hospital who were of school age and unable to attend for education at school, rested with the Secretary of State for Social Services. Schools were provided at the hospitals, and the teachers and other staff were appointed and paid by the hospital authorities. The Education (Handicapped Children) Act 1970 brought within the education system on 1st April 1971 those children in England and Wales who, under previous law, were determined as unsuitable for education at school, and also provided for staffs, buildings and facilities already in existence to pass to local education authorities. Arrangements were made for the necessary transfer of staff to new conditions of service.

The Local Authority Social Services Act 1970 implemented the principal recommendations of the Seebohm Report. The main purpose of the Act was to provide a unified system of personal services in partnership with an integrated National Health Service. The personal services come under one department headed by a Director of Social Services under a Social

Services Committee. Functions of these committees include all those responsibilities which were formerly under the mental, children's and welfare committees.

The mental welfare officer has many important functions under the Mental Health Act 1959. What has happened in practice is that the mental welfare officers have become social workers, and the term "generic" has been applied to all social workers under the Social Services Committee. The National Health Services Act 1977 requires local authorities "as regards persons suffering from mental disorder within the meaning of the Mental Health Act 1959" to appoint officers to act as mental welfare officers under that Act. In most local authority areas, social workers in addition to those who were formerly mental welfare officers are now authorised for this purpose.

Mental nursing homes and residential homes

The expression "mental nursing home" is defined for legal purposes by section 2 of the Nursing Homes Act 1975:

(1) In this Act "mental nursing home" means, subject to subsection (2) below, any premises used, or intended to be used, for the reception of, and the provision of nursing or other medical treatment (including care and training under medical supervision) for, one or more mentally disordered patients (meaning persons suffering, or appearing to be suffering, from mental disorder), whether exclusively or in common with other persons.

(2) In this Act "mental nursing home" does not include any hospital as defined in subsection (3) below, or any other premises managed by a Government department or provided by a local authority.

(3) In subsection (2) above "hospital" means—
  (a) any hospital vested in the Secretary of State by virtue of the National Health Service Act 1946;
  (b) any accommodation provided by a local authority, and used as a hospital by or on behalf of the Secretary of State under the National Health Service Acts 1946 to 1973 [now 1977]; and
  (c) any special hospital within the meaning of section 40(1) of the National Health Service Reorganisation Act 1973.

The definition of registration authority for these homes was changed under the N.H.S. Reorganisation Act 1973. Section 41(1) of the 1973 Act makes "the Minister" the registration authority, and the responsibility is, therefore, with the Secretary of State for Social Services and not the local authority.

The Mental Health (Registration and Inspection of Mental Nursing Homes) Regulations 1960 give details of the form registration will take, and provides for six-monthly inspections of these homes.

Section 3 of the Nursing Homes Act 1975 states that any application for registration in respect of a mental nursing home, shall specify whether or not it is proposed to receive there any patients who are liable to be detained under the provisions of the Mental Health Act 1959. Where the home is registered to receive such patients the fact shall be specified in the certificate of registration, and the particulars of the registration shall be entered by the registration authority in a separate part of the register. It is a condition of registration that the number of persons kept at any one time in the home (excluding persons carrying on, or employed in, the home and their families) does not exceed such number as may be specified in the certificate of registration (s. 8, 1975 Act). The registration authority may include any conditions regulating the age, sex or other category of persons who may be received in the home. Section 8 also states that a person carrying on a home shall be guilty of an offence if any condition imposed is not complied with, and the penalties are prescribed in this section. Apart from fines, the registration may be cancelled. No regulations have yet been made under the 1975 Act, but the following regulations have effect as if made thereunder: Mental Health (Registration and Inspection of Mental Nursing Homes) Regulations 1960 and Conduct of Mental Nursing Homes Regulations 1962. The Conduct of Mental Nursing Homes Regulations 1962 came into operation on September 13, 1962, and require the managers of mental nursing homes to provide accommodation, care and staff of a satisfactory standard. The managers of these homes shall:

(a) provide for each patient efficient nursing care and for this purpose employ by day and night suitably qualified and competent staff in numbers which are adequate having regard to the size of the home and the number and condition of the patients received there;

(b) provide for each patient in the home by day and night reasonable accommodation and space having regard to his age and sex and the nature and degree of the mental disorder or other illness or disability from which he is suffering;

(c) provide adequate and suitable furniture, bedding, curtains and, where necessary, screens and floor covering in rooms occupied or used by patients;

(d) provide appropriate and suitable medical and nursing equipment, having regard to the condition of the patients received there;

(e) provide for the use of patients a sufficient number of wash-basins and baths fitted with hot and cold water supply, a sufficient number of water-closets and any necessary sluicing facilities;

(f) provide adequate light, heating and ventilation in all parts of the home occupied or used by patients;

(g) keep all parts of the home occupied or used by patients in good structural repair, clean and reasonably decorated;

(h) take adequate precautions against the risk of fire and accident, having regard in particular to the mental and physical condition of such patients as are received there;

(i) provide sufficient and suitable kitchen equipment, crockery and cutlery, together with adequate facilities for the preparation and storage of food;

(j) supply adequate, suitable and properly prepared food for every patient;

(k) arrange for the regular laundering of linen and articles of clothing;

(l) arrange as may be necessary for the provision for any patient of medical and dental services, whether under Part IV of the National Health Service Act 1946, or otherwise;

(m) make suitable arrangements for the safe keeping and handling of drugs.

Section 1 of the Residential Homes Act 1980 defines a residential home for mentally disordered persons. Subsection (3) provides:

> "In this Act "residential home for mentally disordered persons" means any establishment the sole or main object of which is, or is held out to be, the provision of accommodation, whether for reward or not, for mentally disordered persons, but does not include—
>
> (a) any hospital within the meaning of section 147(1) of the Mental Health Act 1959;
>
> (b) any mental nursing home within the meaning of the Nursing Homes Act 1975; or
>
> (c) any other premises managed by a government department or provided by a local authority."

Sections 37 to 40 of the National Assistance Act 1948 (which relate to the registration, inspection and conduct of homes for disabled persons and old persons) apply in relation to residential homes for mentally disordered persons as they apply in relation to homes to which those enactments applied immediately before the commencement of the 1959 Act.

Section 20 of the 1959 Act, and the National Assistance (Registration of Homes) (Amendment) Regulations 1960 detail the Conditions of Registration, and the National Assistance (Conduct of Homes) Regulations 1962 cover the requirements for these homes. The conditions are similar to those for mental nursing homes and penalties are similarly prescribed for breach of conditions of registration. It will be noted that these residential homes do not include "provision of nursing or other medical treatment" which is a requirement for mental nursing homes. Under Section 22 of the 1959 Act a mental welfare officer may

> "at all reasonable times, after producing, if asked to do so, some duly authenticated document showing that he is such an officer, enter and inspect any premises (not being a hospital) in the area of that authority in which a mentally disordered patient is living, if he has reasonable cause to believe that the patient is not under proper care."

Special hospitals

Special hospitals for the purposes of the Act are institutions provided by the Secretary of State for Social Services under the provisions of section 4 of the National Health Service Act 1977 for persons subject to detention under the Mental Health Act 1959, being persons who, in the opinion of the Secretary of State, require treatment under conditions of special security, on account of their dangerous, violent or criminal propensities. These hospitals are controlled and managed directly by the Secretary of State.

In 1959, a working party considered the role of the special hospitals (Broadmoor, Rampton and Moss Side) and in 1961, the Ministry of Health gave advice on "Treatment of Psychiatric Patients under Security Conditions" (HM Circular (61)69). It was made clear that National Health Service Hospitals should provide services in hospitals for mentally disordered persons to deal with certain types of violent and dangerous patients. Admission to special hospitals should only be used if it is reasonably clear that a patient cannot be treated elsewhere. Special units at some psychiatric hospitals cope with many of these difficult patients, and regional health authorities are required to make provision for psychiatric treatment under secure conditions. It is not necessary for a patient to have been before the courts to be admitted to a special hospital, but the needs of the individual will decide which type of accommodation is most appropriate for treatment. Admissions to special hospitals are approved by the Secretary of State for Social Services, and requests for admission or transfer should give full details of the patient's disorder and say why other accommodation is unsuitable.

Part VII of the 1959 Act laid a duty on the Minister of Health to "provide such institutions as appear to him to be necessary for persons subject to detention under this Act, being persons who, in the opinion of the Minister, require treatment under conditions of special security on account of their dangerous, violent or criminal propensities."

Regional secure units

Following publication of the Butler Report in 1976 (Report of the Committee on Mentally Abnormal Offenders, Cmnd. 6244) the Government made available £17.2 million for the construction of regional secure units. These psychiatric units are now in the course of planning or building in each health service region. They are for mentally disordered patients who require more security than can be provided by local hospitals but not of the degree provided by the special hospitals.

The so-called "criminally disordered" may at some time later than their original detention be transferred from a special hospital (and the point will no doubt apply also in respect of transfers from the regional secure psychiatric units when they are operational) to a local hospital. It will normally be the practice that such a patient is first interviewed to assess suitability in relation to the receiving hospital.

II

The Responsible Medical Officer

In section 59 of the Mental Health Act 1959, the "Responsible Medical Officer" means:

    (a) in relation to a patient liable to be detained by virtue of an application for admission for observation or an application for admission for treatment, the medical practitioner in charge of the treatment of the patient;

(b) in relation to a patient subject to guardianship, a medical officer authorised by the local authority to act (either generally or in any particular case or for any particular purpose) as the responsible medical officer.

The chief duties of the R.M.O. in relation to hospital patients are powers to grant leave of absence, powers of discharge, power to make a report barring discharge by nearest relative and power to make statutory reports which renew authority for detention. All hospital patients should be under the care of a senior medical officer (normally a consultant) who is in charge in the sense that he is not responsible or answerable for the patient's treatment to any other doctor. This doctor will usually be the R.M.O., and it is necessary for another senior doctor to be made responsible for certain functions whilst the normal R.M.O. is away due to leave, sickness, etc. A guardian appoints a "nominated medical attendant" and this may be a medical officer of the local authority, but the responsible medical officer will always be appointed by the local authority. For patients in hospital on an informal basis, the term "medical practitioner in charge of treatment" is substituted for R.M.O.

Duties of the Responsible Medical Officer

In Part IV of the Act the following provisions refer to duties of R.M.O.s in relation to patients liable to detention under that part:

s. 36: Correspondence addressed to or sent by a patient may be withheld under certain conditions;

s. 38: the R.M.O. may reclassify a patient's form of mental disorder;

s. 39: the R.M.O. may grant leave of absence subject to such conditions as he considers necessary;

s. 43: report on the need for continued detention (see also, now, Mental Health (Amendment) Act, 1975);

s. 44: report on psychopathic or subnormal patients within two months of reaching age of 25 years;

s. 45: report on patients (if necessary) absent without leave when liability to detention is due to cease;

s. 47: discharge of patients may be ordered;

s. 48: a "barring certificate," which makes an order for discharge by the nearest relative ineffective, may be furnished.

Where patients are detained under a court order (Part V, 1959 Act) without restrictions, the R.M.O.'s powers and responsibilities are the same as those for patients liable to detention for treatment under section 26. If a restriction order is in force, or for prisoners transferred to hospital, the R.M.O. reports to the Home Secretary. He is required, however, to keep such patients under view, and report to the managers not less frequently than he would under section 43. Forms are prescribed for the various reports by R.M.O.s. Under section 30(2) the medical practitioner in charge of treatment may issue a report which has the effect of detaining a patient for three days, and the doctor in charge of the patient's treatment is then the responsible medical officer. The point is here that the patient is informal, but the doctor thinks he should be subjected to compulsion.

Mental health review tribunals

A mental health review tribunal has been appointed for each of the 15 regions in England and Wales in accordance with section 3 and the first schedule of the Act. Offices and staff for the tribunals are provided by the Ministry of Health. The tribunal consists of legal members, medical members and persons with administrative experience and knowledge of social services or such other qualifications as are considered suitable. Appointments are made by the Lord Chancellor, after consultation with the Minister of Health except for legal members. One of the legal members of each mental health review tribunal is appointed chairman by the Lord Chancellor and any three members may exercise the jurisdiction of the Tribunal provided that one member is drawn from each of the classes described above.

Persons aggrieved by any order may, under the Mental Health Act 1959, in circumstances described in the Act and within time limits provided, appeal to a mental health review tribunal. Such persons will be patients subject to detention and relatives of such patients whose request for discharge has been refused. A tribunal shall then hear the appeal and may cause such enquiries to be made as it thinks proper. After hearing the appeal the tribunal may make an order (a) to discharge the patient if satisfied that it is not necessary for him to be detained; or (b) to adjourn the inquiry to another date which seems convenient. A tribunal may sometimes make no order at all in which case the order in force before the appeal continues to be effective. A tribunal also has the power to reclassify a patient to another form of mental disorder.

Sections 122–124 of the Act refer to applications to and powers of tribunals, and provide for rules of procedure to be made by the Lord Chancellor. These rules, the Mental Health Review Tribunal Rules 1960, are concerned with procedures for making and hearing applications, and set out official forms which will be used in all cases. Provision is made for evidence, medical examination and the way in which a hearing will be conducted. The Secretary of State for Social Services may refer an application to a tribunal, and there are provisions in the rules and the Act for the Home Secretary to refer patients to tribunals for advice. Tribunals sit in private unless the applicant requests otherwise. The statement to the tribunal will give reasons why the responsible authority (that is, managers, responsible medical officers, etc.) is not willing to discharge the patient.

Within the Mental Health Act 1959 are the times when detained patients may apply to tribunals, and the rights of these patients to apply are given in leaflets which are recommended for issue to patients and relatives. Tribunals are appropriate only if the responsible medical officer or managers are not willing to discharge, or if the nearest relative is unwilling or not allowed to discharge (s. 48). The main occasions on which applications may be made to tribunals are as follows:

(a) on admission to hospital: s. 31(4);

(b) on reception into guardianship: s. 34(5);

(c) on reclassification: s. 38(2);

(d) on transfer from guardian ship to hospital: s. 41(5);

(e) on renewal of authority for detention or guardianship: s. 43(6);

(f) subnormal or psychopathic patient detained beyond the age of 25: s. 44(3);

(g) on report barring discharge by nearest relative: s. 48(3);

(h) by nearest relative having been deprived of his power of discharge by court order: s. 52(6).

These provisions give the various time limits for applications by a patient himself or by the nearest relative. Patients detained under court orders without restriction have rights of appeal to tribunals. Those with restrictions under section 65 have no rights of appeal, but after 12 months can ask the Home Secretary to refer their case to a tribunal. This is for advice and the Home Secretary is not bound to accept the advice of the tribunal (s. 66).

Mental health review tribunals took over one of the functions held by the Board of Control as an independent authority looking after the rights of the individual. Tribunals usually meet to deal with applications at the hospital where the patient is detained, and although it has been suggested that some staff feel that a tribunal is enquiring into the conditions at the hospital, the relationship between tribunals and hospitals is generally clearly understood.

The Mental Health Review Tribunal Rules require that applications to the tribunal will be made on a prescribed form and require the tribunal or the responsible authority to supply a form on request to any patient or relative who has a right to make an application. Hospitals in which patients are detained and local health authorities in whose area there are patients under guardianship, should hold stocks of the prescribed forms which can be obtained from the Stationery Office. When the application is received at the offices of the mental health review tribunal a copy of the application will be sent to the responsible authority, with a request for information, both factual and opinion. If the applicant has a right to apply, the tribunal will then arrange for the necessary hearing. The medical member of the tribunal will examine the patient prior to the hearing and form an opinion on the patient's mental condition.

At the hearing the responsible medical officer will usually be present to answer any questions put to him by the tribunal, and other persons, for example, social workers, may be brought as witnesses when necessary. Legal representation is unlikely to be necessary but under the new legal aid scheme in 1973 it is possible for a patient or his nearest relative who is subject to eligibility on financial grounds, to have assistance as well as advice in the case of an application to a tribunal. Legal aid would not include representation at the hearing.

Management of patients' property and affairs

Sections 100–121, Part VIII, Mental Health Act 1959, are concerned with the management of property and affairs of patients.

HM(60)80 to hospital authorities and Circular 23/60 to local authorities amplify the provisions of Part VIII, Mental Health Act 1959, and Form P.N.1A. issued by the Court of Protection explains what should be done when a mentally disordered patient has assets which need to be protected or which cannot be used for his benefit (or when necessary the benefit of his dependants) because he is incapable of managing his own affairs. There is no presumption that because a person is a patient in a psychiatric hospital he is *ipso facto* incapable of managing his own affairs; the decision is dependent on each individual patient's mental capacity.

The Court of Protection continues as an office of the Supreme Court. The functions of the Court expressly conferred on a judge are exercisable by the Lord Chancellor or by any judge nominated by him, or by the Master or Deputy Master of the Court, or by any other officers nominated by the Lord Chancellor to act for the purposes of Part VIII, Mental Health Act 1959. There may be limitations in the powers of the Master and Deputy Master by the Act or Rules made thereunder and of other officers by the instruments by which they are nominated.

The Administration of Justice Act 1960, s. 12 provides that:

"The publication of information relating to proceedings before any court (including a Mental Health Review Tribunal) sitting in private, being proceedings brought under Part VIII of the Mental Health Act, 1959 or under any provision of that Act authorising an order or application to be made to a Mental Health Review Tribunal or to a County Court, is contempt of court."

The Administration of Justice Act 1969 amended section 103 of the Mental Health Act 1959 to give the Court of Protection powers to authorise the execution of a will on behalf of a patient. The court will require medical evidence that the patient is incapable of doing this himself, and may decide if the patient is to be given details.

Part VIII of the Mental Health Act 1959 prescribes the functions of "Nominated Judges" of the Supreme Court with respect to property and affairs where the judge is satisfied on medical evidence that the person is incapable, by reasons of mental disorder, of administering these himself. Sections 102 and 103 give details of the powers which a judge has in these cases and the way in which provision may be made for the patient, relatives or other persons. There are powers for a judge to act in cases of emergency (s. 104) and to appoint a receiver who will act as directed until discharged by order of the judge.

The Lord Chancellor's Visitors (Medical and Legal) continue as provided in sections 108 and 109. The main functions of these visitors are:

(a) visiting patients in accordance with the direction of the judge;

(b) investigating matters affecting the capacity of the patient in relation to the administering of his property and affairs;

(c) making such reports on their visits as the judge may direct.

Circular HM(60)80, dealing with the protection of patients' property, gave advice on matters connected with the management and protection of the property of mentally disordered patients as a result of the Mental Health Act 1959. The Circular enclosed a copy of a letter which had been sent to all local authorities giving details of the role of the Court of Protection, and advising on the appointment of receivers for patients not considered capable of managing their own affairs. The Circular also enclosed copies of a leaflet headed "Mental Patients possessed of Property" which could be given to all relatives, friends, solicitors, and others who may be requiring information on the subject. It was certainly not anticipated that it would be necessary in every case for someone to act as a receiver for a patient receiving treatment for mental disorder.

The circular points out that patients whose affairs have been placed under the jurisdiction of the Court of Protection should not be allowed to transact any business or sign any documents, which would, of course, include the making of a will. When any patient not under the Court's jurisdiction expresses a wish to sign documents or make a will, the responsible medical officer should satisfy himself that the patient appreciates what he is doing and what its effect will be. If the medical officer has doubts on these matters it will be advisable for him to inform the patient's nearest relative, or the patient's solicitor (if any) or to seek the advice of the Chief Clerk of the Court of Protection.

Mental patients and voting rights

The right, or lack of it, to exercise a vote is not directly affected by the Mental Health Act 1959. Nevertheless an electoral registration officer has a common law duty (that is, independently of any statutory provision) to exclude from the franchise those who were once crudely referred to as "lunatics" or "idiots." Furthermore there is an important provision of the Representation of the People Act 1949 excluding from the franchise (right to vote) certain residents of mental hospitals and similar institutions.

At common law, persons suffering from severe mental illness are subject to an incapacity to vote at an election. Such a person may, however, vote during a lucid interval. Hence it seems that a person suffering from severe mental illness making a claim in a lucid interval to be registered has a right to be registered, so far as regards his legal capacity, but there do not seem to be any judicially decided cases on the subject. It appears to be a question of fact for the presiding electoral registration officer to decide whether the voter is, at the moment of voting, sufficiently *compos mentis* to discriminate between the candidates, and to answer questions about residence and identity in an intelligible way. If, however, a person alleged to be mentally disordered votes, while still in the community, as an absent voter, there appears to be no method by which his vote could be questioned. In order words the duty of the electoral registration officer seems to be impracticable of exercise—he would have to set himself up as an itinerant mental welfare officer and psychiatrist alike, and such would be an impossible task.

An apparently similar, but effectively very different, reason for exclusion from the franchise results from a provision of the Representation of the People Act 1949 in its reference to patients in mental hospitals. It was only in 1976, as a result of a decision of the Warrington County Court in Lancashire, that the practical injustices caused by section 4(3) of the 1949 Act became the subject of a judicial ruling.

On November 28, 1975 the provisional electoral register for Warrington was published. It included the names of 574 inmates of Winwick Hospital, a large mental hospital on the outskirts of Warrington. Objection was taken to the inclusion of the 574 on the register by the Liaison Officer of the Newton Constituency Conservative Association on the grounds that the hospital was "an establishment maintained wholly or mainly for the reception and treatment of persons suffering from mental illness or other mental disorder" (note that this statutory provision differs from the common law exclusion by including also mental handicap). And the Representation of the People Act 1949 provides that patients in such an establishment shall not be treated as *resident* there for electoral purposes. Thus the hospital inmates could only register to vote if they had other residences.

Following the complaint by the constituency Liaison Officer the Electoral Registration Officer, acting in accordance with the regulation 19 of the Representation of the People Regulations 1974 (a statutory instrument) decided to delete all the names from the register. Now inmates of mental hospitals, in common with inmates of general hospitals, are apt to complain from time to time. A nursing officer at Winwick Hospital, inured to complaints about the food, temperature or weather, was soon after the events just described asked by an inmate why she could not vote, and the question appeared to be asked very lucidly, especially in the light of other statements of political opinion made by this inmate. As a result, the Electoral Registration officer held a hearing to consider the objections of five patients, brought together for the purpose of a test action by a senior psychiatrist.

The registration officer turned down the complaints about exclusion from the electoral register, and the inmates, represented by MIND (the National Association for Mental Health) appealed against the officer's decision to the Warrington County Court, and the appeal was heard on June 15, 1976: *Wild and others* v. *Electoral Registration Officer for Warrington and another.*

The judge ruled that the five were not to be regarded as "patients" resident in the hospital for the purposes of the statutory exclusion, and that they were therefore entitled to vote. The decision was based on evidence showing that the appellants were in Winwick Hospital only because they had no other home to go to. The Department of Health and Social Security considered this a case of great importance, as indeed it is both numerically and on grounds of principle. They issued a health notice to all area health authorities informing them of the judgment. Estimates vary greatly as to the number of inmates who could thus legitimately be enfranchised, but some put the number as high as 50,000. Much depends on the way in which surveys of inmates are carried out by staff, in particular their reasonableness and regularity see HN(76)180.

The decision does not serve to enfranchise a patient who is in hospital on a formal basis, having been compulsorily detained, for the rationale of "having no where else to go even if the inmates wanted to go there" could not apply in the case of formal patients. An interesting footnote is that the numbers of the long-stay informal patients, or others without an outside home, are apt to be sufficiently large to control the parish vote in the place where mental hospitals are situated.

Control of correspondence

Sections 36 and 134 of the Mental Health Act 1959 make provision for control of incoming and outgoing correspondence of patients. Section 36 relates to patients liable to detention or subject to guardianship, but section 134 applies the controls to "any patient who is receiving treatment for mental disorder in a hospital or mental nursing home, *having been admitted for that purpose*, but not being liable to be detained therein." The provisions do not apply to patients not detained who may receive some psychiatric treatment in hospital but who were admitted primarily for other treatment. The right to open or examine correspondence is limited in section 36(3) to cases where the responsible medical officer or guardian believes the patient to be suffering from mental disorder of a kind likely to lead him to send communications described in s. 36(2)(b)). It is not considered necessary to display notices drawing attention to the provisions of this section, as only exceptionally will letters be opened or withheld and patients will be told when restrictions are in force.

The opening of incoming correspondence is limited to those cases where the responsible medical officer or guardian considers that "the receipt of the postal packet would be calculated to interfere with the treatment of the patient or cause unnecessary distress." Such letters would be returned to the sender if possible. "Postal packet" includes letters, postcards and parcels which might be sent by post even if, in fact, delivered by hand. It also includes telegrams. Section 36(2) states that:

Subject to the provisions of this section, any postal packet addressed by a patient so detained and delivered by him for dispatch may be withheld from the Post Office
- (a) if the addressee has given notice in writing to the Managers of the hospital or to the responsible medical officer requesting that communications addressed to him by the patient should be withheld; or
- (b) if it appears to that officer that the packet would be unreasonably offensive to the addressee, or is defamatory of other persons (other than persons on the staff of the hospital) or would be likely to prejudice the interests of the patients.

It is provided that this subsection does not apply to any postal packet addressed as follows, that is to say:
- (i) to the Minister;
- (ii) to any Member of the Commons House of Parliament;
- (iii) to the Master or Deputy Master or any other officer of the Court of Protection;
- (iv) to the managers of the hospital;
- (v) to any other authority or person having power to discharge the patient under this Part of this Act;
- (vi) at any time when the patient is entitled to make application to a Mental Health Review Tribunal, to that Tribunal.

III

Absence from hospital

Section 39 of the 1959 Act authorises the responsible medical officer to grant leave to a patient, who is for the time being liable to be detained, either indefinitely or on specified occasions or for any specified period. He may impose such conditions (if any) as he considers necessary in the interests of the patient or for the protection of other persons, and he may grant extensions of leave in the absence of the patient.

The patient may be directed to remain in custody during his absence, and he may be kept in the custody of any officer on the staff of the hospital or of any other person authorised in writing by the managers of the hospital.

The responsible medical officer may, if he considers it necessary in the interests of the patient's health or safety or for the protection of other persons, revoke the leave of absence and recall the patient to hospital, but the patient may not be recalled after he has ceased to be liable to be detained.

Where a patient who is for the time being liable to be detained under Part IV of the Mental Health Act 1959 is absent without leave or fails to return from approved leave or is absent from a place where he should be when on approved leave, he may be taken into custody and returned to the hospital. This may be done by any mental welfare officer, any officer of the staff of the hospital, any constable, or any person authorised in writing by the managers of the hospital: section 40. Similar considerations apply to guardianship. Patients cannot be taken into custody after the expiration of the following periods:

(a) In the case of a patient over the age of 21 liable to detention or guardianship as a psychopath or subnormal patient: six months.

(b) Any other cases: 28 days.

Again these conditions do not apply to patients subject to restriction orders.

It should be remembered that patients subject to hospital orders with restrictions under section 65, should have their leave of absence approved by the Home Secretary. The Home Secretary's final decision as to the *discharge* of restricted patients was noted and discussed in Chapter 13. It may well be that the question raised about the legitimacy of the finality of the Home Secretary's discretion in relation to ultimate discharge would apply also to leave of absence for a restricted patient.

It will be noticed above that a patient who is absent without leave from hospital may be returned to hospital by a mental welfare officer, the police or an officer of the hospital or someone so authorised. There is no particular requirement in the Act that any of these persons should take the necessary action, but it is generally accepted that the main responsibility falls upon the health authority who, under the Act, were exercising the power of detention from which the patient has escaped. Accordingly, the hospital or authority will normally arrange the provision of escorts and transport for the patient. However, where the patient's physical or mental condition is such that conveyance by ordinary public transport is out of the question, the local health authority for the area where the patient was can be called upon to provide suitable transport under the provisions of the National Health Service Act 1946. Hospital and health authorities are not authorised to bring back to hospital any patient who is there informally. In these cases, where it is considered necessary for the patient to be returned to hospital, the necessary action will be taken by the mental welfare officers.

Further reference to patients absent without leave is in section 135 which deals with occasions when a patient is believed to be on premises to which admission has been refused. Under section 135(2) a Justice of the Peace may issue, on information laid on oath by a constable, mental welfare officer or other approved person, a warrant authorising a named constable to enter the premises and remove the patient. The constable may use force if necessary, and may be accompanied by a medical practitioner or mental welfare officer or officer of the hospital or health authority.

Protection of others against dangerous patients

The actions of a great many mental patients are remarkably predictable, and it would be wrong to suppose that, once outside the confines of a mental hospital or institution, such patients are apt to run amok. Some detainees, however, act unpredictably, and if such patients are also violence-impulsed the danger exists that an innocent third party might be harmed.

In an analogous case, the subject of a decision of the House of Lords (*Home Office* v. *Dorset Yacht Company* (1970)), damages were recovered against the Home Office on account of the negligence of prison officers at an open Borstal. Officers at the Borstal on Brownsea Island, off the South Coast, failed to exercise adequate supervision with the result that a number of detainees were able to abscond. In their flight they damaged a boat belonging to the Dorset Yacht Company, and this damage was held to be a foreseeable result of the original negligence of the supervisors. The Home Office was sued as principal, the actual negligence being that of its agents or employees.

Liability for negligence is based on the foresight of a "reasonable man" or, simply on reasonably foreseeable consequences. There is no general duty to prevent harm by someone else to a third party; such a duty may, however, exist, if the potential offender is in some way under restraint or supervision. Supervisors may become liable for damages if they do not supervise properly. Clearly, not every error suffices to produce legal liability if damage or injury ensues; but, equally clearly, the greater the degree of risk, the greater the corresponding duty of care. In this respect, violence-impulsed patients present special problems, especially if they are "criminal lunatics."

The case of *Holgate* v. *Lancashire Mental Hospitals Board* (1937) concerned negligence in releasing on licence a patient who had a criminal record, who had a mental age of nine and who was described as a "moral imbecile." Insufficient attention was paid by the officers of the institution to the grant of a licence, and they (with the institution as principal) were held liable for damages when the patient caused severe physical injury to a woman whom he visisted. This was a case in which the officers had a *discretion* as to how they should act, and it was held by the court that they were so negligent as to have failed to act within the proper confines of their discretion. The case was specifically referred to in these terms by Lord Reid in the *Dorset Yacht Company* case.

Some cases—the Borstal case is one—do not involve discretion, for the question is simply one of detention or proper supervision. Lest it be thought that mental institutions admit dangerous or unpredictable patients at their peril, or that it is harsh to attach liability to those to whom Parliament has entrusted a difficult task, the words of Lord Reid should be emphasised: "Parliament cannot reasonably be supposed to have licensed those who do such things to act negligently in disregard to the interests of others so as to cause them needless damage." Those acting in pursuance of statutory authority will be liable to compensate victims of their carelessness.

Protection of patients against themselves

A word on patient care may be added, in this instance in respect of the harm which any patient, but especially a mental patient, may do to himself. The issue resolves itself in the last analysis into a particular application of the general principles of negligence, the sole apparent difference being that the resultant damage is self-inflicted.

An illustrative case if *Selfe* v. *Ilford and District Hospital Management Committee* (1970). A 17-year-old patient had been admitted to what was in fact a general ward after having taken an overdose of sleeping pills. He was put in a ground floor ward with an open window at the back of his bed, which was grouped with the beds of three other suicidal patients. He escaped through the window and climbed some steps onto a roof from which he threw himself, sustaining serious injuries. His claim in negligence against the authority was successful, it being held by the judge that the duty of those in charge of such a patient included the duty to avoid actions of the patient which could foreseeably occur and cause self-inflicted harm. The magnitude of the risk in the case of a patient with known or suspected suicidal tendencies is sufficiently pressing to impose a high standard of surveillance, the absence of which would amount to breach of the duty of care and therefore, in cases resulting in harm or injury, to negligence.

There had been three nurses on duty in Selfe's ward and each knew that he was a suicide risk and had to be kept under constant supervision. Besides the charge nurse, there was another nurse who, just before the occurrence giving rise to the action, and without a word to the charge nurse, had gone to the lavatory. The third, a nursing auxiliary, went to the kitchen, neither of those nurses being able to see into the main ward. The charge nurse answered a call for assistance by a patient and went to him. Thus, no one had an eye on Mr. Selfe, who was able to get out of bed. The judge thought that the charge nurse had been let down by the other two nurses. The incident should never have been allowed to happen, should not have happened, and would not have happened if three, or even two, nurses had been in the ward keeping Mr. Selfe under observation.

Immunity for acts done in pursuance of the 1959 Act

Protection for acts done in pursuance of the Mental Health Act 1959, or *purporting* to be so done, is given by section 141 of the Act. To qualify for protection the act in question must not have been done in bad faith or without reasonable care. Leave of the High Court is required before any civil action can be taken.

This section does not apply to offences committed under the Act, but proceedings for the offences which are created by the Act require the consent of the Director of Public Prosecutions.

IV

Propsects for law reform

There has during the last few years been an upsurge of interest, both official and unofficial, in the state of the law relating to the treatment of mental disorder and to connected issues. A variety of lobbies and interest groups is represented, not least the mentally disordered themselves. It cannot please all the people all the time. In its *Review of the Mental Health Act 1959* (Cmnd. 7320) published in September 1978 the Department of Health, together with the Home Office (see in particular the so-called "criminally disordered"), the Welsh Office and the Lord Chancellor's Department (see judicial management of patient's property and affairs, and "visitors"), presented a survey containing both exposition of the present law relating to the treatment of mental disorder and associated issues, and also proposals for changes in the existing law and practice consequent thereon. The White Paper was published in September 1978.

An interdepartmental committee was established in 1975 to review the 1959 Act, and started from the general premise that on the whole it had worked well but that some improvements were needed and that amendment would benefit all concerned. It considered proposals suggested both before and after its establishment, published a Consultative Document in 1976 which it followed with a well-attended one-day conference. Among other contributions published after the Consultative Document and which were considered by the Committee were the second volume of MIND's "A Human Condition" on offender patients and the British Association of Social Workers' "Mental Health Crisis Services—A New Philosophy." The White Paper is the result of this consultative exercise. Most of its proposals were intended by the Government for prompt legislative enactment, but some were more tentative. The most important of these topics is what compulsory powers if any are needed outside hospitals. Part VIII of the Act, which concerns the management of the property and affairs of patients, was not covered in the White Paper; the Lord Chancellor is considering separately whether any changes are desirable. The general philosophy behind the proposals is stated to be "the need to strengthen the rights and safeguard the liberties of the mentally disordered whilst retaining a proper regard for the rights and safety of the general public and of the staff."

One of the difficulties which now faces the legislator was the very product of the strong emphasis placed on informality of admission and treatment by the 1959 Act. For while almost 90 per cent. of those admitted to mental illness and mental handicap hospitals and units, and nearly 95 per cent. of those resident there at any given time, are informal patients, the line between the situation of those who still possess the wit to have themselves admitted or (more usually) consent to or at least go along with an admission put in train by someone else (relative, social worker), and those who are "sectioned" can be so fine as to be non-existent. Chapter 1 contains a useful survey of the existing position of informal patients and makes the point, so important to civil libertarians as well as to the patients themselves, that the taking of compulsory powers also brings with it safeguards (application to a mental health review tribunal etc.) which are not at present available to the vast majority of patients, the informal ones.

The *Review's* standpoint on mental handicap is this:

> "The Government has considered whether there should be a separate Act for the mentally handicapped. Whilst this would have the advantage of avoiding confusion, there would seem little point in having separate Acts of Parliament for mental illness and for mental handicap unless their content is to differ significantly. Most of the areas discussed in this White Paper concern both the mentally ill and the mentally handicapped, and it is proposed to maintain the powers and safeguards within the same Act but to ensure that distinctions are made where appropriate."

Chapter 2 deals quite fully with what is called "Compulsory Admission to and Detention in Hospital" (though *formal* admission would perhaps have been more terminologically accurate if not also practically representative). In paragraph 2.3 the *Review* expresses a "hope" that the increasing development of 24-hour crisis intervention services will reduce recourse to section 29 of the 1959 Act (emergency admission, 72 hours' duration). A new type of holding power exercisable by, *inter alia*, Registered Mental Nurses, is mooted. Furthermore, comments received in response to the 1976 Consultative Document showed strong support for the removal of age limits in relation to section 26 orders on subnormals (handicapped) and psychopaths. This would give even further legislative credence to the policy expressed in the Mental Health (Amendment) Act 1975 in relation to extended powers of detention for certain patients so classified. In response to fears and doubts expressed about the section 136 power of a policeman to restrain someone he thinks is mentally disordered, in a public place, and take the person to a "place of safety," it is proposed to retain the power but to issue guidelines emphasising that a police station should be used as a "place of safety" only as a last resort. Throughout Chapter 2, the requirement of "likelihood of benefit from treatment" is emphasized. This could be more hollow than it sounds. Who would detain a non-offending handicapped or psychopathic person if there was no likelihood (prospect?) of benefit. And anyway, "treatment" can be so widely defined as to make it a foregone conclusion that this requirement will be satisfied whenever detention or restraint is proposed. The small but vital amendment of the criterion for detention under section 26 of the 1959 Act, from "protection of other persons" to "protect others from harm" is a most welcome proposal.

Chapter 3 contains two points of particular interest. "Nearest relative" is to be amended from the section 49 definition to the first in a list of relatives to be caring for the person concerned or to be doing so immediately after his admission. Secondly, "approved social workers" continue to be treated as a whole (see Seebohm Report 1968) even though individuals specialise within the overall genre. It is high time this position was officially admitted. Chapter 4, on which further comments are invited, concerns the extension of compulsory (formal) powers to non-hospitalised patients.

Safeguards for patients are discussed in Chapter 6, and attention is not unexpectedly given to the role and duties of mental health review tribunals and also to the vexed issue of consent to treatment. As for mental health review tribunals, the Government believes that the best answer is for greater use to be made of the existing power to appoint a fourth tribunal member, but not to make it a statutory requirement either that a social worker be appointed as fourth member or that a social worker should replace the third "lay" member. The exposition of the existing law on consent is a welcome and indeed essential inclusion in the *Review*, but in one respect it is unsatisfactory. The important question is "consent to what?" Attitudes to treatment, whether clinical psychological, mental or "whole person" treatment directly affect the rights and liberties of the patient. There is scant evidence in the *Review* as to what our attitudes should be.

Chapter 7 preserves a happy equilibrium by discussing safeguards for staff, an area in which C.O.H.S.E. and the other health service unions have been particularly (and justifiably) vocal. A point which also affects patients in this chapter is the important expression of the hope that it will be made clear that section 141 (the wide immunity provision in the 1959 Act) does not apply to informal psychiatric patients. In Chapter 8 the uncontroversial proposal to repeal section 134, at present allowing the withholding of correspondence to and from informal patients (formal patients are covered by section 36, which will stay) is a welcome proposal.

Finally, Chapter 9 (Resource Implications) is a necessary finale, but the implications for better treatment, care and integration make it clear that this is not a conclusion but the start of a further important debate. A clearly enunciated philosophy is now as urgently needed in the field of treatment of mental disorder as it ever has been.

INDEX

329

UNFAIR DISMISSAL—*cont.*
  retiring age and, 66
  status and, 65
  wrongful dismissal, distinguished
    from, 56–57
UNFAIR DISCRIMINATION, 72–78
  compensation for, 75
  International Labour Organisation,
    and, 72
UNIVERSITIES
  representation on RHAs, 8
UNLAWFUL DETENTION, 196–198
  defences to, 196
  unknown to detainee, 198
UNLAWFUL DISCRIMINATION
  advertisements and, 74
  areas of, 73, 74
  exceptions to, 74, 75
  midwives, application to, 74
URINE SPECIMEN
  police obtaining, in hospital,
    206–207

VATICAN
  euthanasia, view on, 270
VICARIOUS LIABILITY, 48, 81–82
  "actual or ostensible authority"
    and, 89
  additional liability, as, 80
  application to hospitals, 94–96
  course of employment and, 81,
    83–89
  criminal and fraudulent acts for,
    88–89
  economic reasons behind, 80
  enterprise liability, as, 96
  express prohibitions and, 84–88
  getting the job done, 86–88

VICARIOUS LIABILITY—*cont.*
  negligence in course of employment,
    for, 83
  scope of employment and, 81, 83–89
  theft and, 89
VIOLENCE
  injuries from, 105–108
  patients, by, 192–195
  reports of incidents involving, 107
VIOLENT PATIENTS
  care of, 193–195
  treatment of, 29
VISITOR
  duty to, by hospital
VISITORS
  refusing to leave, 201–202
  trespassers, as, 201–202
VOLUNTARY HOSPITALS
  distribution of, 3–4
  employment law, and, 48
  means of support, 3
  taken over by NHS, 4–5
VOLUNTARY WORKERS
  status of, 49
VOTING
  mental patients, by, 316–318

WHITLEY COUNCIL
  "Conditions of Service", 70
  redundancy schemes, and, 68, 70
WHITLEY COUNCILS, 42, 54
WORK RULES, 49–50
  communication to employee, 50
WRITTEN PARTICULARS OF EMPLOYMENT,
    50–53
WRONGFUL DISMISSAL
  unfair dismissal, distinguished
    from, 56–57